Celluloid Colony

Celluloid Colony

Locating History and Ethnography in Early Dutch Colonial Films of Indonesia

Sandeep Ray

NUS PRESS
SINGAPORE

Published by:

NUS Press
National University of Singapore
AS3-01-02, 3 Arts Link
Singapore 117569

Fax: (65) 6774-0652
E-mail: nusbooks@nus.edu.sg
Website: http://nuspress.nus.edu.sg

ISBN 978-981-325-138-0 (paper)

National Library Board, Singapore Cataloguing in Publication Data

Name(s): Ray, Sandeep, 1969–
Title: Celluloid colony: locating history and ethnography in early Dutch colonial films of Indonesia/Sandeep Ray.
Description: Singapore: NUS Press, [2021] | Includes bibliographical references and index.
Identifier(s): OCN 1164350389 | ISBN 978-981-325-138-0 (paperback)
Subject(s): LCSH: Indonesia--History--20th century. | Indonesia--History--20th century--Sources. | Indonesia--History--Archival resources. | Ethnology--Indonesia--History--20th century. | Ethnology--Indonesia--History--Sources. | Ethnology--Indonesia--Archival resources. | Motion pictures--Indonesia--History--20th century.
Classification: DDC 959.80223--dc23

Cover image: Simon Buis in Flores with local actors. Photo courtesy of PASVD, Teteringen.

Printed by: Integrated Books International

Contents

List of Figures

Acknowledgements

First, I thank Timothy P. Barnard of the Department of History at the National University of Singapore. His stewardship and advice during my time at the university, and after, have been invaluable. I have gained much from his knowledge of Southeast Asia, both on and off screen.

Barbara Andaya reassured me that my fledgling, insecure idea of pursuing film as a primary source material was a bona fide history project. She counselled me first in class and later again as I worked on this book. I also thank Jan van der Putten for sharing his knowledge of the Dutch colonial era. I acknowledge the collegiality of the extended community of the History Department at NUS and the generous Lee Kong Chian fellowship that enabled me to be a part of it. Pointed comments from Maitrii Aung-Thwin and Susie Protschky at the end stages of my formal studies helped me edit and situate my work in the fields of Southeast Asian Studies and Visual Studies.

From earlier in my life, I turn to Abraham Ravett at Hampshire College for nurturing my first exploration of the celluloid format. A subsequent multi-year apprenticeship with ethnographic filmmaker John Marshall led to hands-on experience of working with archival footage. I am grateful to Nancy Florida for turning me on to Indonesian Studies in 2008 at the University of Michigan. Rudolf Mrazek remains a juggernaut of experience and knowledge; I thank him for beseeching me to try to 'touch the past'. My year as a Luce post-doctoral fellow at the Chao Center for Asian Studies at Rice University provided me much required time and resources to work on the manuscript. I am grateful for the centre's support. I thank the Humanities, Arts and Social Sciences Department at Singapore University of Technology and Design for giving me sufficient respite from my teaching duties to work on this book and bring the project to a close.

Research for this book was conducted, intermittently, in the Netherlands between 2012 and 2017. I am indebted to several people and institutions in that country. At the film archives of Beeld en Geluid and the Eye Filmmuseum, I thank Bas Agterberg and Rommy Albers respectively. Both Bas and Rommy were extremely helpful in guiding me through the collections while I worked in their offices for months on end, asking numerous questions, gratefully drinking many cups of free coffee. They remained supportive even after my departure, honoring my email requests and sending me DVD copies of archival material and related information. Another institution, one that unexpectedly became a frequent location, was the University of Utrecht. After befriending Dafna Ruppin, a fellow researcher who patiently taught me how to navigate the labyrinthine Koninklijke Bibliotheek in The Hague, I inveigled my way into participating in the graduate film seminars of the Department of Media and Culture Studies led by Frank Kessler. Here I also met Lisabona Rahman, an Indonesian film restoration expert with overlapping interests, and lively discussions ensued. I acknowledge the contribution of Carinda Strangio, whose own early research had led her to scour the minutes of the Colonial Institute's meetings, an exercise that proved to be of great value to me as I pieced together institutional histories. While the work progressed, Jacqueline Hicks and Sarah Maxin invited me to present my ongoing findings at the KITLV in Leiden and UC-Berkeley respectively, bringing me into dialogue with scholars whose feedback I noted closely. Dorrette Schootemeijer at the Eye Filmmuseum was helpful and instructive with her vast knowledge of the collections and, in the last stages of this book, in helping me with stills. Marie-Antoinette Willemsen was selfless with her time and helped locate images during the pandemic lockdown that prevented travel to the Netherlands.

My time in Amsterdam was pleasant because of Kiki Post, my landlady, friend and colleague who showed me how to navigate the city and to live within my limited means. Her generosity will not be forgotten. During a trip to the Netherlands in 2014 to present at the KITLV in Leiden University, I was fortunate to be able to meet Vincent Monnikendam, the veteran Dutch documentary director and maker of *Mother Dao*, the film that sparked the desire in me to explore colonial films. Mr. Monnikendam's many helpful emails and conversations about the original footage have found their way into *Celluloid Colony*. Also communicative and generous with his time was Karel Steenbrink, who watched films with me through his vastly knowledgeable eyes and drove me to the SVD archive in Teteringen to help dig up information on the Catholic priests who had made films in the 1920s.

Once a manuscript had been drafted, Peter Schoppert at NUS Press took charge and helped place it with the right reviewers, whose feedback helped shape the final version. They remain resiliently anonymous. Sunandini Arora Lal of NUS Press was an inspiration. Observing her attention to detail in copy-editing was an exercise in humility. Michiel Baas helped with eleventh-hour translation checks.

I reserve the final acknowledgement for Nico de Klerk. An expert on the colonial film archives and a researcher with a prodigious knowledge of early non-fiction cinema, he is one whose scholarship and kind, collegial attention I have deeply benefited from. In our fortnightly meetings at the lounge of the Lloyd Hotel in Amsterdam, I spilled forth my many questions and insecurities, to be met with clear advice and direction. I aspire to live up to his exacting standards of scholarship. There would be no book without his encouragement.

There are several others—kindred souls who are now no more—on whose tedious endeavours this exploration fundamentally rests. Like me, they too traversed the Indonesian archipelago with cameras, trying to capture a changing world. But they did so a hundred years ago, when it was infinitely more difficult. While I am critical of their art and politics in this book, I cannot but readily admit that it is only because of their hard work and pioneering spirit that we are able to see shards of the complex, receding colonial past. It is as close as we can come to touching it. I thank all the filmmakers whose works I reference and the archivists who came after who meticulously annotated and restored them.

I remain indebted to my companion and partner, Robin Bush, for her support and example. Finally, I dedicate this book to my parents, who were both born in the colonial era, experienced its many upheavals and yet lived long enough to see a time of relative peace. Like these old films, their memories flicker on in the digital century.

INTRODUCTION

A Case for Outcasts

Hilversum, a municipality near Amsterdam, has been a hub of the Dutch radio and television industry for almost a century. In 2007 the *New York Times* ran a story describing a new building in this town—the spectacular offices of Nederlands Instituut voor Beeld en Geluid (Netherlands Institute of Sound and Vision).[1] Alighting at the train station, one is just a few hundred metres across from this tall, striking structure with vivid, colourful cast-glass panels. Inside this ultra-modern enterprise, technicians and archivists hunch over, decoding machines connected to large digital servers. They are converting old film to a viewable electronic format. Much of that information at the time of writing this book was already accessible on the vast network database at Beeld en Geluid. The encoded images on those computer servers are the primary sources for this study.

In 2006 a project titled 'Images for the Future' secured a grant of 154 million euros from the Dutch Fund for the Reinforcement of Economic Structure to digitize archival film material.[2] It was an effort to create a publicly accessible repository of Dutch media in all its forms, from the earliest days of its inception. In this era of instant new media proliferating on television broadcasts and palm devices in high resolution, 'old media' has surprisingly been given a compelling makeover here.

[1] Nicolai Ouroussoff, 'Heaven, Hell and Purgatory, Encased in Glass', *New York Times*, 26 May 2007.
[2] Giovanna Fossati, *From Grain to Pixel: The Archival Life of Film in Transition* (Amsterdam: Amsterdam University Press, 2010), p. 175.

Anyone can walk into Beeld en Geluid and view film footage from a century ago. Some of the material has also been uploaded to the internet for remote viewing from around the world. A sliver of this mammoth archive is a propaganda film collection from the Netherlands East Indies. Between the celluloid holdings at Beeld en Geluid and those at the Eye Filmmuseum in Amsterdam (both beneficiaries of the substantial Images for the Future grant), several hundred short silent films—varying from a few minutes to an hour in duration—are digitally available for research. In the 1910s and 1920s these films were used to persuade the Dutch population that their country's ongoing rule in the East Indies was justified. The public who viewed these films in lecture halls and theatres were receiving their government's version of conditions and events. The films portrayed colonial rule as benevolent and well received, leaving out those administrative challenges that would emerge in the early decades of the 20th century and eventually derail the Dutch stranglehold over the enormous archipelago.

Through a close reading of these early colonial non-fiction films that were produced from 1912 onwards, this study uses motion picture as a source to explore the historical milieu of the era and contribute to our knowledge of developments in early-20th-century cinema. The study continues to 1930, marking a robust period of filmmaking. The issues covered in these short films run a wide range of topics—agriculture, healthcare, urban planning, infrastructure, arts and crafts, transmigration, and religion, among others. While hundreds of films were produced all over the Indonesian archipelago, there has been no methodical study exploring the historical and ethnographic value of this material. Accordingly, this book researches the ethnographies constructed via film on indigenous communities in the Netherlands East Indies, and questions how this information could help us better understand the colonial encounter. Over the next several chapters, I rehabilitate historical moments that have remained unexplored in the archives, demonstrating that the effort of locating history in the propagandistic films commissioned by a diversity of agencies—the colonial government, multinational corporations and the Church—is worthwhile. A salient point of this study is the observation that histories of ethnography in Indonesia rarely mention non-fiction film. In all, this study spans about two decades. Several dozen films, carefully selected from an archive of hundreds and illuminating aspects of an under-represented historical or ethnographic point of view, will be analyzed and discussed.

While research on this topic and period is limited, there has been inquiry into the representation of Dutch colonial rule in propaganda films. Gerda Jansen Hendriks' PhD dissertation, 'Een voorbeeldige kolonie: Nederlands-Indië in 50 jaar overheidsfilms, 1912–1962' [An Imagined Colony: Netherlands East Indies in 50 Years of Government Films, 1912–1962] (2014), systematically looks at government complicity in creating a visual represenation of pre-Independence Indonesia that appeared unnaturally peaceful and well managed:

> The recurrent public outcry over the Dutch colonial policy can be partly explained by the existence of an idealized image of Dutch colonialism derived from these films. Exploitation of laborers, summary executions or the burning of villages were never shown. Rather, viewers were treated to an unending visual stream of Dutch colonial benevolence and alleged expertise, making it hard to imagine that Dutch men could be responsible for gruesome deeds.[3]

The primary time frame for the gruesome deeds mentioned in the excerpt above was 1945–49, when the Netherlands fought tooth and claw to hold on to the East Indies. Though my study halts at 1930, it has resonance with Hendriks' work in that it acknowledges the lack of political or socio-economic analysis of issues the teeming, and often seething, colonial subjects faced. The charade of a peaceful colony is indeed selectively constructed; dissatisfaction is rarely explored in these films. While this rankles, it ought not surprise us. It was the job of film-makers, often hired professionals, to depict the colony in this manner—their primary client, after all, was the Dutch colonial government and its vested collaborators. This study, however, adds another dimension, and this is where it significantly departs from Hendriks' exploration: even though the films were propagandistic, relatively simple in their depiction of colonial life, and geared towards maintaining a visually appealing image of the East Indies, there is still a significant amount of footage and documentation that can be unpacked through closer readings of the films. To elaborate on this point, I draw upon the observations of veteran film editor Dai Vaughn, who frames this argument

[3] G.A. Jansen Hendriks, 'Een voorbeeldige kolonie: Nederlands-Indië in 50 jaar overheidsfilms, 1912–1962' (PhD dissertation, University of Amsterdam, 2014), p. 389.

in somewhat dramatic but effective terms. When considering documentary footage that is deliberately manipulated, even to the point where it shows us the *exact opposite* of what was pro-filmic, he remarks, 'today's lie, differently regarded, may be tomorrow's evidence'.[4] His contention is that documentary footage, unlike fiction, places a significant burden on the viewer to determine what is of value in it. Hence the habit of many ethnographic filmmakers to preserve every frame of their material with the hope that at some future date 'researchers yet unborn' would benefit from them. Accordingly, I insist that we cannot dismiss out of hand these films as informationally flawed and biased propaganda. In fact, very often, the tensions between colonial rule and native life surface in these films. The intention may have been to depict benevolence, but today, with refined understandings of how colonial systems worked, much of what we see in these films smacks of servitude and the co-option of an entire native class. If the field of colonial studies today tends to avoid a binary narrative of opressor-versus-oppressed, then these films will help shed light on much of that overlapping space. Accordingly, this book offers a substantial and nuanced consideration of these films as both historical as well as ethnographic expositions of early-20th-century Netherlands East Indies. Despite their propagandistic slant and their limitations in projecting a realistic picture of conditions in the colony, the films are steeped in primary sources that can be reappraised. Dutch archivist and film scholar Nico de Klerk incisively sums up the connection between colonial film and the possibilities of historical enquiry within the material when he states, 'Colonial filmmaking is not colonial all the time.'[5]

In order to argue this concretely, I will excavate from the film archive several examples of such sources and subject the visual excerpts to robust textual cross-referencing. The films in this archive, because of their sheer scale and scope of coverage—unrivalled by any other colonial power—allow for in-depth analyses and cross-referencing with written primary sources. Although fairly accessible, the collection has

[4] Dai Vaughn, *For Documentary: Twelve Essays* (Berkeley: University of California Press, 1999), pp. 81–2.

[5] Nico de Klerk, 'Home Away from Home', in *Mining the Home Movie: Excavations in Histories and Memories*, ed. Karen L. Ishizuka and Patricia R. Zimmermann (Berkeley: University of California Press, 2008), p. 11.

not piqued much interest among historians involved in the study of Indonesia. De Klerk has written trenchantly on the odd lack of exposure of this material:

> To illustrate the absurdity of this, let us look, for example, at the largest, most systematic transcultural enterprise ever undertaken by the Dutch film industry. It consists of those films made and shown in the former Dutch colonies, the West-Indies and, particularly, the East-Indies (now Indonesia). This enterprise was large, because it involved thousands of films: on the one hand, predominantly documentary footage shipped from the colonies for screenings in Holland.... This enterprise was systematic, because the *making* of the films in the colony was carefully planned, often in coordination with the government and/or business community, either in Holland or overseas. The *screening* of these films in Holland was systematic too, in the sense that they were exhibited under specific conditions, preferably in non-theatrical venues and often bracketed by introductions.... This enterprise, this involvement, which lasted for over 30 years, has not found its way into Dutch national film historiography [emphases in original].[6]

The omission of film as bona fide primary source material is not limited to scholars studying the Netherlands East Indies. Despite the wealth of such material, academic programmes, and in particular history departments, have rarely delved into film sources to study the past. Jane Landman and Chris Ballard observe: 'Cinema—as a source for writing about history, and as a particularly powerful medium for communicating the past—commands the attention of historians, but is not yet a field in which historians have developed a particularly rigorous or robust set of analytical methods.'[7] In this book, in addition to drawing attention to this particular collection, I will also suggest a general set of analytical tools to tackle film, in this case specifically non-fiction film, as historical and ethnographic source material. The methodology can be summed up in four steps. First, an identification is made of filmed material that historians and ethnographers would generally classify as 'primary sources'. Second, that footage is cross-referenced with existing sources, mostly

[6] Nico de Klerk, 'Tesori nascosti: ritrovare I film coloniali'/'Dark Treasures: Rediscovering Colonial Films', *Cinegrafie* 17 (2004): 436.
[7] Jane Landman and Chris Ballard, 'An Ocean of Images: Film and History in the Pacific', *Journal of Pacific History* 45, 1 (2010): 2.

text-based, that help to authenticate and situate the material. Third, the films are closely reviewed for sections that could be relevant as micro-histories, even though they could possibly go against the grain of the broader theme of the film. Finally, an effort is made to understand the commercial, cultural and political influences on the makers of the films. While these approaches are not unusual or new in the study of the colonial era, they have yet to be utilized rigorously for the study of non-fiction film from this period in Southeast Asian history and ethnography. In this sense, this book aspires to contribute to the early stages of what could be a useful historiographical approach in the study of colonialism—the search for history and ethnography embedded in non-fiction film.

While film is still underappreciated as a historical source, still images have played an important role in studying the colonial era. That intensity of analysis, however, has not carried over to motion picture, which arguably involves a more acute simulacrum of visual representation. While much dialogue has been opened up by the engagement of innovative visual methodology in the studies mentioned above, the exploration of history and ethnography via non-fiction motion picture remains lacking, especially in the Southeast Asian context.[8]

A Brief History of Looking at History through Film

While the consideration of film as a source of historical research remains a relatively underdeveloped approach, academics have been arguing for its inclusion for decades.[9] James Chapman's *Film and History* (2013)

[8] Jean Gelman Taylor's essay 'Ethical Policies in Moving Pictures' (in *Photography, Modernity and the Governed in Late-Colonial Indonesia*, ed. Susie Protschky [Amsterdam: Amsterdam University Press, 2015]) does explore some aspects of early colonial filmmaking in the Netherlands East Indies. I will discuss her contribution in more detail later. Dutch cultural historian Pamela Pattynama has also researched the connections between film and colonial history. Her work, however, focuses on fictional cinema, unlike the non-fiction sources being explored in this book. See her '(Un)happy Endings: Nostalgia in Postimperial and Postmemory Dutch Films', in *The Postcolonial Low Countries: Literature, Colonialism, Multiculturalism*, ed. E. Boehmer and S. De Mul (Lanham: Lexington Books, 2012), pp. 97–122.

[9] Polish photographer Boleslas Matuszewski is the first known advocate for film as 'a new source of history'. See Boleslas Matuszewski, Laura U. Marks and Diane Koszarski, 'A New Source of History', *Film History* 7, 3 (1995): 322.

details an impressive overview of this burgeoning movement. In an essay titled 'Film as a Historical Source', he traces the origins of the advocacy for this subfield to the late 1960s.[10] In 1968, simultaneous articles in the French journal *Annales* and the British *University Vision* encouraged the close study of film as a historical source. The establishment of the Inter-University History Film Consortium at the University of Leeds followed these publications. The consortium's mandate was to 'produce archive compilations to teach modern history'.[11]

About a decade later, in 1980, noted French sociologist Pierre Sorlin wrote an impassioned essay bemoaning historians' continuing lack of the study of film. In 'How to Look at an "Historical" Film' he opined bluntly, 'Historians must take an interest in the audiovisual world, if they are not to become schizophrenics, rejected by society as the representatives of an outmoded erudition.'[12] Using 1960 as a rough date marking the start of the 'audiovisual age', when the advent of television and the widespread use of portable equipment had started in-depth coverage of social and political events, Sorlin insisted that it would behoove academics to look at films more closely. There seemed to be little interest in the larger community, however, in trying to develop a new approach. In 1988 film historian Robert Rosenstone commented contentiously, 'the chief source of historical knowledge for the majority of the population—outside of the much-despised textbook—must surely be the visual media, a set of institutions that lie almost wholly outside the control of those of us who devote our lives to history'.[13] In the 1990s, frustrated by the continuing lack of traction of these earlier ideas within the academic community, art historian W.J.T. Mitchell implored that a new reorientation, the 'pictorial turn', was needed urgently.[14] Pointing to the 'linguistic turn' that had altered the study of humanities

---

[10] James Chapman, *Film and History: Theory and History* (Basingstoke and New York: Palgrave Macmillan, 2013).

[11] Ibid., p. 75.

[12] Pierre Sorlin, *The Film in History: Restaging the Past* (Oxford: Basil Blackwell, 1980), p. 5.

[13] Robert A. Rosenstone, 'History in Images/History in Words: Reflections on the Possibility of Really Putting History onto Film', *American Historical Review* 93, 5 (1988): 1174.

[14] W.J.T. Mitchell, *Picture Theory: Essays on Verbal and Visual Representation* (Chicago: University of Chicago Press, 1995).

a few decades earlier, Mitchell now called for a 'de-disciplined humanities' that looked closely at images, including films.[15] According to Mitchell, it was vital that the value of visual evidence proliferating in the world be investigated, acknowledged and integrated on its own terms. He was not necessarily singling out historians to commandeer this new era of visual reintegration; he was appealing to the academic community at large. The importance of historians in a pivotal role was, however, emphasized.

While a call for that 'pictorial turn' has been made repeatedly since the late 1960s by academics from different fields, not all film material was assumed to be relevant. Most limiting for scholars of the 20th century was perhaps Sorlin's own nomenclature of visual material. Dividing films into two categories, 'fictional' and 'informational', Sorlin expressed little optimism about the availability of relevant documentary or 'informational' footage pre-1960. He was blunt in his denunciation: 'I am going to criticize this kind of document. My proposition is that the informational film is of undoubted but extremely narrow value, and that for the period we are dealing with, that is, for the years *before 1960*, the most original source is the fictional film.' According to Sorlin, events such as Hitler's accession to power in the 1930s had little visual evidence as compared to events that received extensive coverage in subsequent decades—for example, the Vietnam War. He categorically dismissed early- to mid-20th-century newsreels as viable sources of history. According to Sorlin they were 'of limited value, although they are not entirely worthless'.[16] Calling them 'directed images of society', he argued that newsreels rarely held any more information than what was already known from written sources about important events. Consequently, he concentrated on fiction films for methods of locating history from that period.

Sorlin was not alone in his lack of interest in newsreel type of archival footage from the first half of the 20th century. Most contemporary scholars who take an active interest in resurrecting films vis-à-vis the study of history typically focus on fictional films. Discussion of documentary evidence is limited; colonial films and newsreels at best

---

[15] See review by Sol Cohen, 'An Innocent Eye: The "Pictorial Turn," Film Studies, and History', *History of Education Quarterly* 43, 2 (2003): 250–61.
[16] Sorlin, *Film in History*, p. 15 (emphasis in original).

get a cursory nod. Yet, despite his lack of interest in non-fiction film, Sorlin did make one very reassuring concession:

> Newsreels illustrate diplomatic and military history, but they might also be useful in another way if we are prepared to consider them as ethnological documents ... in this respect films are a potentially useful source of evidence, but we are perhaps still too close to the period and should leave research of this sort to the historians of the twenty-first century.[17]

Unfortunately, he did not give us pointers as to how future historians ought to look at informational films. This book, written well into the 21st century, will attempt to unpack this suggestion. But first one needs to explore the conditions and expectations with which filmmakers produce images—filmmakers' intentions and the historical insights gleaned from their filmed material may differ considerably.

While the makers of newsreels, *actualités* and propaganda films may not have consciously chosen to produce ethnological documents, they might have inadvertently done so. Were the creators of these potential historical sources always aware of their precise roles in the construction of historical events? Historian Arthur Marwick has separated 'witting' from 'unwitting' testimonies. According to Marwick, unwitting testimony in a document is quite simply the 'unintentional evidence that it also contains'.[18] Taking this idea a little further and considering that film could fall within the category of historical documentation, film theorist Karsten Fledelius commented, 'Often the most interesting evidence is the "unwitting testimony" of cinematographic recordings, all those incidental aspects of reality which have just "slipped" into the camera without being consciously recorded by the cameraman.'[19] This theory

[17] Ibid. Sorlin also describes a workshop where the Open University selected some short sequences from newsreels that were devoted to the precise aspect of social life. This was to glean their ethnographic value.

[18] Arthur Marwick, *The Nature of History*, 3rd ed. (London: Macmillan, 1989), p. 216.

[19] James Chapman quotes Karsten Fledelius in *Film and History*. See Karsten Fledelius, 'Film and History: An Introduction to the Theme', in *History and the Audio-visual Media*, ed. Karsten Fledelius et al. (Copenhagen: University of Copenhagen, 1979), p. 9.

of an unwitting coverage of history is very relevant to the current study. In the films that we shall delve into presently, there are numerous instances of both deliberate ethnography as well as the unwitting or inadvertent capturing of ethnographic-historical evidence. When he categorically denounced non-fiction film as not being historically useful, Sorlin might not have been aware of the existence of such an unusual and exhaustive archive as the one we are exploring in this book. Indeed, ethnography, documentary and various subgenres of early non-fiction film fill the Dutch East Indies collection with rare historical coverage—well beyond the standard newsreel shows of 'important events'.

There have been outright opponents of the idea of using film as source material. In *Eyewitnessing: The Uses of Image as Historical Evidence*, Peter Burke (2008) mounts a lively, well-argued campaign against the use of film and other visual sources for the study of history. Arguing that cinema is mostly constructed and that its interpretation is highly subjective, Burke maintains that the cornerstone of historical analysis is accuracy and that the innate 'verisimilitude in details' of cinema disqualifies it as a source material.[20] His criticism of film as a source is particularly focused on ethnographic film, a subgenre that proliferates the visual archive of the Netherlands East Indies. Burke insists that ethnographic films contain innumerable layers of artifice and offer too many ways in which readings can be distorted. He points out that ethnographer Franz Boas filmed night dances of the Kwakiutl during the day and Robert Gardner used several scenes of different fights of Dani warfare rituals to reconstitute what Burke calls a semi-credible account of 'reality being instantaneously covered'.[21] Burke also criticizes the ordering of knowledge related to sequencing. The exact sequence of events during the making of a film, he points out, is almost never known after the fact. He does, however, acknowledge that British newsreels have been credibly used as sources of history about the Spanish Civil War and films made by the British army were used in the Nuremberg trials in 1945. Oddly, Burke also argues (in favour of the approach in this book) that 'if tape recorded oral history is taken seriously as source, it would be odd to take videotapes any less seriously'.[22]

---

[20] Peter Burke, *Eyewitnessing: The Uses of Images as Historical Evidence* (Ithaca: Cornell University Press, 2008).
[21] Ibid., p. 156.
[22] Ibid., p. 155.

In the case of early Dutch colonial films, because the medium of film in and of itself was relatively young, recreations and deft editing were often self-revealing; they lacked the seamlessness of films produced later. Log entries of the early films actually indicate a number of versions for each film—these early practitioners and those who commissioned their works were evidently struggling to get the 'right' tone across. Just as we look for cues of exaggeration and imprecision in textual documents, cinema too lends itself to a variety of ways in the assessment of veracity. And very often, while the general thrust of a propagandistic film may be manipulated and biased in its construction, there might be a singular shot or scene that documents a moment in history that could be referenced as a useful source. This crucial idea is often overlooked in the discussion of film as a historical source—a distinction needs to be made between the context and the content of filmed material. The context of the filming and its subsequent construction into a film is indeed important as it is telling about the circumstances of production and cultural expectations of the creators and their audiences. Yet, the problem I am alluding to is the tendency of film historians, even those who are open to the idea of investigating film as a possible historical source, to attempt to see the entire film as a cohesive body. History can lurk in isolated moments. Thus, the content of a shot, disconnected from the larger sequence it is woven into, may often reveal something historically useful, unencumbered by the biases in the larger body it is a part of. While Burke's scepticism about the manipulated works of Gardner and Boas has merit, it does not justify the complete omission of an entire genre of cinema. Accordingly, embedded in my analysis of Dutch colonial films is the strategy that we may be able to review archival films—be they newsreel based or informational—and select from them what engages and challenges us. In other words, there may be just one or two scenes in an entire propagandistic film that have ethnographic importance—deliberate or inadvertent. We may be able to disentangle the production process to see through manipulation and reconstructions.

In most books debating and arguing for the inclusion of film in historical discourse, there tends to be a chapter titled 'Documentary' that looks at sources that are not fictional. Robert A. Rosenstone's *History on Film/Film on History*, Marnie-Hughes Warrington's *History Goes to the Movies*, and Philip Rosen's *Change Mummified* all have a section devoted to a critical analysis of the documentary form. They discuss the ethics of production, the psychoanalysis of interpretation, the derailing influences of politics, and the perils of commercialization.[23] The trend is to look at the film, or even the genre, as a whole. Many non-fiction films, if considered on the basis of whether their overall purpose was to project a position of inaccurate propaganda, would not rank very high. While Leni Riefenstahl's *Triumph of the Will* may be propagandistic, there are moments in it that are extraordinary as primary sources. Scenes of films from the Netherlands East Indies, albeit biased, are far less problematic than Nazi propaganda.

This method of search and analysis is, of course, painstaking; one has to dissect a film in very discrete segments and hunt for relevant sequences. To put it differently, it would be akin to salvaging sections of those films that have inadvertently become part of an existing canon of 'salvage ethnography', a genre that did not become identified as such till the mid-1950s.[24] Such an approach, however, should not be problematic with historians. Simply put, it is similar to the standard approach historians employ when dealing with texts: they often search for the piece that ought to be scrutinized closely, regardless of the larger context. Why would we not do the same with film? Once the compelling sections in the filmed material have been identified, we could apply to them the same rigour with which we would approach a textual source. Hayden White incisively addresses lingering doubts in the minds of historians who are sceptical about film as a source when he writes, 'Every written history is a product of processes of condensation, displacement, symbolization and qualification exactly like those used in the production of a filmed representation.'[25] The Dutch collection discussed in this book, when looked at collectively, is often swiftly dismissed as propaganda. It is the search of the sections within that enormous corpus that makes the task rewarding to the historian. That

---

[23] Robert A. Rosenstone, *History on Film/Film on History* (Harlow: Longman/Pearson, 2006); Marnie-Hughes Warrington, *History Goes to the Movies* (New York: Routledge, 2007); Philip Rosen, *Change Mummified: Cinema, Historicity, Theory* (Minneapolis: University of Minnesota Press, 2001).

[24] Salvage ethnography can be said to have dominated that period of early visual anthropological film started by Jean Rouch, continued by John Marshall and Timothy Ash.

[25] Hayden White, 'Historiography and Historiophoty', *American Historical Review* 93, 5 (1988): 1197–8.

is the work emphasized in this study. And, needless to say, the comprehension of what these films in their unedited totality reveal about the colonial mindset at the time is invaluable.

This book will, therefore, focus on the study of film in the Netherlands East Indies between 1912 and 1930 and meticulously analyze overlooked primary sources that add to our knowledge of the colonial encounter. In order to organize the staggering amount of Netherlands East Indies archival material, I attempt to merge the chronological developments in filmmaking along with the origin of the resources that led to the making of these films. I also attempt to classify the regions where films were being made during these time frames. But first, a few fundamental considerations: What is it about the Dutch collection that sets it apart from other colonial documentaries from a similar period? Does this archive particularly lend itself to a study of this nature?

What's Special about the 'Dutch Colonial' Non-fiction Collection?

The styles of films adopted by colonizing nations, not surprisingly, evolved within their own political, cultural and scientific orientations. Towards the end of the 19th century, right around the time when cinema was being born, Western anthropologists made a decided shift from the sedentary 'armchair' perspective to a more hands-on 'fieldwork' approach.[26] European chroniclers of culture and society were expected to traverse their colonies and return with evidence to corroborate the theories they presented. Hence, it is no surprise that the advent of the movie camera around this time was utilized in the pursuit of illustrating the lives and habits of natives, especially of 'primitive' groups around the world. The camera was a new tool to probe, measure and codify races. The impulse for producing films was often under the aegis of such scientific projects. But in time films also became tools for colonial expansion. They allowed us to see different forms of colonization—industrial, economic, cultural, religious—and the different roles film played across this historical period. Just as in the Netherlands East

[26] David E. Cooper engages in a lively discussion comparing *a priori* anthropology with anthropology conducted in the field. See David E. Cooper, 'Anthropology and Translation', *Proceedings of the Aristotelian Society* 86 (1985–86): 51–68.

Indies, filmmaking began in limited form in British, French and German colonies in the early 1900s and took the form of rough documentaries by the 1910s, the period when this study starts.

There are several key differences between the Dutch East Indies films discussed in this book and films produced by other colonial systems. First, although colonial production in the East Indies began in 1912, after filming had already begun in Africa (by German and French camera operators) and in the Philippines (the United States had an early presence there), we find a plethora of propagandistic films from the East Indies—significantly more than from any other colony. The Dutch colonial government and its corporate affiliates continued the funding of informational films about the colony for almost two full decades. A staggering number of films, although often with repetitive themes, were produced and provided wide visual coverage of life and activity in the colony. It is noteworthy that even though the makers of these films came from different backgrounds—the government, private production companies, independents and evangelists—there was a general uniformity in their styles over the two decades. The films in this collection are typically slow and deliberate. They often hover over close details of technical processes, cultural performances and depictions of nature. There is an unhurried, observant and stately feeling. There are title cards that explain the scenes, but they are not interruptive or word heavy. It is this generally less subjective approach and quotidian aesthetic that makes the collection stand out and also gives it a far greater ethnographic texture than many of the other existing colonial film production systems of that era.

An important factor contributing to this unhurried, less 'pushy' approach of societal depiction might be that the Netherlands had remained neutral during World War I. The Dutch government took the position that they did not have enemies they needed to vilify, or allies to persuade with propagandistic film. They not only avoided producing war-related films, they even lacked a robust national propaganda machine related to wartime efforts. One exception is Willy Mullens' 1917 *Holland Neutraal: Leger en Vlootfilm* [Holland Neutral: The Army and Fleet], a 2.5-hour film advocating armed Dutch neutrality. The film, though popular, was atypical. In general, no war movie industry came into being. In this manner, the Netherlands differed significantly from other European colonial powers. As Hendriks states:

> Because of its neutrality in World War I, the Netherlands was an exception to the 'universal practice'. It did not set up a propaganda service. The Netherlands held stubbornly to the idea that it had no enemies and therefore did not need to cast enemies negatively, as other foreign propaganda services during the war years had done with great zeal.[27]

Herein lies an interesting paradox. Martin Loiperdinger has persuasively made the case that it was Britain's push to make compelling propaganda during its war effort that led to the first documentaries.[28] If we are to consider the unpleasant notion that the necessity to create compelling works of propaganda arose out of World War I, and that those films could be considered 'documentary', is it possible that the Dutch had a handicap then, having no demonstrable need to make wartime films? I am of the opinion that they did. And yet, herein lies the contradiction: they were better ethnographers for that very reason. My conjecture is based on the observation that the push to make documentaries—that restructuring or 'cooking' of short, reel-based *actualités*, in order to create a more dramatized narrative that would have wider appeal—is precisely what took away from the ethnographic strength of American-influenced non-fiction films in the 1920s.

The Colonial Institute's (Vereeniging Koloniaal Institute's) early austerity with its simple instructions to not make 'popular' films had an untampered authenticity. Even though Dutch cameramen did not capture a comprehensive image of their colony, and there were huge omissions in their depictions of society, class and politics, their films were rarely embellished or sensationalized. Given the political reach of the British Empire combined with a strong American influence, an Anglophone preference was clearly visible in informational and educational constituencies internationally. The Dutch were a relatively limited colonial power; the style and reach of English-language films predominated internationally. By the 1930s, John Grierson's championing of what he publicized as 'documentary' became the standard by which the

---

[27] Hendriks, 'Een voorbeeldige kolonie', p. 36.

[28] Martin Loiperdinger, 'World War I Propaganda Films and the Birth of the Documentary', in *Uncharted Territory: Essays in Early Nonfiction Film*, ed. Daan Hertogs and Nico de Klerk (Amsterdam: Stichting Nederlands Filmmuseum, 1997), p. 26.

quality of non-fiction came to be judged; the publicity of *Nanook of the North* contributed to this end. In that environment, the films of Dutch camera operators were not evaluated as being particularly important or 'with the times'. They tended to be slower, had non-complicated or absent plots, and were too quotidian for the excitement that was sought from documentaries. The legacy of this oversight lingered throughout the 20th century. This might also explain the lacunae in the study of this material, and pre-Grierson non-fiction in general. Simply put, the films were less scintillating and film historians ignored them. And yet, in their ordinariness they managed to often capture moments and sequences that were far more authentic or pro-filmic in content and temporality.

The second difference between the Dutch East Indies films discussed in this book and films produced by other colonial systems is there were no colonial fiction films produced in the East Indies during this period. Moviegoers in Europe did not see any Dutch-produced melodrama or tales of colonial romance-adventure during the 1910s and 1920s. Surprisingly, there were two very famous novels—*Het Leven in Nederlandsch Indie* [Life in the Netherlands East Indies] (1900) and *De stille kracht* [The Hidden Force] (1900)—in wide circulation during this period, but they were not adapted for screen until much later. Although there were some smaller films in the late 1920s, it was not until as late as the mid-1930s that larger productions began.[29] In the years to come this would change, and fiction films made in the East Indies would start to be seen in theatres both in the Netherlands and in the colony. The lack of early large-scale cinema with actors and dramatic stories contrasts strongly with the French and British filming activities during the same period—France and Britain had switched to rather sophisticated feature film production by the 1920s, drawing interest and investments from an extended international finance community.[30] The focus in the East Indies remained on non-fiction propaganda.

---

[29] Karl Heider, *Indonesian Cinema* (Honolulu: University of Hawai'i Press, 1991), p. 15.

[30] The first major Indonesian-language motion picture to make a healthy profit was *Terrang Boelan* [Bright Moon] in 1937, created by the team that had made *Pareh* [Rice] in 1936. As the Indonesian language was accessible to the wider Malay-speaking population, the former film's popularity sparked the start of the Malay-language film industry. See Timothy P. Barnard, 'Film *Melayu*: Nationalism, Modernity and Film in a Pre-World War Two Malay Magazine', *Journal of Southeast Asian Studies* 41, 1 (2010): 57.

Third, the 'adventurer' genre that preoccupied much of the colonial cinematic effort by the French in Africa was limited in the East Indies. While colonial propaganda documentary petered out in both French Indochina and the French colonies in Africa, two other genres appeared in Africa: 'explorer' films and large-budget fiction feature films. Both of these styles addressed colonialism obliquely. These films exploited a Western preoccupation with the 'primitive' when it came to African lives rather than Asian. Widely circulated, *La Croisiere Noire* [Black Journey] was a record of Citroen engineer Georges-Marie Haardt's journeys across Africa in specialized vehicles. A stunning public relations coup, the films actually revealed the limitations of technology in rough African terrain (the team went from Algeria all the way across the Sahara to the Indian Ocean)—we see hundreds of African porters dragging the vehicles through rivers and swamps. By the film's end, after a series of harrowing travel adventures, a huge assortment of art objects is delivered to the Trocadero Museum of Ethnography in Paris. This type of cinematic construction was virtually absent in the East Indies. Once again the focus remained on slower, undramatic non-fiction films.

Though *Flores Film* and its accompanying *Bali-Floti*, made by the Societas Verbi Divini (SVD) Catholic priest Simon Buis and his collaborators, did have some elements of travel and discovery, they were minor. Aspects of the explorer style are seen also in Protestant evangelical films made in the eastern islands, such as Celebes, Sumba and Papua, by I.A. Ochse. It is in these narratives of missionary journeys that we find some semblance of the heroic traveller who braves odds to accomplish his goal of reaching a distant people. In Africa the stories were often about physical feats of endurance and overcoming the terrain and encounters with large animals. In the East Indies they were about travelling through uncharted territories to reach the less fortunate and help them with an introduction to a modern, Christian life. Adventure for its own sake was rare—save one long sequence of hunting a Komodo dragon in *Flores Film*; it was not a priority in the East Indies collection. Machismo and conquest of terrain was muted in Dutch colonial films.

Finally, some of the Dutch colonial filmmakers may have actually been somewhat anti-propagandistic in their filming, uncovering aspects of colonial rule that did not flatter the Dutch government. This makes for unique archival documentation in the context of the colonial encounter. Dutch films were generally rigorous in their factual construction and tended not to have elaborate narrative plots. Answering a call driven by the Ethical Policy set into motion in 1901, in order to document the efforts towards 'the elevation of the people', the Colonial Institute in Amsterdam saw film as a useful way of providing both evidence of the state of the colony, as well as a means to persuade civilians in the Netherlands to take pride in developing the East Indies. While this is not unlike the contents of the several propagandistic films both French and German filmmakers made in response to their directive of the 'civilizing mission', considering the level of detail in the Dutch material, one is clearly exposed to a far more descriptive, intimate and seamy side of colonialism. The Dutch cinematic simulacrum of the colony, often motivated by either a liberal-political or a paternal-evangelistic outlook, resulted in the need to be somewhat introspective and expository. The scenes are often meant to generate sympathy as much as they are meant to show progress. And possibly, simply by virtue of the sheer high volume of Dutch films, we are invariably exposed to a more detailed impression of native life. Apart from the visceral reality of seeing colonialism, there are moments of tremendous moral and ethical lucidness of the injustice of these larger systems that is difficult to experience otherwise. In the ensuing study I shall rehabilitate unscrutinized footage from this vast collection now available to us.

Unlike colonial film productions in other parts of the world that were often not organized under any cohesive oversight, there was a reasonably robust and integrated production system in the Dutch East Indies. After the first films were commissioned by the Colonial Institute in 1912, every few years a new cameraman would film in the archipelago and send back the material for screenings in order to raise awareness about issues in the colony. Specialists would curate films from different sources and organize screenings. Newspapers frequently printed reviews of the films and the reaction of audiences. The productions were closely followed and very often accessed by institutions or film societies as part of lectures. The commercial companies Polygoon, Haarlem and Nederlands-Indische Filmmaatschappij (NIFM) collaborated closely with the Colonial Institute and relied on a common system of outreach and dissemination. Though the process was labour intensive, it was ultimately possible for archivists to bring together the surviving material in a common repository. This explains why there is a well-maintained archive of the material in the two institutions (Eye Filmmuseum and Beeld en Geluid) responsible for their stewardship. Researchers whose scholarship involves studying colonial filmmaking in other countries often have to scour numerous archives with varying rates of success.[31] One distinct feature of the Dutch East Indies archives is that it is remarkably easy for a researcher to access it. Yet, there has been little investigation of this material. Despite the increasing availability of such material, there are inherent problems, both cultural and epistemological, when considering archival films and their connections to colonial history—especially when historians attempt to connect the dots many decades later. This book is about that endeavour.

As this book is intended for a readership interested in Asian history as well as cinema studies, it is important to clarify the terminology used by film historians, documentarians and archivists when discussing film. Accordingly, chapter 1 eases us into the many identifiers used in cinematic classification—*actualités*, documentary, non-fiction, ethnographic, propaganda—and considers the vantage points through which the Dutch East Indies archives and other archives can be sourced for historical research.

---

[31] Donald Wilson comments that France's National Center for Cinematography does have several prints from Indochina and its small staff update a library in Bois d'Arcy, France. But in his experience, 'In order to view films at CNC [French National Centre for Cinematography], a long administrative process is necessary to obtain permission and assistance.' Very few of the colonial-era films there have been restored, and most are not in viewing condition. Donald Dean Wilson Jr., 'Colonial Việt Nam on Film: 1896 to 1926' (PhD dissertation, City University of New York, 2007), p. 15.

CHAPTER 1

Situating Early Non-fiction Film in Colonial Studies

> I have hundreds of all kinds of books: Photo albums, touristic books, novels, essays, political and historical books. I read a lot. But almost each of the two thousand documentary (propagandistic) films lets us see what no book evokes. This is the unique force of film, of cinema.
>
> – Vincent Monnikendam, director, *Mother Dao* (1995)[1]

Cinema is a relatively new medium. This might explain why, despite protestations by a small group of academics, considering film as a primary source is not an approach most historians are comfortable with. Those who do study the history of film, however, have long been exploring the evolution of cinema and the genesis of its various genres since it began in the late 1800s. I am making a distinction here between historians—scholars primarily within the academic field of history, typically involved in research at history departments—and film historians, those involved in the discipline usually called film studies. This chapter will compare how both groups have approached the connections between film and history, in order to help us understand how they impact our investigation of the Dutch propaganda films mentioned in the Introduction. I will also classify and demarcate the various types of film and consider where they lie in our investigation of historical source materials suitable for study of the late-colonial era.

[1] Vincent Monnikendam, personal email communication, 17 Dec. 2013.

As in any discipline, film studies scholars write reviews, academic articles and monographs on a variety of current issues in cinema as well as on its complex, fascinating history. Textbooks on film history—fiction and non-fiction—are required reading for many college-level courses in film studies. But if historians, the group that typically study the past based on text, were to turn to those expert historians of film for information on early colonial cinema, they would find limited reference to this material. The historiography of colonial cinema, a substantial global undertaking in the early 20th century, has come to be recognized as an area of study only in recent decades. While there have been some notable publications since the 1980s, they are still few and far between.[2] In fact, some of the most revered authorities on film history have mostly avoided discussing non-fiction film, colonial or otherwise, produced before the 1920s.[3] Film scholar Tom Gunning deplores, 'After a ceremonial nod to the Lumière brothers, the enormously rich period of

[2] For a selection of writings on colonial cinema, see: Pamela Pattynama, *Bitterzoet Indie: Herinneringen en nostalgie in Literatuur, Foto's en Film* (Amsterdam: Prometheus, Bert Bakker, 2014); Luc Vint, *Kongo made in Belgium: Beeld van een kolonie in film en Propaganda* (Leuven: Kritak, 1984); Nick Deocampo, *Cine: Spanish Influences on Early Cinema in the Philippines* (Manila: National Commission for Culture and the Arts, 2003); Clodualdo Del Mundo, *Native Resistance: Philippine Cinema and Colonialism, 1898–1941* (Manila: De La Salle University Press, 1991); Peter Bloom, *French Colonial Documentary: Mythologies of Humanitarianism* (Minneapolis: University of Minnesota Press, 2008); Janekke van V. Dijk, Jaap de Jonge and Nico de Klerk, *J.C. Lamster, an Early Dutch Filmmaker in the Netherlands East Indies* (Amsterdam: KIT Publishers, 2010); Panivong Norindr, *Phantasmic Indochina* (Durham: Duke University Press, 1996).

[3] It must be mentioned here that there have been some developments in this subfield since the 1990s. In addition to Gunning, the following have contributed to lively scholarship about this era of non-fiction filmmaking: Charles Musser, *The Emergence of Cinema: The American Screen to 1907*, Vol. 1 (Berkeley: University of California Press, 1994); Roland Cosandey and François Albéra, *Cinéma sans frontières: 1896–1918* (Lausanne: Payot Lausanne, 1995); Stephen Bottomore, *The* Titanic *and Silent Cinema* (Hastings: Projection Box, 2000). Important symposiums such as 'Cinema Turns 100' in New York in 1994 and the Amsterdam Workshop the same year at the Nederlands Filmmuseum focused on this period and produced anthologies of articles. But the publications of these authors remain outside the realm of popular textbooks; Erik Barnouw and Karl Heider still dominate the college syllabus. In Gunning's own words, 'But even with these contributions, I believe these authors would agree that nonfiction filmmaking remains not only less thoroughly studied than early fiction filmmaking, but also less theorized' (Gunning 1997).

nonfiction filmmaking before Flaherty basically remains undiscussed, as if shrouded by a collective amnesia.'[4] The Lumière brothers began their pioneering film experiments in the late 19th century, and Robert Flaherty produced *Nanook of the North* in 1922. This constitutes a lacuna of almost three decades in the history of cinema. The late film historian Erik Barnouw perpetuated this problem with a mere passing reference to 'colonial films' in his widely read *Documentary: A History of the Non-fiction Film*: 'The leading film-producing countries of this period were nations with colonial empires. Not surprisingly, their work reflected the attitudes that made up the colonial rationale.... Most "native" shots probably gave western audiences a reassuring feeling about the colonial system.'[5]

While these films would include some of the early efforts of Dutch filmmakers in the East Indies, Barnouw does not mention them. This is especially problematic because most university students wishing to read about early non-fiction cinema would very likely be assigned this book. The title of Barnouw's monograph, too, might be a source of categorical confusion.

'Non-fiction' was not a term synonymous with 'documentary' during the 1910s and 1920s. In fact, it truly came into its own only in the 1990s. Directors made films; some had actors in them, others did not. The term 'documentary', found in some early catalogues of the French film-producing and -distributing company Pathé, was widely publicized by the filmmaker and critic Grierson as late as 1926, in reference to Flaherty's second film, *Moana*.[6] It was not intended to describe all non-fiction activity. The term was devised to distinguish it

---

[4] Tom Gunning, 'Before Documentary: Early Nonfiction Films and the "View" Aesthetic', in *Uncharted Territory: Essays in Early Nonfiction Film*, ed. Daan Hertogs and Nico de Klerk (Amsterdam: Stichting Nederlands Filmmuseum, 1997), p. 12.

[5] Erik Barnouw, *Documentary: A History of the Non-fiction Film* (Oxford: Oxford University Press, 1983), p. 23.

[6] Film scholar Nico de Klerk has located use of the phrase '*scène documentaire*' in Francophone regions of Pathé film distribution. Two Belgian handbills of 1911 specify LES FRONTIÈRES DU THIBET and LES SPORTS D'HIVER À CHAMONIX as '*film documentaire de la Société Éclipse*' and '*Film documentaire des Etablissments Gaumont*', respectively. See Nico de Klerk, 'Sand Proft pour Eux: Dierenopnamen in vroege commerciële cinema, 1891–1911', *Tijdschrift voor Mediageschiedenis* 12, 2 (2009): 83–104.

from films made from 'natural material' such as newsreel and scientific or educational materials. Today, we classify these films collectively as non-fiction—productions that are not overtly fictionalized accounts of people's lives, or produced with actors as intermediaries.

The demarcation between fiction and non-fiction was certainly prevalent during the 1910s. Thus, it is no surprise that J.C. Lamster, the first filmmaker sent to the Dutch East Indies, had explicit orders to refrain from any filming that was arranged or manipulated. Although he did on occasion stage events in order to effectively convey some exemplariness, the scenes were never fabricated. In contrast, some of the materials Catholic missionaries filmed in eastern Indonesia in the late 1920s were staged. They were composed based on actual events, but there was a great deal of 'scene setting', an approach that will be explored further. Regardless, this would not disqualify them as documentaries per the practices of the time. By his own account, Flaherty staged several scenes in the famous *Nanook of the North* and later reordered the chronology of the footage to create a cohesive and compelling narrative structure.

Several early Dutch colonial films were produced under unusually difficult conditions, often far from laboratories and studios that could have provided technical support during the filming. We might perhaps do better to compare them with films that were made in areas removed from production studios and were conceived around a need to tell a story of the racial 'other' with minimal scripting and acting. Films of this category, typically made in the developing world, were later classified as 'ethnographic'. Arguably some of the early East Indies films might qualify as ethnographic as they were invested in bringing to their mostly Western audiences the habits and cultures of people that such audiences would otherwise never see. While the very term 'ethnographic' has been rigorously debated, it is generally accepted that any non-fiction film having some amount of anthropological content could be considered as having ethnographic value.

Karl Heider, a foundational figure in the study of ethnographic film and a specialist on Indonesia, surprisingly does not mention the Dutch East Indies collection in his canonical academic textbook *Ethnographic Film*, revised in 2006.[7] In his 1991 book *Indonesian Cinema*, Heider

[7] Karl Heider, *Ethnographic Film* (Austin: University of Texas Press, 1976, 2006).

writes rather bewilderingly, 'Although documentary films *apparently* [emphasis added] were being made in the Dutch East Indies from the turn of the century, the local production of fictional feature films came relatively late.'[8] Heider was correct, but the statement reflects a refusal on his part to locate, establish and view those early documentary films. Heider, like most film historians, predictably marks Flaherty's *Nanook of the North* (1922) as a major turning point for both ethnographic film and documentary cinema. In *Ethnographic Film* he traces several films that operated within that tradition, stating that 'few other films ... that were made before 1922 may be mentioned in passing'.[9] He mentions the Hamburg South Sea expedition of 1908–10 that produced a 20-minute film on dancing, Gaston Melies' 'documentary romances' in Tahiti and New Zealand of 1912, and a 1914 film by Edward Curtis about the Kwakuitl Indians called *In the Land of the Headhunters.* Heider also acknowledges the works of Martin and Osa Johnson, the glamorous adventuring American couple who filmed in several locations around the world, including the Solomon Islands, Malayan Borneo and various destinations in Africa starting in 1918. While the anthropological value of early colonial films in the East Indies can be debated (as can that of the sensational and often caricature-like Johnson films), it is peculiar that these films do not even get a mention in a fairly recent write-up of early ethnographic efforts. Like Barnouw, Heider too has omitted much of early non-fiction, notably colonial non-fiction.

Why, we may wonder, has this compelling footage from the Dutch East Indies been completely ignored by 'documentary' historians or those studying ethnographic records? In none of the broad studies of Indonesian cinema does a single one of the numerous productions from 1912 onwards find mention. Was it because the films were typically propagandistic in nature, having been produced by the colonial government? Or perhaps because, at times, these were amateur films made by individuals who had few ties with the larger industry? De Klerk in his essay 'Dark Treasures' writes pointedly about this problem:

> Typically, the colonial era, presented as something alien, receives a dismissive treatment in just a couple of pages. Reception and exhibition—

---

8 Heider, *Indonesian Cinema* (Honolulu: University of Hawai'i Press, 1991), p. 15.

9 Heider, *Ethnographic Film*, p. 18.

> which would imply the screening of foreign films, too—are only beginning to be considered. But location hardly is (which is important in this context, as the films shot by Dutch crews contain the oldest extant footage of the Indonesian archipelago).[10]

De Klerk suggests two primary reasons for this oversight and lack of exposure. First, these films were, until recently, not readily available for film historians to study, especially scholars from Indonesia, as they were stored in various locations in the Netherlands and were difficult to access. Second, there was perhaps a sense of guilt associated with such colonial projects. A filmic expression of the colonial past can swiftly be dismissed as biased, less authentic and politically problematic. A third, far more pervasive, issue faced by scholars worldwide in attempting to delve into this era of non-fiction is the still-lingering notion that such films do not have much value in and of themselves—they are useful only in how they may situate fiction film of that era. In his essay 'An Archival View', Paolo Cherchi Usai writes with regret:

> Every now and then we have heard that, oh yes, non-fiction films are worth looking at as well. Why? Because, it is argued, their expositional strategies do often contain stylistic devices and technical choices that were bound to become standard practice in fictional films. In these terms, non-fictional films [*sic*] still doesn't have a value in and of itself; its role in the evolution of fiction films is perceived as some sort of justification for its potential interest.[11]

What, then, are the considerations of situating these non-fiction propagandistic films within academic discourse, now that we have access to them for historical scrutiny? Do they merit a place in the search for primary sources or does an overwhelming sense of bias still remove them from discussion? To answer these questions, we first need to cover some elementary aspects of film, its general categories, and establish what might validate films as historical sources. While this exercise will be mostly pedagogic, it is crucial to our understanding of the precise types of material which we will be immersing ourselves in in the following

[10] De Klerk, 'Dark Treasures', p. 437.

[11] Paolo Cherchi Usai, 'An Archival View', in *Film and the First World War*, ed. Karel Dibbets and Bert Hogenkamp (Amsterdam: University of Amsterdam Press, 1995), p. 242.

chapters. It will also perhaps help us to determine why the Dutch East Indies colonial film archive has remained in relative academic obscurity.

Categorizing Film, Scrutinizing Footage

Film, as we know well, in its most elemental unit is composed of still frames, individual images akin to still photographs. And a continuous succession of these images moving forward in time make up a shot. Shots are edited together to create sequences. The term 'footage' refers to a length of film. All films thus are some amalgamation of footage. Footage may refer to scenes in completed films, unedited material, or outtakes of a film—the shots that fall on the editing room floor. These extra shots may or may not be archived. The ratio of the amount of pre-edited or 'raw' footage to the length of the completed film tends to be significantly higher in a documentary film than in narrative films. Nowadays, with the advent of portable digital technology, it is not unusual for this ratio to be as high as 1:100 or even more. This trend was observed even in films dating back to the 1910s and 1920s but not with as high a differential. It is important to mention this aspect of unused footage because some of the archival footage discussed later in this book is from such sources.

The boundaries of non-fiction and fiction film can, of course, be blurred. There are fiction films set in original locations, and thus some of the scenes may have actually occurred, e.g., the inclusion of moments filmed at an actual riot. Similarly, documentary films very often have a 'doctored' aspect to them—the subjects in the film could be asked to express themselves in a certain way to make the point the filmmakers are trying to put across. Currently, these lines between fiction and non-fiction are often indistinguishable. The technology and artistic skills with which these genres can fluidly blend into each other are remarkable and perhaps somewhat worrying for a historian looking for visual 'evidence'. The evolution to these complex hybrid forms occurred quite swiftly.

There was in the earliest days of cinema, the *actualités*, or composites of single shots of film. A scene was recorded for as long as the hand-cranked camera could run without being depleted of raw stock. At that time this would be for less than a minute. Scenes were then edited together with some thematic coherence. *Actualités* were primarily descriptive in nature. They were often edited as travelogue films—moving visual postcards of distant places. At times they showed us the process of something being manufactured or crafted. These *actualités* evolved into what we define as the 'documentary'. Gunning considers this evolution of the *actualité* to have occurred when filmmakers 'embedded its images in a larger argument and used those images as evidence to substantiate or intensify its discourse'.[12] In Grierson's simple terms, documentaries were 'the creative treatment of actuality'.[13]

The propaganda film, the material we are primarily concerned with in this study, originated in the middle of this evolution from *actualités* to documentary. It was the link between the two. However, this very transformation of early non-fiction film—from the Lumière productions at the turn of the 20th century to Flaherty's documentary films—is generally overlooked by film historians. *Actualités*, early travelogues and the propaganda film, all genres explored in this study, do not feature much in textbooks. The problems created by the long absence of these early films in academic discourse should not be underestimated—for one thing, the absence has made a study such as this one far more difficult to establish. Gunning has identified this as a gaping hole in film history:

> The most frequently given reason for this neglect, the belief that this early material remained too raw, too close to reality and bereft of artistic and conceptual shaping (compared to the more 'cooked' documentary), does not take us very far.... The voyeurism implicit in the tourist, the colonialist, the filmmaker and the spectator is laid bare in these films, without the naturalization of dramatic structure or political argument.[14]

At the time of this research, an unusual rehabilitation of this rather 'raw' tradition that attempts a 'purer' and less tempered recording of places and society was being conducted by the Dutch academic organization Koninklijk Instituut voor Taal-, Land- en Volkenkunde (KITLV; Royal Netherlands Institute of Southeast Asian and Caribbean Studies). In 2003, in collaboration with Indonesian filmmakers and scholars, KITLV began its 'Recording the Future' long-term audiovisual research

[12] Gunning, 'Before Documentary', p. 21.
[13] Paul Rotha, *Documentary Film* (New York: Hastings House, 1952), p. 70.
[14] Gunning, 'Before Documentary', p. 24.

project in Indonesia. One of its key methodologies is to film from a fixed spot in several predetermined locations over time:

> The procedures for filming these locations are bound to strict rules, in order to facilitate comparisons over time. In each place we chose two locations, or 'fixed points'—a crossroads, a street, a square, or a market, in short: public spaces—where we make shootings from 5.30–6.00 in the morning (at sunrise), 8.00–8.30, 11.30–11.00 [*sic*], 13.00–13.30, 15.30–16.00, 17.30–18.00 (sunset); 20.00–20.30 and 22.30–23.00.[15]

In addition to fixed locations, filming is also done from atop a moving vehicle as it passes through selected landscapes. A third method is to conduct interviews while the filmmakers travel across a pre-charted area for three to four hours without stopping the camera. The composite of these three styles provides the researchers with their objective of a longitudinal study of society and its changes. This pre-documentary spirit, harking back to the earliest and elemental methods of filming the world, is directly referenced in the project's operating manifesto: 'Looking at our recordings made from a fixed position; it seems at first sight as if our project follows the very first experiments of pioneer film makers like the Lumière brothers.'[16] Indeed, the attempt to return to a sort of pre-fictive, pre-manipulated era of cinematic exercise seems to be the *raison d'être* of the project. It appears to be a contemporary, technologically driven version of that original *actualité* in its refusal to turn into or abet the making of a more 'cooked' documentary motivated by the dramatic structure of a political argument.

What is most relevant for this book is the investigation of whether any, or all, of these myriad styles, and their interpolated expressions, can be legitimate primary sources for historians. Unlike Barnouw, who championed the documentary form exclusively, I will consider *actualités*, propaganda, documentary—and all hybrids, such as the academic project described above—as subsets of non-fiction film. While we are concerned almost entirely with non-fiction in this study, it would be useful

[15] Henk Schulte Nordholt and Fridus Steijlen, 'Don't Forget to Remember Me: An Audiovisual Archive of Everyday Life in Indonesia in the 21st Century', *Indonesia Studies Working Papers* 1 (2007): 11.
[16] Ibid., p. 7.

as an exercise in contrasts to situate that other behemoth category of cinema as we try to understand existing practices of studying history through film: fiction.

The Fiction of History

Most of the attention on using film as a source to study history is related to fiction film. Robert A. Rosenstone's *Visions of the Past: The Challenge of Film to Our Idea of History* (1995) and Marnie-Hughes Warrington's *History Goes to the Movies* (2007) substantially engage with this persuasion. Both authors delve deeply into the social phenomenon of history as it exists in society through cinematic retelling. They contend that films tell us as much about the society and era in which they were made as they do about the stories and issues they attempt to recreate. Fiction films are more easily accessible. Unsurprisingly, historians teaching at different levels urge students to look at movies in order to gain a better understanding of the society they depict.[17] It is not, for example, uncommon for a high school instructor to assign students a viewing of Richard Attenborough's *Gandhi* (1982).[18] Most university students of Middle Eastern politics have watched Gillo Pontecorvo's *The Battle of Algiers* (1966).[19] Indeed, the complexities of historical events, distilled for us in dramatic scenes through persuasive acting, are often the images with which we associate key events from the past. Fiction films can illustrate key moments in history, provided the information in them

[17] Robert A. Rosenstone, *Visions of the Past: The Challenge of Film to Our Idea of History* (Cambridge: Harvard University Press, 1995); Warrington, *History Goes to the Movies*.

[18] A quick search finds the world history curriculum for tenth graders at the Co-operative Arts and Humanities High School in New Haven, Connecticut, utilizing the film. Yale-New Haven Teachers Institute, 'Mohandas Gandhi: The Art of Nonviolence', Unit 98.03.05, http://www.yale.edu/ynhti/curriculum/units/1998/3/98.03.05.x.html, accessed 4 Jan. 2021.

[19] 'America and Middle Eastern Wars' instructed by Juan Cole at the University of Michigan (2007) and 'Cities of the Middle East' offered by Sofian Merabet at the University of Texas at Austin (2011) are examples of classroom use of the film. The introductory undergraduate course on Southeast Asian history at the National University of Singapore screens the French production *Indochine*, directed by Regis Wargnier.

is corroborated to be accurate. Accordingly, many makers of epic films denoting historical figures often advertise their detailed research efforts.

The 2001 Thai production of *Suriyothai* serves as an example. The film is an epic, big-budget, purportedly historical period film based on the legend of a supposed 16th-century queen turned warrior. It was publicized widely that seven years were spent in researching the script for historical accuracy. *Suriyothai*, being lavishly produced, has a number of scenes from the Thai royal past: baroque palaces, ceremonies, battles—the entire gamut of episodes expected from a period film about royal honour and its excesses. In an essay about the film, Thai scholar Amporn Jirattikorn points out that 'a number of Thai historical chronicles, including the stories of great leaders and heroic wars, were written or rewritten during the reign of King Rama IV (1851–1868) as part of a strategy of nation building'.[20] Citing the few inconclusive references to Suriyothai in the archives, Jirattikorn dismisses any historical credibility to this myth. The thrust of her article, however, is not to challenge or disprove the existence of Suriyothai. Rather, she investigates why the film *Suriyothai* was produced in 2001 and the reasons behind its popularity. Simply put, the article is a historical analysis of the making of *Suriyothai* the film, not of Suriyothai the mythical queen. In this sense, *Suriyothai* provides Jirattikorn with a primary source, as her interest lies in the very making of the film. But is it a historical source for those interested in the period of Thai history depicted in this film? Can we learn anything about life in the kingdom of Ayutthaya?

The film may have realistic portrayals of 16th-century Thai life. For example, there is an important scene of elephants being trapped. Research quickly reveals several primary sources from the 17th, 18th and 19th centuries describing the ceremony and details around such an event.[21] The makers of *Suriyothai* plausibly read these, or similar, accounts as

[20] Amporn Jirattikorn, 'Suriyothai: Hybridizing Thai National Identity through Film', *Inter-Asia Cultural Studies* 4, 2 (2003): 300.

[21] Eric Cohen, *Explorations in Thai Tourism: Collected Case Studies* (Bingley: Emerald Group Publishing, 2008), p. 147: 'The round-ups, though they served a "real" purpose, were also a major spectacle during the Ayutthaya period, the classic age of Siamese history (1351–1767), and even beyond it.' Cohen goes on to quote historians David K. Wyatt and William Warren and French Jesuit priest Abbe de Choise, in their descriptions of the detail and ceremony around these popular events.

they designed the re-enactment, which seems to fit very well with other textual primary source descriptions. Thus, while the reconstructed scene above cannot be a primary source about the trapping of elephants in the court of Ayutthaya, it can hold up to historical scrutiny as a plausible representation of the event as corroborated by other primary sources; it could be used as a secondary source. This example is key in understanding a distinction that I draw between illustration and evidence, between fiction film as a secondary source and non-fiction as a possible primary source.

Not all historians are, however, keen on demarcating a primary/non-primary divide in their assessment of fictional historical films. They have, on occasion, argued for their evidentiary inclusion. Historian Syed Muhd Khairudin Aljunied focuses on the films of the famous Malay actor P. Ramlee to make a case for 'film as a source of social history'.[22] Arguing that P. Ramlee's productions, particularly the 1961 film *Seniman Bujang Lapok*, contain a wealth of materials about Malay customs and history, Aljunied observes, 'In their pursuit of linear narratives written from vantage points of a selected few, such genre of historians have often overlooked alternative sources, which could give an illuminating insight into the social history of the Malays.' Aljunied stresses that one should look at 'the background of the creator or producer of such films' when trying to 'justify it as a useful historical source'. Aljunied's research indicates that P. Ramlee was 'indirectly portraying to his audiences the realities of life in which he was an organic part'. Classifying such a genre of films as 'realistic films', Aljunied argues that P. Ramlee's commitment to bring to screen the realities of his personal life is evident in the themes that he chooses to discuss—poverty, Malayan modernity, the Japanese occupation, and situating Islam within Malay society of that period.

There are two issues I raise with this method of locating historical merit in fiction films. First, I do not agree with the conjecture that when the social background of an artist appears to mirror the content of his or her artistic expression, it necessarily indicates historical authenticity. Artists, for a myriad of reasons, may choose to distort society.

[22] Syed Muhd Khairudin Aljunied, 'Films as Social History: P. Ramlee's "Seniman Bujang Lapok" and Malays in Singapore (1950s–60s)', *Heritage Journal* 2, 1 (2005): 1–21.

They could well imbue their creations with idealized notions and produce inaccurate depictions. These recreations could be compelling as stories (and perhaps sell tickets), but they may not be historically accurate. Second, Aljunied's use of the term 'alternative source' to describe P. Ramlee's films suggests that these films are used in lieu of documentation on the subject via other sources and indicates that the veracity of these films perhaps cannot be corroborated by other sources. For a fiction film to be valid as a historical illustration, its contents ought to be verifiable by other primary sources. An artistic recreation of society in and of itself cannot stand the test of being historically plausible. To call certain productions 'realist fiction', based on the notion that their creator may have tried to reproduce the realities of their own lives, while somewhat compelling, is not sufficient to give the films the status of being 'historical' films.

My criticism of Aljunied's approach notwithstanding, there is always the possibility that P. Ramlee's films do indeed have a high degree of historical accuracy. We can determine this only by further research of sources other than the films themselves, to lend the latter some authenticity. Should such evidence come to light, these films could indeed be viewed as historically illustrative. The paradox here is that for a fiction film to be relevant to historians, there need to be sources outside of the film to confirm its veracity. The lack of corroborable archival material only diminishes the historical value of a fiction film. By the conclusion of his article, however, Aljunied seems to have modified his initial reasoning. He writes:

> Films can be a useful addition alongside other sources of social history such as oral records, memoirs, newspapers, coroner's records and governmental reports. The essential task of a historian (and perhaps anthropologists as well as sociologists) is thus to tease out persuasive evidences [*sic*] from such films, cross-examining it with other sources and providing rational interpretations of varied aspects of Malay society in a given period.[23]

Indeed, should P. Ramlee's films stand up to the rigours of such cross-examination, and not the mere premise that he produced realistic films

[23] Ibid., p. 16.

because of his life's experiences, they should be used in classrooms to study that era of Malayan history. This is also the basic methodology that could be used while studying films that present themselves as primary sources. Engaging as fiction may be, primary sources remain the bedrock of any historian's methodology of analysis and unpacking. While I join a devoted group of academics clamouring for the inclusion of different genres of film in the study of history, in this book I limit my agenda to the confines of non-fiction film.

Non-fiction Film as Primary Source

Michael Galgano, in *Doing History: Research and Writing in the Digital Age* (2007), defines a primary source as 'Any record contemporary to an event or time period. Primary sources may be written, oral, visual, or physical.'[24] The American Library Association adds an extended temporal caveat: 'Original records created at the time historical events occurred or well after events in the form of memoirs and oral histories.'[25] While definitions found in other publications vary slightly in their listing of criteria that qualify as primary, they concur on the notion of 'original records' being a basic criterion for a primary source. Can we, however, consider all portions of non-fiction films as being original records? To be fair, it has almost never been claimed by any film historian that a documentary film showed the truth. Even Grierson, who so championed Flaherty, coined that clever phrase, 'a creative treatment of actuality'. Can we evoke a methodology to unpack those layers of artifice and treatment to try to find dynamic material for historians? For the purposes of this exercise it is necessary to digress momentarily from the silent era in order to create a more relatable and inclusive discussion.

In a standard television documentary, there are often un-staged portions of some aspects of real life unfolding in front of the camera that are verbally described. The narrating track is typically rehearsed and recorded in a studio. Most significantly, the narration is often not in the first person, creating a blurred credit of authorship. It is likely that

---

[24] Michael J. Galgano, *Doing History: Research and Writing in the Digital Age* (Stamford: Cengage Learning, 2007), p. 57.

[25] American Library Association, 'Primary Sources on the Web: Finding, Evaluating, Using', http://www.ala.org/rusa/sections/history/resources/pubs/usingprimarysources, accessed 11 Nov. 2020.

Figure 1. Still from *Indonesian War of Independence 1945–1949*[26]

a voice-over artist performs the lines based on someone else's script—actor Peter Coyote narrating Ken Burns' *The Vietnam War*, a multi-part documentary on Netflix, is an example. In such instances, the intent, conditions of recording, and authorship of narration are often not evident to us, making it difficult to categorize the source as an original record, a memoir or oral history. Now let us consider another style of documentary film, which is typically seen on television in a reportage-style programme, where a subject answers questions asked by an interviewer. The transcripts of such interviews would certainly constitute primary sources as they are individual accounts of an episode—even if created after the event. The people are usually identified, and the reasons for their narratives are often straightforward. All narratives or memoirs, be they written in a diary format or filmed as interviews, can, of course, be investigated further for veracity and accuracy. But generally speaking, this is the sort of material that is acceptable as a primary source.

[26] *Indonesian War of Independence 1945–1949*, *YouTube*, https://www.youtube.com/watch?v=8U2QImMSzwE, accessed 11 Nov. 2020.

Another type of primary source is newsreel footage. Typically filmed live to capture current affairs, and screened in movie theatres soon after, newsreels were eventually replaced in the 1970s by television broadcasts. But they are often reused, even decades after the fact. The still in Figure 1 is from a newsreel filmed in 1949, the last year of Dutch rule in the East Indies. It captures the moment Sukarno and his family leave their residence as they are exiled to Bangka. It is a powerful scene, depicting the peaceful but forcible removal of the president of a nation the colonial government does not recognize. A clip of it surfaced again, in 2014, in *Indonesian War of Independence 1945–1949*, a documentary sympathetic to the native resistance. It is not uncommon for the same footage to be repurposed in varying contexts, depending on the intentions of the producer. Regardless of the larger narrative it is embedded in—a colonial government's newsreel or a historical documentary—the scene in and of itself resiliently remains a primary source. A historian, aware of its milieu, could note from the footage details that would be hard to capture in a written account.

Another category of documentary, and one that we are most concerned with in this study, is propaganda films. It is important to note that any film, regardless of genre, can have propagandistic aspects. In this book, when I mention the term 'propaganda film' I am specifically concerned with those *non-fiction* films, bearing some structural similarities to what we conventionally call a documentary, produced by governments or large agencies for the purposes of furthering their image. Many propaganda films, even if manipulated via voice-over, editing and other production variables, often capture real scenes. A good example of this from the former East Indies can be found in Japan's extensive propaganda efforts during World War II. In the film *Berita Film Di Djawa: Disinipoen Medan Perang!* [Java Film News: Here Too Is a Battlefield!] (see still-frame sequence in Figure 2), Japanese-trained Indonesian troops drill and General Yamamoto talks about a pan-Asian solidarity movement led by Japan against the Allies. We also see Sukarno, who would later become the first president of the republic, urging Indonesians to help the Japanese in a fight that would 'destroy the American and English forces'. While these materials were certainly propagandistic in the sense that they were produced to motivate Indonesians to join with the Japanese and stir a feeling of pan-Asian solidarity, the fact remains that Sukarno did give that particular speech in the film and that the Pembela Tanah Air (Defenders of the Homeland) troops were

Figure 2. Still from *Berita Film Di Djawa: Disinipoen Medan Perang!* [Java Film News: Here Too Is a Battlefield!], produced by Nippon Eigasja Di Djawa, c. 1944[27]

indeed a big part of the Indonesian anti-Allied efforts. In that sense these scenes are authentic and are undeniably primary sources. Today, they provide us with exact transcripts of what Sukarno said to aid the Japanese war campaign.

With all the shaping, 'cooking' and sculpting of the footage filmed on location to create a product driven by doctrine, there is inevitably material that is rejected. Just like the field notes of a journalist, or an anthropologist pursuing an ethnographic account, much of the material that does not quite fit into the larger narrative of the project remains unused. As mentioned before, documentary films are often shot with a very high raw-footage-to-used-footage ratio. And should the raw footage be preserved properly in an archive, it can be invaluable to researchers. In the ensuing chapters of this book I shall provide examples of out-takes from the Dutch East Indies projects and describe how they furnish

---

[27] *Berita Film Di Djawa: Disinipoen Medan Perang!*, *YouTube*, http://www.youtube.com/watch?v=bJ-rhWRJD00, accessed 11 Nov. 2020.

us with useful historical knowledge. What is left out is often as significant as what is included.

Documentary and Propaganda: Kindred Genres

I have touched upon possible ways in which non-fictional, documentary footage might be of use to a historian. While not all documentary films can be considered primary evidence, some of them could be, regardless of whether they are features, newsreels, visuals with voice-over tracks, or even obvious propaganda. All of the examples above, in some manner and moment, fit the American Library Association guideline established earlier of being 'Original records created at the time historical events occurred or well after events in the form of memoirs and oral histories'. Even the footage in a propaganda film, despite inherent bias, can be a valid primary source as it does often capture actual events before narration and editing (the creative treatment) distort them. Yet, film historians have often left out any systematic study of non-fiction film in the pre-Flaherty era, a time when propaganda proliferated. According to Gunning the specific juncture when *actualités* turned into documentaries was during World War I:

> I propose that we use the already existing terms for these different periods in nonfiction filmmaking: 'actuality' referring to this practice before World War I and 'documentary' reserved for the practice that begins with the later period of the war. The dates for this periodization are certainly provisional, an area which calls for further discussion. However, I believe that World War I itself plays an important role in the transformation of nonfiction filmmaking.[28]

Film theorist Loiperdinger has further argued that the propaganda film gave birth to the documentary. It was the crucial link between *actualités* and documentary. This observation is radical, as propaganda has often been relegated to the status of a lesser or B-grade documentary, giving it little credibility and thus frequently excluding it from the historiography of non-fiction film. Loiperdinger builds his case by first chastising the two most canonical non-fiction film historians—Robert Barsam and Erik Barnouw—for overlooking almost everything that happened in

[28] Gunning, 'Before Documentary', p. 11.

the development of non-fiction film from the Lumière brothers until the point of Flaherty. Observing that subsequent scholars adopted this flawed chronology *en masse*, he contends, 'Flaherty ranks undisputed as the first documentary film director. But that certainly does not mean there were no nonfiction films worth mentioning before Flaherty or that documentary actually began with Flaherty.'[29] Loiperdinger goes on to posit that a historical turn of events (the Allied victory over Nazi Germany) gave the term 'propaganda' a 'stigma of reprehensibility'. Noted film historian Brian Winston is in agreement, observing that structurally speaking, Leni Riefenstahl's classic Nazi propaganda film *Triumph of the Will* is really not any different from what Grierson claims to be a documentary film. Loiperdinger quotes Winston handily: 'As with Nanook's winter excursion, so with Hitler's trip to Nuremberg. The point is not the mendacity or otherwise of the final film; it is simply that the material has been "treated"; it has been dramatized.'[30]

Loiperdinger observes that the form of documentary, then, has no real inventor. It grew out of a need to create convincing narratives, with dramatic effect, to rally patriotism among wartime audiences. Real scenes restructured cleverly and treated with intertitles to drive forward a narrative become a documentary. In his words, 'paradoxical as it may sound today, it should be regarded as an indication of how closely documentary and propaganda have been related all along'.[31] Propagandistic film is thus perhaps far more integral to the very understanding of the documentary form. Its analysis would therefore be of interest not just to those involved in the search for remnants of primary sources, but to film historians as well.

Outcasts

The archival material from the Netherlands East Indies that we are scrutinizing here covers almost every stage of the development of non-fiction film as outlined in this chapter. We find in the earlier works many examples of the *actualités* or 'view' film. These sometimes resemble travelogues. As the filming and editing began getting sophisticated, the

[29] Loiperdinger, 'World War I Propaganda Films', p. 26.
[30] Brian Winston, *Claiming the Real: The Griersonian Documentary and Its Legitimations* (London: British Film Institute, 1995), p. 109.
[31] Loiperdinger, 'World War I Propaganda Films', p. 31.

films produced by the Colonial Institute began to resemble propaganda film. Soon many of the propaganda films actually seemed to be rather like documentaries. And by the 1930s some of the documentaries had innovative fictional elements integrated into them. Given the vast diversity of material that was filmed in the Dutch colony, film historians might take note that the entire structural evolution of the non-fiction film can be studied in this one archive. The numerous cameramen who made these films adapted to the changing formats of consumption around the world. J.C. Lamster and L. Ph. De Bussy's Colonial Institute commissioned forays into filmmaking in the 1910s remind one of the Lumière brothers and the many non-fiction filmmakers that followed—trying to invent a language of cinema to meet evolving expectations. In this case it was to create appropriate propagandistic materials—not for war, but for convincing viewers that colonial rule was required and justified. The early Dutch filmmakers demonstrated both enterprise and innovation—filming the world around them with bulky, unwieldy equipment and developing the raw footage under difficult conditions to make it comprehensible to a wider audience. The improvements were swift. Isidor Arras Ochse, who filmed in the 1920s, was tremendously skilled, and the quality of his filming was possibly on a par with the best in the world of known documentarians. Father Simon Buis' innovative ways of filming on location and having actors cast from local villagers in Flores remind us of Robert Flaherty and even Jean Rouch from several decades later.

Despite their innovations, these pioneers are outcasts from the collective history of non-fiction film. The digitized collection available to us now will serve not only historians of the former colony but also any scholar of cinema interested in the evolution of the non-fiction form. In fact, one might argue that it would perhaps behoove us, scholars of colonial studies, to help pry open the door of the investigation of early non-fiction cinema. As it turns out, both historians, and historians of film, will have a lot to gain from it.

CHAPTER 2

Obscurity and Rehabilitation of the Dutch East Indies Propaganda Film Collection

On 24 April 1912, the following brief announcement appeared in the *Nieuwe Rotterdamsche Courant*: 'To a Captain in the Ordnance Survey in the Netherlands East Indies, J.C. Lamster, ... our union [the Colonial Institute] makes available funds for making cinematographic and photographic images for a term of one year or less as necessary.'[1] This signalled the start of the process that would document several decades of the Dutch presence in the East Indies, as well as some of the darker consequences of Dutch actions. The beginning of active, voluminous filmmaking, the documentation process had a social and political purpose. The impetus to produce early colonial films originated from a very specific set of sociopolitical circumstances. This chapter will identify those origins and the fate of the rapidly accruing collection.

The early 20th century was an opportune time for the Dutch government to educate its population about conditions in its colony in the East Indies. Historian George Gonggrijp states pithily, 'One could say that between 1904 and 1914 the East Indies changed more than it had in the preceding three hundred years.'[2] The colony in the East

[1] *Nieuwe Rotterdamsche Courant*, 24 Apr. 1912.

[2] Quoted in George Francois Elbert Gonggrijp, *Schets ener economische geschieldenis van Nederlands-Indie* (Haarlem: De Erven F. Bohn, 1949).

Indies needed Dutchmen with specialized knowledge in the fields of agriculture, forestry, railways, waterworks and roadways. But the extreme exploitation of native labour, due to unfair and ill-managed policies of the previous century, worried many. Segments of the Dutch population became concerned about their moral core as a European-Christian nation. A speech from the throne in 1901 sent a clear message about the need for a new colonial direction. Queen Wilhelmina stated, 'As a Christian Power the Netherlands is ... to imbue the whole conduct of government with the consciousness that the Netherlands has a moral duty to fulfill with respect to the people of these regions. In connection with this the diminished welfare of the population of Java merits special attention.'[3]

Although there was no singular document or charter that outlined the Ethical Policy's mission and modes of application, this period is regarded as the dawn of the program. Historians differ somewhat on the origins and the thrust of this new era of reckoning. Amry Vandenbosch, writing in 1942, saw it as arising from the new Christian coalition that came to power in 1901. The new policy, according to Vandenbosch, galvanized around a Christian penetration determined to uplift the peoples of the colony. Strong lobbying from Conrad Theodor van Deventer, a leading and influential liberal who had long been arguing that the Netherlands was honour bound to repatriate some of its earlier profits, influenced the coalition. J.S. Furnivall, writing around the same time, acknowledged Van Deventer's enormous role in the matter—especially in his article 'A Debt of Honour', which had shaken up the country with its scathing criticism of Dutch exploitation and commercial unscrupulousness.[4] Furnivall, however, saw the turn more as economic rationale—a consensus in Parliament (partly based on Van Deventer's mathematical modelling) that a capitalist system that did not look after the welfare of its workers was essentially ensuring its own extinction.[5] Differing perspectives aside, it was a mandate that had the

[3] Amry Vandenbosch, *The Dutch East Indies: Its Government, Problems and Politics* (Berkeley and Los Angeles: University of California Press, 1942), p. 64.
[4] J.S. Furnivall, *Netherlands India: A Study of Plural Economy* (Cambridge: Cambridge University Press, 1939), p. 231.
[5] Ibid., p. 232.

rare, unified agreement of the throne, Parliament, corporations and the Church. The state would now have to intervene.[6]

The Colonial Institute was established in 1910 to assist with the 'elevation of the people', a motto not too different from the general thrust of the Ethical Policy. The institute saw in making films a promising way of providing visual evidence of the state of the colony, as well as a means to persuade civilians in the Netherlands to take pride in the development of the East Indies. It aimed to collect data and disseminate knowledge about the colonies. It is significant that the institute was founded on the initiative of a business-minded person—J.T. Cremer, a former minister of colonies and president of the Dutch Trading Company. Cremer and H.F.R. Hubrecht, a member of the House, had the backing of a number of large companies, making the venture an early example of a public-private partnership.[7]

It was in the early discussions of the Colonial Institute that the novel notion of using film as a tool to create informational programmes was developed. Carinda Strangio has followed the evolution of this process in detail. Her research uncovers that three Dutchmen—S. de Hammer, F. Roggerath and A. Prell—requested support for filmmaking efforts as early as 1910 but were denied.[8] Soon afterwards, however, it was deemed to be a useful idea and the institute went ahead with sanctioning funds, if somewhat reluctantly.[9] A statement in the minutes of the Colonial Institute records:

> These films will be made to serve a wide action to spreading knowledge of our colonies in the Motherland. The first action will be to organize various series of lectures held on ... the Indian nature and natural phenomena, household and company life, Europeans and natives, the traffic system, education and mission, trade and industry, the great

---

[6] Among the most comprehensive coverages of the Ethical Policy is Elsbeth Locher-Scholten's, *Ethiek in fragmenten: vijf studies over koloniaal denken en doen van Nederlanders in de Indonesische archipel, 1877–1942* (Utrecht: HES Publishers, 1981).

[7] Carinda Strangio, 'Standplaats Soekaboemi: De Lamster-collectie van het Filmmuseum', *Tijdschrift Voor Mediageschiedenis* 2 (1999): 23–35.

[8] Ibid.

[9] Strangio's article mentions that the secretary of the new institute, H.P. Wijsman, was not very keen on the idea and felt that it would not gain support in the academic community.

> cultures, the army and navy, the household of the natives, the natives hired by various companies, the foreign Orientals etc.... A serious and thorough handling thereof shall be deemed guaranteed.[10]

After employing two filmmakers, J.C. Lamster and L.P.H. de Bussy, who made several dozen films, the Colonial Institute withdrew from active film production in 1922. It did, however, continue to screen and promote films that were subsequently backed by corporations and made under the banner of large production houses such as Polygoon and Haghefilm.

It is not easy to establish the degree of penetration of these films in the 1910s and 1920s. While there are records of the minutes of the Colonial Institute's meetings that provide us with details of almost every discussion and every screening, it is difficult to assess the demographics of the people attending, or their reactions. Leading newspapers of the time, from both Holland and the Netherlands East Indies, provide some insights. What are most valuable from the hundreds of film reviews that appeared in print are the reactions of the public to the films and the opinions of the journalists and art critics who covered issues dealing with the East Indies. We get a strong sense of the sociopolitical effect of these films on the Dutch filmgoing class, although they remain anonymous. The films are described not just as works of art but also as a key cultural bridge between the kingdom and its colony. Four magazines dedicated to the arts, some specifically to film—*Geschiedenis Beeld & Geluid*, *De Filmwereld*, *Nieuw Weekblad voor de Cinematografie* and *Het Weekblad Cinema et Theater*—provide us with records of titles, feature articles on some of the projects, and the artists involved.

A more recent source of information is the ambitious online database project Cinema Context (http://www.cinemacontext.nl/). Cinema Context is an open access site, allowing the user to conduct a search for any film going back to 1896 and its creators. The website does not reveal information about its implementers and researchers. In its words, 'Cinema Context contains a wealth of information on film screenings from 1896 to 1940 in various cities in the Netherlands, mostly from Amsterdam, Rotterdam, The Hague, Utrecht, Groningen and Limburg.

[10] Letter Board of Bebeer (KI) to Min. Kol., 7 number I911 (ARA 2.I0.36.04 inv August 8, indexes public verbal 1814–1912).

Each week's film programme has been included, as far as this is documented in the sources we have consulted.'[11] Cross-referencing a vast number of archived online newspapers and magazines, Cinema Context provides the date and location of the screening, including the name of the theatre. While the website is particularly useful for researchers looking up fiction films for wider audiences, data on propagandistic documentaries is limited.

Using a composite of the sources mentioned above, I deduce that the films, while not everyday events in the metropole, certainly occupied a reasonable part of the Dutch cultural and political consciousness. It is important to note that more than 95 per cent of the screenings, in at least the cases I was able to trace, were in the Netherlands. There were hardly any films from this entire collection shown in the colony. In Amsterdam, the Colonial Institute started to screen films as early as 1915, as soon as Lamster's productions were ready to be shown to a wider audience.

The Colonial Institute, however, was a private foundation and lacked the organizational backing for a large-scale commercial dissemination of films. Lamster and De Bussy, the two filmmakers directly employed by the institute, were not professionals. Lamster was a captain in the army and De Bussy an agricultural scientist. They did, nonetheless, produce an impressive and important body of work under trying conditions. Academics in the Netherlands often influenced the footage that Lamster and De Bussy shot. The institute had a specific policy of not showing its films commercially as they were deemed educational. Still, the outreach was significant. The annual report of the Colonial Institute from 1918 records that there were 63 requests for film screenings, in which 314 individual titles were shown.[12] The Colonial Institute's lecture room, where nearly all the initial screenings took place, was, however, deemed a fire hazard, as it was not safeguarded against the dangers of the very flammable nitrate film stock. A project to build a proper auditorium was delayed until 1926 due to interruptions following World War I. A fee was charged for projecting films, and educational lectures were organized. Someone familiar with the material typically stood behind the screen so they could narrate the contents in a loud voice

[11] Cinema Context, 'Film in the Netherlands from 1896', http://www.cinemacontext.nl, accessed 6 Nov. 2020.

[12] Dijk et al., *J.C. Lamster*, p. 57.

(to be heard above the mechanical din of the projector). It was difficult for audiences to follow the films even with these scripts. The screenings in the completed auditorium did not meet with great success.[13]

After the late 1920s, these films were rarely screened. The cans in the Colonial Institute gathered dust. Whereas in 1926 Will Hays, the president of the Motion Picture Producers and Distributors of America, famously asked the large studios to preserve their films so that 'schoolboys of 3000 and 4000 A.D. may learn about us', the flammable documentary nitrate stock from the Dutch East Indies lay dormant with no attempt at preservation.[14] Alarmed by discussions at the Instituut voor de Tropen (the Tropical Institute, the new name for the Colonial Institute) proposing the destruction of the films because of their hazardous nature, an employee hurriedly secured their transfer to an attic. They remained there, untouched for several decades. The fate of the early footage and prints in the repositories of the larger production companies remained uncertain as well. In 1975 they were moved to the Filmmuseum and the Ministry of Development sanctioned their cataloguing.[15]

Mother Dao: A Resurrection

In the late 1980s, Dutch archivist and researcher Rogier Smeele entered the Filmmuseum film holdings to confront the less than ideally archived collection. He recalled, 'I made an inventory at that time of the nitrate films brought down from the Tropenmuseum. They did not know what to do with that material they had.... The vaults of the Filmmuseum were a mess.'[16] Smeele started to reorganize the material: 'We decided to search for everything related to the Netherlands Indies, whatever was in 35mm or materials connected with it, whether in the Netherlands or abroad.'[17] Soon Smeele had put together preliminary excerpts for

[13] Ibid.
[14] 'Films Put on Ice for Fans Yet Unborn. Movies Deemed Peculiarly Worthy of Preservation Will Be Treated to Last Forever. Screen Cornerstones. Films for Fans Yet Unborn', *New York Times*, 24 Oct. 1926, p. 2.
[15] Dijk et al., *J.C. Lamster*, p. 7.
[16] Stef Lokin, 'Een gesprek met beeldresearcher Rogier Smeele, Oude beelden en een nieuwe visie', *GBG-Nieuws* 33 (1995): 35–8.
[17] Ibid.

screening at a visual anthropology conference at the University of Amsterdam in 1989 called 'Eyes Across the Water'. Vincent Monnikendam, a Dutch filmmaker, happened to sit in on a screening of Smeele's montage at that conference. The 20 minutes of arresting images of the Netherlands East Indies mesmerized him. Monnikendam had been aware all his life about the Dutch involvement in Asia, and yet he had never quite seen images like these before. To him they were culturally and politically revealing as well as aesthetically moving. He decided immediately to produce a film. Leaving the conference, he found his way back to his office at Hilversum in a daze. Once there, he telephoned the director of the National Film Archive and requested permission to make a film edited from this historic material. Astonishingly, by midday he had secured a new film project. Monnikendam was given carte blanche to proceed. Sitting in darkrooms surrounded by the nitrate film stock, he and Smeele reviewed 260,000 metres of film (about 120 hours) over the next six years.

They scoured other archives in the Netherlands, including those of long-standing Dutch production companies that had been involved in some of the productions in the colony. There was limited material in the Smithsonian Institution in the United States. In England the duo found footage in the National Television and Film Archive and the Imperial War Museum. They travelled to Indonesia to make audio recordings and were surprised at the extent to which they were able to record some of the natural sounds:

> We visited a number of industrial locations—sugar and tobacco plantations. We also went to oil factories of the Batavian Petroleum Society. A number of these factories still exist and even operate as in the Dutch time. This was a big surprise.... So we wrote letters to Pertamina, the oil company of the State that had taken over the Dutch possessions. We were given free access.... On many plantations were even the steam trains of that time. They cracked and squeaked and whistled. Thus we had a large amount of audio recorded.[18]

Working with this visual material, reconstituting some of the audio from new recordings and layering the collage with Javanese poetry,

[18] Ibid.

Monnikendam released *Mother Dao, the Turtlelike* in 1995.[19] He made archival history by producing the first 'review' of the entire corpus of footage on colonial Indonesia, a staggering amount of visual material. More filmic essay than documentary, *Mother Dao* is 90 minutes long and has no guiding narration.[20] It is a found-footage exercise, an effort to expose history lurking in cans and rolls of unseen film. There is minimal intrusion—we feel as though we are seeing the real thing judiciously and carefully assembled for us. The result is beautiful and, for some, devastating. 'Who would have thought that out of anonymous documentary footage from Indonesia in the first decades of this century, taken by the Dutch authorities, a contemporary Dutch filmmaker could make a film that is both a searing reflection on the ravages of colonialism and a noble work of art,' said renowned art critic and cultural historian Susan Sontag when the film started making its rounds at screenings in museums and at film festivals around the world.[21] While Sontag was incorrect in addressing the footage as being from 'anonymous' sources (the material was already inventoried and logged by then), her reaction to viewing a troubling and enigmatic history of Dutch colonial operations was shared by many. *Mother Dao* was invited to several prestigious festivals and academic forums and broadcast on television. In the credits of the film, Monnikendam lists himself as 'documentary compositor' rather than 'director', which reveals his perceived role in the project. What is somewhat miraculous, given the fragile nature of nitrate film, is that the films were so well preserved—as evidenced by the clarity of the images in *Mother Dao*. The quality of the images is at times extraordinary, arguably better than that of celebrated ethnographic

---

[19] *Mother Dao, the Turtlelike*, dir. Vincent Monnikendam (Nederlandse Programma Stichting, 1995).

[20] Bernard Arps, the noted Javanese scholar, was consulted for the minimal poetic narration and music used in the film. Monnikendam's vision, Arps told me in conversation, was to 'let the images speak for themselves as far as possible' (22 Mar. 2011); see also Jugiarie Soegiarto, 'Wacana Kolonial Dalam Film Moeder Dao, de schildpadgelijkende', *Wacana, Journal of the Humanities of Indonesia* 10, 2 (2008): 317–47.

[21] University of Chicago, Film Studies Center, 'Colonial Imaging: Mother Dao the Turtlelike', http://filmstudiescenter.uchicago.edu/events/1997/colonial-imaging-mother-dao-turtlelike, accessed 7 Nov. 2019.

films made in the 1920s such as Flaherty's classic *Nanook of the North*. Indeed, *Mother Dao* is a visual, historical and ethnographic spectacle. Its concept was unusual, a bold way of assembling a documentary film.

Monnikendam explains that he was convinced that the Dutch colonial film archive was a treasure trove for historical research. Being a researcher and avid reader, he had pored over photographic albums, touristic books, novels, essays and newspaper articles throughout his life. For him the several hundred propagandistic films revealed a world that print material could not recreate. His challenge was to produce an edited film that gradually unpacked the rich material for the viewer. Inspired by French psychiatrist Jacques Lacan, Monnikendam employed what he describes as a strategy of *chaîne signifiante* (chain of signifiers) to structure his narrative logic from left to right, from the start to the end of the reel.[22] This tradition of re-appropriating existing documentary film material, of course, has a rich history. In Vaughn's words, 'Old documentaries are constantly being ransacked for new compilations; yet such recycling seems always to enrich rather than diminish them. Documentary, unlike fiction, welcomes its own displacement.'[23]

Julia Noordegraaf (2009) has described Monnikendam's approach as using 'a specific technology of memory, one that uses montage, or editing, as a tool to intervene in the way we remember the past'. She has written about the types of awareness created in the recontextualizing of filmed images with particular reference to *Mother Dao*:

> As in other compilation films, *Mother Dao* uses propagandistic imagery and turns it against itself: images originally celebrating the production processes in the tobacco factory now mainly show the dirty and dangerous circumstances in which the local workers have to do their work.... Compilation films literally displace the footage they use: images are removed from their original context and represented in a new one. This displacement entails a shift in meaning: in the new context the same images can mean differently.... As such, the displacement and re-editing of archival material in compilation films can be a tool for remembering the past differently.... The film thus constructs a new view on the colonial history of Indonesia: the Dutch invaded

[22] Monnikendam, personal email communication, 17 Dec. 2013.
[23] Vaughn, *For Documentary*, p. 81.

> an unspoilt country and brought hunger, death and destruction in the name of modernization and progress.[24]

I argue that the new context that Noordegraaf refers to is not so much because of the re-editing of the material but primarily because a century has passed between the events occurring in the film and our viewing of them. *Mother Dao* in and of itself does not actually create a new view.[25] The passage of time, new value systems, and a deepening awareness of the brutality of colonialism are what really turned the propagandistic imagery against itself—not the creative compilation. The viewer had changed. To be sure, *Mother Dao* is meticulously and judiciously edited to produce a narrative of doom and destruction in 90 minutes. There are, however, limits to how much re-editing could alter the basic texture of the archive. If one were to pull out one of the more incriminating reels from the film and watch it in its entirety, I doubt that the conclusion would be much different. The filmmakers were intentionally capturing the 'dirt and the dangerous circumstances' at the time—the images just did not seem very exploitative a century ago. After all, a large population in the Netherlands had viewed the same visuals with little outcry.[26]

To his credit, Monnikendam does not just show us one side of the colonial enterprise. We get the impression that many Indonesians,

[24] Julia Noordegraaf, '*Facing Forward* with Found Footage: Displacing Colonial Footage in *Mother Dao* and the Work of Fiona Tan', in *Technologies of Memory in the Arts*, ed. Liedeke Plate and Anneke Smelik (Basingstoke: Palgrave Macmillan, 2009), pp. 175, 180. It is historically inaccurate to suggest that the Dutch invaded an unspoilt East Indies; they were one in a series of successive economic and cultural marauders.

[25] A more recent audiovisual project that reworked archival colonial film material was Peter Forgasc's exhibition at the EYE in 2013 titled 'Looming Fire: Stories from the Dutch East Indies 1900–1940'. Forgasc appropriated home movies and other personal documents for this installation, aiming to recreate a semblance of daily life of Europeans in the Netherlands East Indies, but he admitted that he took artistic and personal licences: 'I make compositions on the basis of the material I have found. They are personal interpretations of history, not documentaries aiming at objectivity' (Forgasc 2013).

[26] Pamela Pattynama (*Bitterzoet Indie: Herinneringen en nostalgie in Literatuur, Foto's en Film* [Amsterdam: Prometheus, Bert Bakker, 2014]) explores in compelling ways the notion that altered contexts for different audiences might reshape the effect of these works over time.

especially members of the elite—given their attire and bearing—were complicit in the arrangement. The country appears to be run by an entire class of local administrators and helpers—figures walking alongside Dutch officials, managers working on estates, and teachers in schools. Colonialism, *Mother Dao* seems to illustrate, is not a one-way stratagem. It involves a significant co-opting of a local class that effectively reaps the economic benefits of a land through the exploitation of a large, easily available workforce. The result of the images these camera operators captured, and Monnikendam's reassembly of them, is ultimately simple —we *see* colonization instead of reading about it.

The filmic material from which Monnikendam assembled his film, saturated with a multiplicity of detail, provides—sometimes inadvertently—much texture about life in the East Indies, its rhythms and quotidian aspects. The idea that films made during this period in the Netherlands East Indies are not necessarily 'colonial' is the key theme in Nico de Klerk's compelling essay 'Home Away from Home', which is a discussion of amateur home movies Dutch families made in the East Indies.[27] The argument is generally applicable to any roll of film from this era. De Klerk warns scholars not to fall into the same traps as some writings about photography in colonial times have in the past. He asks us to be wary of generalized statements akin to 'it was in this way that the western community legitimized its dominance'.[28] Such a simplistic stance is of little value, according to De Klerk. An idea like colonialism is too abstract to read from film images. Add to this the unregulated arrival of modernity and its unpredictable effect on both sides of the race divide and we are suddenly left less confident of the nature of the original colonial gaze. We should not 'fit simple, binary, and above all static colonial schemata' into a society 'that was changing rapidly and people had multiple positions and loyalties'.[29] In 'Difference, Discrimination, and the Discourse of Colonialism', Homi Bhabha too makes a similar critical plea for the recognition of ambivalence both in colonial as well as in reversed, postcolonial vantage points.[30] A stereotype of

[27] De Klerk, 'Home Away from Home', p. 151.
[28] Ibid., p. 160.
[29] Ibid., p. 161.
[30] Homi Bhabha, 'Difference, Discrimination, and the Discourse of Colonialism', in *The Politics of Theory: Proceedings from the Essex Conference on the Sociology of Literature July 1982*, ed. Francis Barker et al. (Colchester: University of Essex, 1983), pp. 194–211.

colonial intentions, without a possibility of any deviation, according to him is a 'fantasy of wholeness'. Simply put, the Dutch camera operators could not have persistently operated in a colonial frame of mind where every cinematic action was motivated by a perfect vision of effective colonial domination. Nonetheless, it can be argued that even if colonialism as a political and societal phenomenon cannot be constantly gleaned from these films, the films are clearly saturated with the sort of information that can help us reconstruct aspects of the colonial era.

The importance of *Mother Dao* in helping us locate and appreciate this archive cannot be overstated. But as mesmerizing as the film is to view because of its diversity of images and scale of coverage, it can be frustrating for a historian seeking cohesiveness or order. Indeed, it might have been very difficult for the filmmakers to carve out a unifying and clear narrative from the voluminous footage. As the film's editor, Smeele, remarked:

> We had been evaluating whether there was a story in it. It was not to be the case because the subjects were very wide apart. You could not tell what the direction ought to be. Vincent did not know, and I didn't either. The binding element was that it was colonial propaganda ... and it was filmed by Europeans and was about the Indies. This was the only consistency.[31]

The main problems for a historian tackling this material are that Monnikendam mixes the chronology as well as the geographic ordering of the film. Although many of the scenes in the film are generally contained within an appropriate time/space rendering, often, possibly for the sake of continuity of action or aesthetic effect, he intercuts scenes from different places and periods. The first few minutes of *Mother Dao* are exemplary of this style. By cross-referencing the images from this excerpt to the original sources in the archives, it is possible to establish details about the individual shots insofar as they were entered into the digital database. In some cases, notes from the curators are extractable. On the following pages are stills from the opening scenes of *Mother Dao* with accompanying information, when available, about the location, date and event.

---

[31] Lokin, 'Een gesprek met beeldresearcher Rogier Smeele', p. 38.

SCENE 1 from *Mother Dao.*
Location: Sumba, 1928

SCENE 2 from *Mother Dao*:
Opening credits

Description:
The first shot of the film is of a young boy looking at the camera. This material is from the outtakes of a film titled *Java-Soemba* shot in 1928 on Sumba Island by cameraman Iep Ochse.[32] According to the description of the footage logged by Smeele and other archivists, it was taken as part of *Java-Soemba,* which provides an overview of the missionary work in the Reformed Churches of Netherlands on the island of Sumba in the Dutch East Indies. The second scene is the opening credits of *Mother Dao, the Turtlelike.*

SCENE 3 from *Mother Dao.*
Location: West Java, 1927

SCENE 4 from *Mother Dao.*
Location: East Java

Description:
The third sequence in the film is from an explosion that occurred in the volcanic caldera of Krakatau, off Java, in 1927.[33] The original can be seen in the film *Mahasoetji,* a multi-part series produced by the film company NIFM. The fourth sequence of the film is from sulphur mines in the Ijen volcano complex, Banyuwangi Regency, East Java.

[32] *Java-Soemba Film* or *Zending van de Gereformeerde Kerken*, dir. Iep Ochse (NIFM Polygoon, 1929), archived in Beeld en Geluid, ID #138829.

[33] *Mahasoetji Act 3*, dir. Iep Ochse (NIFM Polygoon, 1929), archived in Beeld en Geluid, ID #118825.

SCENE 5 from *Mother Dao.*
Location: Netherlands
New Guinea, 1929

SCENE 6 from *Mother Dao.*
Location: Undeterminable

Description:
The fifth sequence is from Netherlands New Guinea (1929). The location of the sixth scene cannot be determined.

SCENE 7 from *Mother Dao.*
Location: Flores, 1930

SCENE 8 from *Mother Dao.*
Location: Nias, 1925

Description:
Several shots from the evangelical fiction film *Ria Rago* (1930, Flores) make up the seventh scene.[34] These were filmed by Father Simon Buis and are an early example of a hybrid of fiction and documentary. The Dutchman addressing an indigenous community in the eighth scene is from footage filmed on Nias Island.[35]

Figures 3.1–8. Opening scenes from *Mother Dao*, 1995, a wide geographic and temporal range

[34] *Ria Rago*, dir. Simon Buis (Soverdi, 1930), print at Eye Film Institute, ID #57030.
[35] Leftover footage on Nias Island, 1925, produced by Polygoon, archived in Beeld en Geluid, ID #530212.

In just the first eight minutes of the film we have been taken to several unidentified landscapes in the East Indies: Sumba, Krakatau (West Java), the Ijen volcano (East Java), Netherlands New Guinea, Flores and Nias. And we have been shuttled through approximately five years.

Monnikendam, of course, had no obligation to maintain any continuity, nor did he ever make any claim that he did so. He developed, while editing the film, a vision of how this material could be rearranged to convey his retelling of colonialism. The montage above was intended to establish the breadth and diversity of the archipelago. Monnikendam insists that it was not his intention to make an 'educative' or explanatory documentary. He deliberately left out a traditional narration track in order to create a composition that evoked the colonial mentality through the available images—a more direct observation of what he called the 'colonial machinery' of the Dutch East Indies. The editing seems to have been driven aesthetically but also politically:

> What was this colonial mentality, how did this feel? It was implanted in an *archipel* of isles. In general, the Dutch didn't understand anything of the different cultures in this huge country. The main aim was: earn money, the more the better. To realize this they (the Dutch) needed manpower, hundreds of thousands. This was not enough and therefore cheap Chinese workers were imported: coolies also—tens of thousands. The scenes show sometimes in detail what the relationship between colonizers and the colonized was by that time. The images 'tell' what no word can express. *This* is cinema! All over the world where the film was shown spectators react almost the same: they *feel* what happens in colonized country. And so the French see in the film their relationship with their former colonies, the Portuguese, Belgians, Germans, English, Brazilians and Americans (what they did with the Indians), and so on. Everybody understood perfectly what the film was about, the essence.[36]

In regard to the film's temporal inconsistency, Monnikendam felt that his decision was justified as he wished to create an impression of a large archipelago that was unified through language and culture. It was not out of place to see it as a whole; the real focus of the film was the Dutch colonial mentality.

[36] Monnikendam, 17 Dec. 2013.

Monnikendam's purpose for making *Mother Dao*, thus, was rooted in a belief that film could evoke a sensibility that the written text could not. Accordingly, neither time nor space is key to this sensibility. This is a position that is hard to argue against: an artistic project that leads us into the colonial experience through a motivated collage of archival images effectively creating a wide vista of political domination. Historians, however, prefer a systematic organization of materials as well as a clearly annotated and accessible data set. If primary sources are a historian's holy grail, then a close sense of time and geographic orientation are key components for organizing sources. A 'sense' of things does not satisfy historians, nor does an artistic exercise 'as a tool that intervenes with the way we remember that past', to quote Noordegraaf describing *Mother Dao*.[37] These devices do not bring the clarity and rigour required to file a document as a valid primary source. 'Displacing' footage, and 'removing images from their original context' to have them represent a new one, are not methodologies typically invoked. While those involved in the field of film studies often look at cinema in all its material and psychological complexities, historians first require documents to be mapped and codified in ways that make them retrievable in a logical and uncomplicated manner—ideally in the original sequencing of their generation. While acknowledging the emergence of a 'filmic turn', Landman and Ballard aptly observe:

> Yet film is not a medium with which most professional historians are comfortable. We are not generally trained either to read or to analyse films; nor are we commonly trained to make them. The theoretical proclivities of film studies specialists—with Marxist, semiotic, formalist and neoformalist, psychoanalytic, post-structural and phenomenological approaches vying for their attention—stand in strong contrast to the high empiricism of much mainstream history.[38]

For historians, primary sources, be they film or text, need to be vetted, corroborated with other documents, examined for bias and chronology, and then archived. They are not particularly valuable if they are strung together as aesthetically driven montages with a general sense of a

[37] Noordegraaf, '*Facing Forward* with Found Footage', p. 174.
[38] Landman and Ballard, 'Ocean of Images', p. 4.

narrative, however well they may be linked together to merit a high degree of *chaîne signifiante*.

In a remarkably germane article in the journal *Film History*, Michèle Lagny (1994) tackles the importance of establishing the basic data in a film and elaborates further on its concomitant social implications. Non-fiction films, according to her, ought to be seen within a sociocultural history, which 'in turn is linked to the general history'.[39] Singling out time and space as important portals towards this pursuit, she lays out a three-point approach. The first step is identifying the date of the film and all the various stages or versions of the film that may have existed. Lagny notes that non-fiction films in particular, because of their weaker status compared to the popular genre of fiction films, need to be closely vetted, as data entry lapses are likely. Second, the rationale of the films ought to be understood: 'Were they made upon commission, as propaganda tools, or were they conceived as an act of good faith in the reciprocal recognition of colonialist values?' As we shall see, the contextualizing of the films discussed in this book will be key to our understanding of their possible accuracy and historical salience. Finally, Lagny insists that we need to know more about the audiences that viewed the films—'the sociocultural context within which they were experiencing them ... and whatever their social status and political beliefs'.[40] Indeed, the films that Catholic missionaries made in the Dutch East Indies highlighting social ills in tribal groups were produced specifically for a churchgoing audience, a group different from the general Dutch population who watched films about the construction of bridges, hospitals and roads.

Monnikendam's compilation film does not tell us anything about the sources utilized—their dates, their intentions and their audiences. Without this basic trifecta of information, the miles and miles of footage that he accessed to reconstitute his vision of colonialism would essentially have remained anonymous and impossible to analyze. However, while *Mother Dao* may not satisfy a historian's need for more specific information, the extensive logging and archiving that accompanied it clearly does. The many archivists, including Monnikendam and Smeele,

[39] Michèle Lagny, 'Film History: Or History Expropriated', *Film History* 6, 1 (1994): 30.
[40] Ibid., p. 29.

Uniforme titel	DE TABAKSCULTUUR OP MIDDEN JAVA (***RESTMATERIAAL***)
Titel	DE TABAKSCULTUUR OP MIDDEN JAVA (***RESTMATERIAAL***)
Publicaties	bioscoop ; NIET VAN TOEPASSING ; 13 ' 59 "
Schone inlas	Niet aanwezig
Dragers	
Samenvatting	***Restmateriaal*** van Polygoon cameraman en regisseur Iep A.Ochse, verm. gemaakt voor de documentaire "De Tabakscultuur op Midden Java" van de Nederlands Indische Film Maatschappij (NIFM), een dochteronderneming van Polygoon. Beelden van een proefstation voor tabak in Klaten op Java in Nederlands ***Indië***.
Genre	documentaire , documentaire
Trefwoorden	dakbedekking ; laboranten ; tabak ; zaden ; bestuiving ; proefstations ; stuifmeel ;tabaks planten ; zaaien
Geografische namen	Java ; Nederlands-Indië
Productie	NIFM (producent) NIFM (producent)
Beoogd medium	bioscoop
Opnamen	01-01-1927
Beschrijving	02:00 Proefstation voor de Vorstenlandsche Tabak in Klaten. Europeaan en inlandse laborant registreren monsters. 02:38 + 03:20 Laborant bedient filtermachine voor zaadverdeling, cu van vallend zaad. 03:07 Laborant selecteert zaadjes met een pincet aan een tafel met glazen stolpjes. 03:20 Cu van zaadjes die in een reageerbuis worden gestopt. 03:40 Twee vrouwen, staande op ladders, bevestigen hoezen om de toppen van tabaksplanten na bestuiving. 04:26 Bestrijken van de stamper van de tabaksplant en div. cu's van het afbinden, opensnijden en bestuiven van de stamper. 07:39 Zakjes met stampers worden aan stokken geregen om te drogen. 07:52 Drie vrouwen halen zaadjes uit gedroogde stampers. 08:20 Sorteerwerk van tabakszaadjes onder glazen stolpjes. 08:54 Cu handen kneuzen bloemknoppen en zeven het zaad er uit. 09:31 Koelies tijdens grondbewerking (patjollen) op het veld. 09:55 Koelie buigt zich over het zaadbed met jonge kiemende plantjes en brengt lucht in de aarde met behulp van een bamboestokje (dangirren). 10:19 + 12:31 Koelie met handpomp op de rug besproeit het tabaksbed. 10:40 Verpoten en begieten van jonge tabaksplantjes. 12:42 Het maken van plantgaten. 12:59 Koelie besproeit tabaksbed met behulp van een gieter van bamboe. 13:08 Bedekken van jonge aanplant met klapperblad (rodongen).. 14:27 Uitstrooien van zaad over nieuwe tabaksbedden en het weghalen van de vlakverdelingen. 15:08 Koelies vullen bamboe-gieters en besproeien de bedden. 15:39 Het afdekken van de tabaksbedden met rieten zonneschermen (pajongans).
Rechten	Herkomst: Inventarisatie Rogier Smeele en Vincent Monnikendam. "Handboek voor Culluur- en Handelsondernemingen in Nederlandsch ***Indië*** (1927) Uit: Bibliotheek Koninklijk Instituut voor de Tropen. Opdrachtgever: Tabaksbedrijf van de N.V. Klattensche Cultuur Maatschappij, verm. in samenwerking met het Koloniaal Instituut in Amsterdam. Rechten: Polygoon
Overige opmerkingen	Vermoedelijk is de film gemaakt tgv de Koloniale Tentoonstelling in Parijs (1931). Bron: brief van P.H. Middelburg, zoon van de voormalige directeur van het proefstation in Klaten. De N.V. Vereenigde Klatensche Cultuur Maatschappij was eigenaar van div. ondernemingen in Nederlands-Indië en had haar hoofdkantoor in Den Haag.
Taak ID	527395

Figure 4. Sample log. Footage from *De Tabakscultuur op Midden Java* [Cultivation of Tobacco in Central Java], filmed by I.A. Ochse for Polygoon. Inventoried by Vincent Monnikendam and Rogier Smeele. The notes say that the film was probably commissioned for the Colonial Exhibition in Paris in 1931. The database is archived at Beeld en Geluid with a unique ID (527395).

who handled the raw film material and saw it through its many transformations into the existing database worked in a manner that is tremendously beneficial to the historical community. An example of their dedication to annotating the material can be seen in the unedited excerpt in Figure 4 from the archival log entries at Beeld en Geluid. Much of the footage I will be discussing in the subsequent chapters has had the benefit of having been described and inventoried as in Figure 4 and merits a sample representation.

The well-annotated descriptions, such as the one in Figure 4, in addition to being tagged with key words and relevant production data such as the intended audience of the film, have made the work of researchers significantly easier. In my case, these thorough logs reduced to about a year what could have been several years of archival viewing and note taking.

Thus, while one may be critical of the ahistorical structure of *Mother Dao*, it is crucial to remember that old film footage is not valuable as a historical source if sitting in archives, unexposed and unanalyzed. It was this act of bringing an awareness of the richness and scope of these films, through an artistic sleight of hand as well as a tenacious dedication to annotation, that will forever mark Monnikendam as the filmmaker who forced historians of Indonesia to take note of a rich archive that had existed for decades, untapped, understudied—occluded by the politics of art and history.

In 1990 the Royal Tropical Institute (formerly the Colonial Institute) and the Nederlands Filmmuseum (renamed the Eye Filmmuseum) were granted modest state aid to preserve a large collection of propaganda or 'informational' films made in the Dutch East Indies. About 300 titles were painstakingly inventoried, annotated and preserved. It was these films that were later digitized and made electronically available with generous support from the Images for the Future grant in 2006 mentioned in the Introduction.[41]

The process of analyzing and codifying the Dutch East Indies repository was long and laborious. It began with the filmmakers' field logs—letters and correspondence describing the working conditions and limitations. It then moved on to the early stages of annotation back at the filmmakers' commissioning centers. The work of annotation might

[41] Fossati, *From Grain to Pixel*, p. 175.

A N A K W O D A

De lotgevallen van WODA'S KINDEREN
'n Ware geschiedenis en ter verfilming gespeeld mpxhex in het dorp
,, BOAWE ,, Eiland Flores N.O.I.

,, EEN S O V E R D I FILM,, van het Missiehuis Maria Middelares
HEIDE-Kalmthout by ANTWERPEN

DE G E S C H I E D E N I S

Malaise!!!Ook de bewoners van Flores hebben ze in de laatste jaren geducht gevoeld. Tusschen de jaren 1915 en 1925 bracht een pikol kokos-noten-vleesch van 10 tot 16 gulden op. Sinds 1925 ging de prys steeds omlaag en nu zyn de arme inlanders bly, wanneer ze een ryks-daalder voor 'n pikol krygen.

Vele familie's, voorheen welgesteld, moeten thans de tering naar de nering zetten, vele ook hebben hun geld verloren en moeten zelfs geld gaan leenen, om nog eenigzins volgens hun stand te kunnen leven.

Ook WODA van BOAWE, stond er finantieel slecht voor. Hy was een voornaam en zeer gezien heiden. Met Pater Heerkens leefde hy op beste voet; zyn oudste dochter Trudi had reeds te Todabeloe de meisjes-school doorloopen, zyn eenigste zoon NICO was by de Paters op de Standaardschool, z'n tweede dochter Nelly was by de Zusters en de kleine ROSA nog by Moeder Potjoe thuis, in Boawe.

Trudi was een knap, braaf en ernstig meisje zorgvuldig alle gevaren vermeed, waaraan zy in het heidensch dopp Boawe was bloodge-steld.
Nico was een vroolyke, levenslustige muzikale jongen met genoegzaam voldoende talenten en vrome aanleg.Hy droeg in Z'n hart het kleine gehei van zyn roeping; Priester wilde hy worden.
Nelly ontving de laatste voorbereidingen voor de eerste H. Communie en de lieve Rosa werdt door haar oudste zus onderricht en kon haar gebeden al vlot opzeggen, als de missionaris op bezoek kwam.

Gelukkige kinderen!!! zeker... zeker.... maar Vader Woda had geen geld meer en moest gaan leenen by z'n vriend Resi. Resi liet zich niet onbetuigd in de meening dat hy het geld weldra weer terug zou krygen. Al vaker had hy tevergeefsch by Woda aangeklopt. Resi wilde tenslotte niet langer wachten en dwong Woda het geld maar by iemand anders te gaan leenen. Woda dacht aan den missionaris en toen Pater Heerkens dien dag de familie kwam bezoeken, werdt hy natuurlyk door Woda aangeklampt. Woda hoopte, dat de missonaris hem uit de geld-verlegenheid zou helpen; hoe groot was zyn teleurstelling, toen de Pater hem verze-kerde, dat hy zelfs z'n allerbeste inlandsche vrienden nooit met GELD kon of(ook mocht helpen). Woda werdt boos.

'n Paar huisjes verder had HADJI ABDHOEL 'n mahomedaan, dat gesprek afgeluisterd. '' Prachtig , dacht ie, Woda heeft geldgebrek, de missionaris kan het voorschieten , nu zal ik in de bres springen.'' Heel onnoozelnadert hy Woda, nadat de missionaris is heengegaan en vraagt hem , waarom hy zoo beteuterd kykt.

Figure 5. Example of typed-up treatment for *Anak Woda*, produced by Soverdi. The original film, made in 1930, is lost.

INTERNATIONAL ASSOCIATION
FOR RUBBER- AND OTHER CULTIVATIONS IN THE NETHERLANDS INDIES.

OIL - PALM FILM.

First Part.

Made by Willy Mullens, The Hague Holland.

2. House and grounds of the Manager of the Rubber Cultivation Company "Amsterdam".

3. Head Office of the R.C.C.A.

4. Clearing the primeval forest.

5. Coolies on the way to work at the clearing.

6. Cutting down the under-growth.

7. The heavy timber being felled.

8. Piling up and burning the felled timber.

9. Clearing "lalang" (grass) land.

10. The burning of a "lalang" territory.

11. "Lalang" burning, working with "tjancols" (native handplough) and forking.

12. Plant-material.

13. Nursery beds. Recently sprouted seed and plantable specimens.

14. In the midst of the plant-material.

15. Planting of the oil-palms.

16. The plantation.

17. Tracts of 1000 "bouws" are cleared in one year.

18. Roads through a young plantation.

19. Control-paths through a young plantation.

20. Panorama from a tree-stump over two year old plantation, with view of assistants-quarters, factory premises, manager's house, office and native clerk's - quarters.

21. View of a 4 year old plantation.

22. Glimpses of a 6 year old plantation.

23. The blossoming.

24. The male blossom is full of pollen.

25. Female blossom.

26. The harvest.

Figure 6. Shot list for *Palm Oil*, 1927, for Haghefilm

have been efforts of the Colonial Institute, which produced and edited much of the early works, or some of the private production companies that sent filmmakers to the colony such as Polygoon, Haghefilm and the Catholic missionary film producer Soverdi. These early logs were gradually improved upon as more archivists reviewed and inventoried them.

The 1990 state grant enabled people to be employed to codify the films with even more accuracy. Researchers thus inherited several decades of detailed and painstaking annotations. The Filmmuseum in Amsterdam also occasionally curated seminars and exhibitions from this material. Most notably, in 2002 it showcased a programme of screenings and lectures—'Van de kolonie niets dan goeds' [All's Well in the Colony]—in which several films from the Dutch East Indies collection were screened, featuring a mix of promotional, ethnographic and amateur films.[42] Today, when one accesses this footage at the research terminals of the Eye Filmmuseum or at Beeld en Geluid, one sees descriptions that have been generated over decades of inventory management and a uniformed system of database entry after the implementation of the Images for the Future project. Indeed, there are several unsung heroes in the backstory of this large film archive that provides us with the fruits of a process that started in 1912.

[42] Julia J. Noordegraaf and Elvira Pouw, 'Extended Family Films Home Movies in the State-Sponsored Archive', *Moving Image* 9, 1 (2009): 87.

CHAPTER 3

The Colonial Institute and Propaganda Film (1912–13)*

> Have we, then, never failed in our colonial government? Yes, more than once. To learn of this one has but to turn to our books of history. But we find that neither our government nor our governors, nor our historians have ever flinched from laying the finger when necessary on the weak spots regardless of persons. And for that reason we never have had anything to conceal. We can say to every unprejudiced expert, come investigate. You will find that we, like everyone else, have been, in the course of the centuries, children of the spirit. This is one of the secrets of our colonial rule. The result of the policy has been that among both the studied and the simple villagers of the interior there is a very large percentage who, as the Easterner typically expresses it, feel happy and contented under the shadow of the Dutch flag.
>
> – J.C. Lamster[1]

In 1911 the search was on for a filmmaker of 'scientific' disposition who was also knowledgeable about the colony and could withstand the climate and the arduous travel needed for the task. According to the minutes from the Colonial Institute, they were seeking someone with the following attributes:

> The leader of the executive tasks should be completely familiar with the Indies and Indies states. He will be someone totally reliable in his

* An earlier version of this chapter was published as 'Inadvertent Ethnography in Propaganda: J.C. Lamster's Films (1912–13)', *Indonesia* 106 (2018): 137–56; reprinted with permission.

[1] J.C. Lamster, *The East Indies: Giving a Description of the Native Population of Netherlands-Indies and of Its Civilization* (Haarlem: Droste, 1929), p. 152.

> scientific talent and with certain prestige within Europeans and natives ... moreover withstand the Indies climate and against the fatigues of an ambulatory life, even in remote areas.[2]

Army veteran J.C. Lamster came highly recommended.[3] Though Lamster was contracted at the time by the Koninklijk Nederlands Indisch Leger (Royal Netherlands East Indies Army, KNIL), the situation was quickly resolved.[4] Being a well-travelled army man with a facility for local languages, he was a good fit and was certainly vested in the aims of the Ethical Policy. Championing the Dutch presence in the East Indies, Lamster penned the quote that begins this chapter. It was published much later in his career, as the closing lines of a coffee-table-style book of essays and images. The publisher was the Droste chocolate manufacturer, a purveyor of chocolate bars lined with collectible cards depicting East Indies scenes, which could be pasted into the large, colourful book. A surviving copy in the Tropenmuseum library in Amsterdam has the full collection. The descriptions, like the cards, are meant for popular consumption. They take the reader through basic themes of life in the colony. The book clearly addresses its propagandistic aim. The publishers, simultaneously straddling a commercial and humanistic line, opine:

> Why have we chosen the Netherlands Indies? Because we hope, apart from our propaganda, to further what our country stands so much in need of: interest in and love for that other Holland to which our Holland is so inexpressibly indebted and which is such a particularly favourable field of activity for the enterprising and energetic young men among us.[5]

---

[2] Letter from Board of Management Kolonial Instituut to Minister of Colonies, 7 Nov. 1911.

[3] Minutes of meeting of Directors of the Colonial Institute record, 15 Jan. 1912: 'In order to be able to find a suitable person to act as a leader of work in the Indies, former Governor-General Van Heutz's feelings on the matter were obtained. Attention was drawn to the captain at the Topographical Corps in the Ned. Indie, J.C. Lamster. The officer was very favorably reviewed by his last boss and personal acquaintance, Colonel Enthoven.'

[4] The Colonial Institute has this on record on 7 September 1911: 'An objection to this appointment is that Lamster is still in active service in the Dutch-Indische army and that he is on leave in the Netherlands. Acceptable as long as he is again available after end February 1912.'

[5] Lamster, *East Indies*, p. 3.

There is clearly, on the part of the chocolatiers, an acknowledgement that they owe 'that other Holland' a debt of gratitude in return for the profits they have secured.

Such sentiments were a widespread theme of colonial concern in the Netherlands in the early 20th century. Government and private entities alike were engaged in propagandistic efforts to project an image of solidarity and, at times, indebtedness towards the East Indies. The term 'propaganda' did not have a negative connotation. In the pre-war period, it simply meant informational.[6] Droste used Lamster as a spokesperson. In this chapter we shall study his contribution to information about life in the colony in the early 20th century. I will attempt to demonstrate that Lamster's films, despite falling under the broad classification of 'propaganda', provide us with a useful historical and ethnographic window into that era. The films are generally uncontroversial, championing the Dutch presence while depicting native culture respectfully. They touch on several styles of filmmaking—travelogue, educational, propaganda, *actualités*, proto-ethnography and even re-enactments. Some of the boundaries are inevitably blurred.

Lamster was personally responsible for making approximately 76 non-fiction 'propaganda' films on the Netherlands East Indies in 1912 and 1913.[7] He produced films covering art and culture, government programmes, and agriculture. The wide range of coverage can be noted in a quick scan of the titles in the Colonial Institute's catalogue—*Dansen van Bedaja's in den Kraton te Soerakarta* [Dancing Bedaja in the Kraton Surakarta], *Inlandsche Huisnijverheid* [Native Cottage Industry], *Inlandsche Veeartsenschool te Buitenzorg* [Veterinary School for Native Students at Bogor], *Het Leven der Europeanen in Indië* [The Way Europeans Live in the Netherlands East Indies], *Het Leven van den Inlander in de Desa* [The Life of Natives in the Village], *Meisjesschool te Bandoeng* [Girls' School in Bandung], *Offerfeest op Bali* [Sacrifice Feast in Bali] and *Rubbercultuur op Java* [Cultivation of Rubber in Java].

Lamster had not worked as an ethnographer or filmmaker before his assignment in the East Indies; he had served in the army. Arriving in

[6] Loiperdinger, 'World War I Propaganda Films', p. 31.

[7] Lamster made about 55 films himself. Several of these were re-edited later at the Colonial Institute. Seventy-six discrete titles exist today, although there is overlap in some of the content.

the East Indies in 1896 at the age of 24, he fought in Aceh, where one of the longest and bloodiest colonial wars had spanned three decades, beginning in the early 1870s. In Aceh, Lamster served under Benedict van Heutz, the newly appointed governor of the government of Aceh and its dependencies. Placed in charge of military operations, Van Heutz together with Christiaan Snouck Hurgronje, adviser for native affairs, opted for a brutal offensive to 'fix' the Aceh problem. Lamster served on the ground in full-on battle in 1898. Hundreds of Acehnese were killed in this fateful encounter; the resistance was contained.[8] Lamster continued serving in the region and was decorated as a Knight of the Military Order of William in 1899 for his contributions and for surviving bullets and injuries.[9]

In 1902 the Dutch government transferred him to the Ordnance Survey, a division of the army's Topographical Institute, where he performed rote duties, including implementing a triangulated method of measuring land in various parts of Java—Semarang, Magelang, Purwokerto, Bandung and Salatiga.[10] During this period he learned to speak Malay and Javanese fluently, married a Eurasian woman, had three children, and led a peaceful life of service. His military days were behind him, although he would later write admiringly about the courage and tactical brilliance of Van Heutz.

Lamster lived through considerable change in colonial policy. He went from being a soldier embedded in a bloody war to a proponent of a new culture of peace and friendship with the East Indies. His films advocated the government's new programmes in health and education and displayed a reverence for indigenous art forms. His personal journey was emblematic of the swift transition that the Dutch colonial government underwent between the late 19th century and the first decades of the 20th. During this time, the Netherlands attempted to change its image from a mercenary, domineering, colonizing power to a friend of the East Indies—a nurturing parent country invested in the colony's well-being. By the 1920s, after his return home, Lamster was considered a cultural expert, an authority on the East Indies. His closing statement

[8] Anthony Reid, *Verandah of Violence: The Background to the Aceh Problem* (Singapore: NUS Press, 2006), p. 101.
[9] Dijk et al., *J.C. Lamster*, p. 13.
[10] Ibid., p. 17.

in the Droste publication conveys a sense of past uncertainties, possible guilt, and yet a conviction that the Dutch had finally become responsible rulers. Lamster attempted to show this on film. He brought to the Dutch people, via the new medium of film, a sense of pride in their involvement in the rapid development of the colony. Despite his prodigious output, Lamster remains relatively unknown in the Netherlands. It was only as recently as 2010 that a thorough and well-researched Dutch-language biography was published.[11] I will thus focus more on discussing some aspects of his films and attempt to understand the context of the era in which they were produced. How did Lamster see the colony? To what extent did the films participate in shaping cultural notions about life in the East Indies in the early 20th century?

After attending a short course at the Pathé studios in Paris, Lamster began his work in Java and Bali in 1912 equipped with a camera, adequate film stock and an operator.[12] The early months proved to be complicated both technically and artistically. Film production was still at an early stage, and there were no established templates to refer to. The Colonial Institute's thorough directive of producing topic-by-topic lecture-based programming must have been somewhat open to interpretation and adaptation to local conditions. Anyone producing a film in 1912 was, to some extent, making up his own rules. Given the high cost of film stock and the requirement of bright light for proper exposures, many rituals and sequences of social life had to be collapsed in time. According to film archivist and historian De Klerk:

> The Pathé company's camera that it [the Colonial Institute] had purchased had a narrow field of vision of only 18°. In any overview of activities that involved co-operating workers, as on plantations, it gave Lamster almost no option but to *arrange* them in order to make them simultaneously visible; hence his deep staging by, for instance, having workers in the field work *behind* each other rather than side by side. The lack of artificial lighting, furthermore, forced him to record events that traditionally took place at night during daytime, such as classic Javanese court dances, or moving activities that usually took place inside into the open air and the burning sun.[13]

---

[11] Ibid.

[12] Ibid.

[13] Nico de Klerk, 'A 1912 Cinematographic Reconstruction of the 1898 Pedir Expedition, Aceh', read at 'Sight and Sound: Challenges and Ethics of Visual Representations of War and Conflict in Asia' conference, Singapore, 29 Mar. 2018.

The need to travel, film in appropriate conditions, be economical with the footage, and conceive film projects with unheralded strategies proved to be a challenge. Lamster and his French operator Octave Collet, who had come from Paris, processed the film using locally filtered water between one and six in the morning in the elevated district of Sukabumi, in Java, where the temperature was cooler. They ingeniously kept the precious film stock cool and dry by storing it in cans filled with rice grains.[14] And yet Lamster and Collet travelled to distant locations, at times as far as Bali, in order to cover a visual simulacrum of cultural life in the East Indies. A celluloid colony was being born. And at the same time the duo were inadvertently becoming ethnographers.

Lamster travelled the breadth of Java and filmed assiduously. But due to the lengthy time for processing film and sending back reports to the Netherlands, this was not initially evident. Not surprisingly, given the amount of travel Lamster was doing, the Colonial Institute lost contact with him towards the end of 1912 and reported him missing. H.P. Wijsman, the institute's secretary, eventually tracked him down. Wijsman, who had initially expressed doubts about the entire film undertaking, reported that Lamster's work was disappointing. Not fully grasping the practical and technical considerations that filmmaking demanded, he complained that Lamster had made Sukabumi the base of his operations and seemed to travel back and forth from there. This was not the plan that the institute had had in mind for its rugged, location-based cameraman.[15]

Wijsman's position, however, softened when he realized that developing film was a complex process and the darkroom that Lamster needed was too complicated to manage portably. He did feel, however, that Lamster might have been overly influenced by his French camera operator's 'bioscope fever' and overlooked the basic difference between films that were meant to illustrate lectures (the type he had been specifically commissioned to make) and films meant to be viewed as standalone programmes that were more common to that era.[16] It has never been entirely clear which films Lamster was the cameraman for in contrast to the ones Collet photographed. The films were all made under Lamster's direction, but the person actually framing the scenes would

[14] Ibid., p. 28.

[15] Colonial Institute logs, travel correspondence Prof. Dr. H.P. Wijsman, Indie, 1912–13, Jan. 1913 (KIT 4314).

[16] Strangio, 'Standplaats Soekaboemi', p. 28.

Figure 7. J.C. Lamster (in black suit, facing camera) on location with equipment and helpers, 1913 (courtesy of Vincent Monnikendam)

have undoubtedly influenced the shape of the films. It is assumed that Collet, given the general trend of the French Pathé of producing *actualités*, or short bursts of newsreel-type scenes, had an inclination for that style. Did Lamster have a style? We do not know for sure—it is very possible that he made up his aesthetic as he went along and likely experimented with the new medium.

The Colonial Institute was determined to carve out a niche for itself. It wanted a certain kind of product, one that could be differentiated from the other avenues of information that were available to the Dutch populace in the 1910s, including films made by other colonial powers that seemed exotic. This led to a certain amount of disagreement and friction with Lamster. Hendriks describes the circumstances:

> The institute was independent, but it did get a yearly subsidy from the Ministry of Colonies, and strong ties existed with that department. The gentlemen who formed the board of the institute were, like most of the elite in those days, suspicious about film. For them it mainly represented amusement for the lower classes. But they did acknowledge

Figure 8. The last frame of Colonial Institute films, showing the building on Linnaeusstraat

> the possibilities of the new medium, especially if it was used in a 'sound' way. They felt that the film should be supportive of a lecture and should not tell a story of its own. Lamster's activities on Java were monitored on this principle and caused some friction because Lamster had begun to master the film trade and did his best to tell stories through the editing.[17]

Lamster's films were re-edited frequently—by himself and others at the Colonial Institute. New scenes from stock footage bought from Pathé, intertitles and still frames were constantly added, making it somewhat of an archivist's challenge to keep the annotations accurate. The record was voluminous as it was complex and provided an arresting visual window on the colony. Later, in the 1920s, each film was released with an image of the institute at its conclusion. This trademark distinguished the Colonial Institute's product (Figure 8).

[17] Hendriks, 'Een voorbeeldige kolonie', p. 371.

Experiencing the Colony

Though cinema was a novel medium, the swift adoption of filmmaking at this juncture of the Dutch engagement with its colony is not surprising. To better understand the environment in which the new films were received and viewed, it would be useful to trace the cultural context in which they emerged.

In his essay 'Romancing the Indies', Joost Coté identifies the late 19th century and the early 20th as a period when there was a spike in interest in colonial matters in the Netherlands.[18] He writes that in addition to the most popular source, the colonial novel, there were several other avenues of information. Significantly, there was also a rise in the emigration of Dutch nationals to the colonies.[19] New networks of family ties were being established rapidly, relaying information back home about life in the East. School textbooks had been republished, and they provided children with ample illustrations of jungles and exotic locations to dream about. Church communities sponsored missionaries, who reported back in parishes across the Netherlands about their work, the life they led, and especially details of native lifestyles. Coté cites Marieke Bloembergen's research on the phenomenon of the increased number of exhibitions about the colony—both at large intra-European events, as well as in sideshows in smaller communities across the country. Europeans, especially the Dutch, were beginning to see the colony represented in various forms—live humans, arts and crafts, reconstituted architecture, food, and photography.[20]

Aiding these new avenues were the rapidly progressing technologies of communication between the Netherlands and the East Indies. Swift industrialization in the colony led to the development of transportation and the use of the telegraph and radio. These created a relay system of

[18] Joost Coté, 'Romancing the Indies: The Literary Construction of Tempo Doeloe 1880–1930', in *Recalling the Indies: Colonial Culture & Postcolonial Identities*, ed. Joost Coté and Loes Westerbeek (Amsterdam: Aksant Academic Publishers, 2005), p. 136.

[19] Ibid., p. 168. According to Coté's research, in 1885 there were 47,000 individuals designated as 'Europeans' living in the Dutch East Indies. These included a high percentage of children of mixed parentage. By 1900 the number had risen to 75,000.

[20] Marieke Bloembergen, *Colonial Spectacles: The Netherlands and the Dutch East Indies at the World Exhibitions, 1880–1931*, trans. Beverley Jackson (Singapore: NUS Press, 2006), p. 107.

information from colony to metropole. A major phenomenon was the advent of the telephone in Java. Rudolf Mrazek situates this moment around a biographical sketch of Kartini, the prolific Javanese princess and intellectual who left an archive of personal letters: 'When Kartini was writing her letters, half a million long distance telephone calls were placed through Java each year. In 1900, there were 925 telephone subscribers in Batavia, 371 in Semarang, 568 in Surabaya, 123 in Yogyakarta.'[21]

All these new modes of communication increased the volume and rate of the transfer of information within Java, and the corresponding expansion of data to be consumed in Holland. In addition to the proliferation of oral histories, letters, schoolbooks, exhibitions, photographs and radio broadcasts, there was also much heightened discussion of political and social issues regarding the colony. The Parliament in the Netherlands had become far more active in its outreach in order to win the support and confidence of the Dutch people. The colony was becoming a concern for the public. But, as Mrazek notes in regard to the high volume of photographs displayed, there was a certain undeniable abstraction to that 'experience' of the colony: 'landscapes were flattened through photographs and maps, and the photographs and maps were placed behind the glass. Faces and places were flattened.'[22] The colony, in spite of all the new conduits of information and imagery, would primarily remain a distant, 'flat' idea for most people. Even though Mrazek writes at length about the works of Hendrik Tillemma, a pharmacist from Semarang who filmed extensively in Borneo, the hundreds of titles of the Dutch propaganda films do not find a place in his exhaustive research on technology and modernity in the East Indies.[23] He may have appreciated the somewhat 'unflattening' aspect of film that is less constricted than photographs in its ability to render a more dynamic perspective of the environment.

While Coté, Bloembergen and Mrazek, in their varied discussions of how the Dutch experienced their colony, did not consider the films

---

[21] Rudolf Mrazek, 'Let Us Become Radio Mechanics: Technology and National Identity in Late Colonial Netherlands East Indies', *Comparative Studies in Society and History* 39, 1 (1997): 3–33.
[22] Rudolf Mrazek, *Engineers of Happy Land: Technology and Nationalism in a Colony* (Princeton: Princeton University Press, 2002), p. 107.
[23] Ibid., p. 132.

of the Colonial Institute, several newspapers reported on this emerging phenomenon in the 1910s and 1920s. In addition to the presence of different avenues to experience the East Indies, film was beginning to play a key role. By various accounts, the first screening of the Lamster films was quite a grand event in the Netherlands. In mid-1914 the Ministry of Colonies became curious as to how the whole film experiment had taken shape. It was at first considered that a commercial venue, a cinema hall, would be chosen for the screenings. Cremer, the chairman of the Colonial Institute, was adamantly against this. The Council Management backed him and insisted that 'the films would not be lent for ordinary cinema performances but only as an illustrative tool in serious performances'. Commercial cinema operators (such as Alberts Freres, who wanted the contract) were not to be associated with a product of the Colonial Institute.[24] The first screenings were to take place in September 1914, but World War I delayed events. Only in April 1915 did the premiere finally occur, three years after initial filming had begun. It took place at The Hague, in the auditorium of the Netherlands Lyceum. Lamster projected the films. Several members of the royal family and almost the entire Dutch Cabinet were present.[25]

The public presentation of Lamster's films was an important event. At the onset of World War I, with every European worrying about their nation's strength and political standing, people were eager to understand their place in the global power hierarchy. The *Bataviaasch Nieuwsblad* reported, in light of the looming war:

> What all this has done to us, the general spirit ... the momentum with which one is ready to defend the colony against whomsoever.... Interest in the Indies is now greater at this end, especially with the interest that both the Queen and Prince Henry show in everything in the Indies. Thus, the Queen attended an interesting demonstration this week at the local Lyceum, movies related to Ned. [*sic*] India and its people. The Colonial Institute organized the event, and the two

[24] Minutes, Board of Trustees, Colonial Institute, 9 Feb. 1914 and 9 Mar. 1914.

[25] Dijk et al., *J.C. Lamster*, p. 33. Newspaper coverage reported, 'By the captain of the Netherlands Indies Army J.C. Lamster, a crafted collection of films on the native life was projected at the Hague Lyceum screened in the presence of the Queen, Ministers and other dignitaries.' *Het nieuws van den dag voor Nederlandsch-Indië*, 23 Apr. 1915.

> princesses appeared surrounded by all kinds of high lords, including ministers and members of the Council of States.[26]

As the hall could accommodate only 120 people, additional public screenings took place after that night. Requests poured in for more screenings in regular cinemas.[27]

What were these films able to add to Dutch people's cognizance about the East Indies that they were not getting from other sources after the turn of the century? Primarily, it was the ability to see what the colony looked like. It was an immersive experience that no novel, painting or still photograph could reproduce. It gave audiences the possibility to imagine the terrains in which the popular novels they read were situated. They saw the expanse of the environment, the humdrum of daily life, and the actual execution of the arts and crafts—far more alive than shadow puppets at a fair or images in a book. Film moved through space. It situated the viewer in a landscape with quotidian physical detail and delivered the experience in a format that was very exciting—especially a century ago. It picked up the range of expressions on a person's face over bursts of filmic time. It displayed bodily motion in a dance performance. Sometimes the sheer novelty of watching a film, any film, was the attraction. One of Lamster's early films, *Autotocht Door Bandoeng* [Car Ride through Bandung], utilized the popular 'phantom ride' shot where a camera is mounted on a vehicle, giving it 'a kinetic experience on par with an amusement ride'.[28] This was one of the early gimmicks of non-fiction film, and it was happening in an exotic location predating similar novel scenes in Dziga Vertov's famous *Man with a Movie Camera* (1929) by 17 years! It was life that had been mostly unseen before, presented in a novel simulation of motion.

Films from distant lands were tremendously popular all over Europe. In a sense, all films made in the colonies, even propaganda, were to some extent travel films—the people viewing them had rarely been to these places. Jennifer Peterson writing about travelogues in the

---

26 *Bataviaasch Nieuwsblad*, 26 Apr. 1915.

27 Minutes, Board of Trustees, Colonial Institute, 17 May 1915.

28 Jennifer Peterson, 'Truth Is Stranger than Fiction: Travelogues from the 1910s in the Nederlands Filmmuseum', in *Uncharted Territory: Essays in Early Nonfiction Film*, ed. Daan Hertogs and Nico de Klerk (Amsterdam: Stichting Nederlands Filmmuseum, 1997), p. 86.

1910s notes that 'they enacted tensions between the exotic and the conventional, thereby exploring a central obsession of Western visual culture from the 19th century through the First World War: images of the Other of other places, images of the changing modern world'.[29] Although these films were broadly classified as colonial or propaganda or sometimes, more neutrally, informational, they undeniably conveyed an aspect of the exotic. And yet the exotic in this case was meant to lure the audience—not to a dangerous travel-adventure but to a meaningful, habitable existence.

The contents of these films were not remotely similar to what was available for the imagination as portrayed in the colonial novels of the time. It would be useful to highlight the most popular works of fiction from this period, as they are a startling contrast to the colonial films. In Louis Couperus' *De Stille Kracht* one reads about the failure of the Dutch to rule sensibly in Java. The main character of this story arrives from the Netherlands for work but gives up when he repeatedly encounters in the East Indies a hidden local mystical force that cannot be comprehended or penetrated.[30] Rampant sexual depravity is the theme of Bas Veth's *Het Leven in Nederlandsch Indie*.[31] Both novels highlight tensions between the new arrivals and the local natives and Eurasians. Another example is F. Wiggers' *Fatima*, a crime novel that deals with the gruesome beheading of a middle-aged local woman that the Dutch detective Sherrif Hinne solves brilliantly. Mrazek observes that the timing of *Fatima's* publication in 1908 was important as it was 'the same year a new political light was lit up in the Indies.... It was a time when "lights" and new lights appeared on a daily basis.'[32] The artificial light of electricity was concomitant with a delayed and yet illuminating penumbra of modernity and new ideas, suddenly ready to come out from under the shadows. A shift was occurring from the more morbid fictive-ethnographies from just a decade earlier. These novels are examples of the popular ideas about the Indies in the Netherlands in the early 20th century. Compared to the novels' complex, exciting and

---

[29] Ibid., p. 81.

[30] Louis Coperius, *De Stille Kracht*, 17th ed. (Utrecht: Veen Uitgevers, 1982), as discussed in Coté, 'Romancing the Indies', p. 138.

[31] Bas Veth, *Het Leven in Nederlandsch Indie* (Amsterdam: Kampen en Zoon, 1900), as discussed in Coté, 'Romancing the Indies', p. 142.

[32] Mrazek, *Engineers of Happy Land*, p. 89.

salacious storytelling, Lamster's films would have felt tame. They were mostly simple motion-postcards with in-line textual descriptions. Yet they were in demand. That was the power of motion picture and the new 'light' of the projection lamp. The Colonial Institute was prescient in sensing this.

Colonial novels of the early 20th century, by and large, had a common theme: the Dutch population in the colony was succumbing to lust and avarice and was losing touch with the people it had come to trade with and eventually rule. It raised the question as to whether they would actually be able to continue to live in the East Indies with a modicum of morality. Or had a distant, bastardized version of their native Christian values calcified with the heady life in the Indies and degenerated them beyond redemption? In Coté's words:

> The new question was whether the European society that had evolved in the East, 'the other Dutch', was capable of exercising that moral responsibility. This was a question that opened up a Pandora's box of fears about national character.... It was an 'end of a millennium' debate about a future in which old values and traditions were being swept aside by the currents of modernity.[33]

In 1900 Veth's *Het Leven in Nederlandsch Indie* was published. It was perhaps the darkest novel of its genre. According to Coté, the author 'was adamant that contemporary colonial society epitomized the degeneration, the ruination of European character'.[34] He classifies this book under a subgenre of colonial literature called 'advice literature'. In this context, Veth's advice to young men seeking to make the journey to work and serve in the Indies was straightforward—they were advised not to go. The book is full of repulsive, sinister characters, lacking moral centredness—boorish, lust-ridden alcoholics with no scruples: 'Good people change into bad ones. All that arrives grows stale, all that blushes becomes pale, all that flourishes withers away, all that sparkles is obscured, all that grows is rendered dull: thoughts, affections, illusions, perceptions.'[35]

[33] Coté, 'Romancing the Indies', p. 140.

[34] Ibid., p. 141.

[35] Bas Veth, *Het Leven in Nederlandsch Indie*, as excerpted in Frances Gouda, *Dutch Culture Overseas: Colonial Practice in the Netherlands Indies, 1900–1942* (Jakarta and Kuala Lumpur: Equinox Publishing, 2008), p. 149.

Veth's book received numerous complaints but was nonetheless (in)famous. To contest this sentiment, a Dutchman named L.C. van Vleuten even printed a pamphlet with his own resources titled 'The Truth about Life in the Netherlands Indies: A Protest against the Book by Bas Veth'. This fear of a colonial population, living among natives and gradually losing their ethical compass, was not limited to the Dutch —it was widespread among most colonizing nations. In her article 'Making Empire Respectable: The Politics of Race and Sexual Morality in 20th-Century Colonial Cultures', Ann Laura Stoler discusses this from the perspective of the British, French and Dutch—colonizing governments that had a substantial European population living in their colonies. Stoler explains that the issue began to be studied closely in the late 1980s:

> There emerged an inquiry within academia that focused on the perception of the colonizing European communities about their own populations living at a distance from their countries of origin and over substantial periods of time. Having focused on how colonizers have viewed the indigenous Other, we are beginning to sort out how Europeans in the colonies imagined themselves and constructed communities built on asymmetries of race, class and gender-entities significantly at odds with the European models on which they were drawn.[36]

Indeed, what was happening in the colony was significantly different from the lifestyles of the 'respectable' class of Dutch back in the Netherlands. There were shifting strategies by colonial governments on how to lower their expenditures while maintaining an appropriate image of white superiority in the eye of the natives. In the Dutch Indies, the higher costs concomitant with having a European wife and family led authorities to discourage or legally ban colonial officers from having wives, especially in the early stages of their careers. Concubines did the household chores, keeping costs low. But soon, in direct contrast with the practical considerations of keeping European women away from the colonies, i.e., lower maintenance costs of officers, were the theories around the new field of eugenics—a pseudo-science that had become popular by the end of the 19th century. Eugenics tended to blame

[36] Ann Laura Stoler, 'Making Empire Respectable: The Politics of Race and Sexual Morality in 20th-Century Colonial Cultures', *American Ethnologist* 16, 4 (1989): 646.

Figure 9. Opening title of *Het Leven der Europeanen in Indië* [The Way Europeans Live in the Netherlands East Indies], 1913

white degeneracy on the mixing of races, both culturally and genetically. It championed a racially hermetic lifestyle, especially in the bedroom. As Stoler notes:

> Eugenic arguments used to explain the social malaise of industrialization, immigration and urbanization in the early 20th century derived from the notion that acquired characteristics were inheritable and thus that poverty, vagrancy and promiscuity were class-linked biological traits.... The 'colonial branch' of eugenics embraced a theory and practice concerned with the vulnerabilities of white rule and new measures to safeguard European superiority.[37]

While this extreme form of race theory did not affect the Dutch population in the East Indies as it did the colonial population of French and

[37] Ibid., p. 644.

German colonies, the Dutch colonial government did alter its policies regarding bringing in white brides and eventually began encouraging officers to have 'wholesome' European families. This was perhaps why the Colonial Institute wished to make a certain kind of film and distance itself from anything populist, sensational and depraved. Lamster's films, with their unambiguous morality, seemed to say that the colony was healthy: the depravity of the late 19th century had been overcome. It is little coincidence perhaps that slightly more than a decade after Veth's *Het Leven in Nederlandsch Indie*, a book on Dutch moral torpor, Lamster produced an 11-minute film called *Het Leven der Europeanen in Indië* (Figure 9). It is a compilation of several scenes of a very tranquil and 'moral' life led by a European family in the East Indies.

Lamster's advice to young men in Holland, conveyed via his films, was to go to the East Indies regardless of what the popular literature of the period might have projected. In the archives of the Eye Filmmuseum is the script of the original narration—the *Toelichting* or 'illustrations' that were read over the screenings of several of Lamster's films (Figure 10). Each document states on the cover page, 'This film includes a detailed Introduction which will be sent on request and will be called back after use.' The documents describe the scenes in a very literal way and add on a second layer of information. The script is timed to fit with the length of each scene.

Het Leven der Europeanen in Indië is straightforward in structure. One or two long shots are edited together and then followed by a title card describing the next scene. First, we are shown a standard European house. A horse carriage travels through peaceful streets. A European man and his wife leave for *Winkelen en Bezoeken Afleggen* [Shopping and Making Visits]. They travel to the home of a friend, and the group of four go to an exhibition of indigenous arts. A retinue of servants help at every step. We are then shown a typical day where three children leave for school by horse carriage while their Dutch mother waves goodbye. A title card reads: *De Europeesche Huisvrouw aan haar Morgenwerk* [The European Housewife and Her Daily Work]. The madam of the house buys various food items from pedlars at her doorstep; she appears to feel completely safe in the company of local men. She then prepares a meal for her children with the help of her native maid in the courtyard within the house. The servants continue with their chores. The next scenes are outdoors in the city. The card reads: *Einde der lesuren; Gymnasium, Weltevreden, vertrek der leerlingen met de gereedstaande trams*

KOLONIAAL INSTITUUT — AMSTERDAM.

Negatief
N.2

N41

TOELICHTING

op de Kinematografische opname van

Het Leven der Europeanen in Indië.[1])

N.B. Van de titels 1 en 2, die aan de Pathefilm 3442 ontleend zijn, is geen negatief aanwezig.

Lengte 170 M.
Gewicht 1.170 K.G.
Tijdduur 12 Min.

1) Bij deze film behoort een uitvoerige „Inleiding", die op aanvraag wordt toegezonden en na gemaakt gebruik wordt teruggverzocht.

Figure 10. *Toelichting, Het Leven der Europeanen in Indië* [The Way Europeans Live in the Netherlands East Indies], 1913

[End of Lessons, Gymnasium, Weltevreden, Students Waiting for Trams]. We see a busy street with tramcars. Dutch boys and girls in uniform exit the gates of what seems to be an all-European school. The scenes are short. However, the guidebook with the 'illustrations' reads rather descriptively. The difference in the level of detail in the film and in the additional material is worth noting closely. Following is an excerpt from the penultimate scene:

> Here we are in Salemba, a lovely district south of Weltevreden, where one finds tall trees and old-fashioned houses. There is a five years' secondary school [meaning it takes five years to the final exam] which had always mistakenly borne the name gymnasium [type of six years' secondary, pre-university school with Latin and Greek], and has been renamed King William III School.
>
> We can only see the headmaster's house, with the school buildings situated in the back. The pupils scurry out; almost all are dressed in white, the girls in bébé ['shapeless, wide gown that falls to the calf or ankle, somewhat similar to a nightgown'], the transitional Indies gown between properly dressed and unproperly dressed. The boys wear a black worsted cap with a gold star and chin strap.
>
> From both directions arrive steam trams that run between the lower town and Master Cornelis. We see no smoke from the chimneys, as the boilers are filled with compressed steam that is being injected after each run. This definitely is a cleaner power supply than the steam trams' own blackening fires.[38]

The 'illustrations' that were narrated to the audiences embellish and add information to what is seen onscreen. In keeping with the theme of images of a tranquil, orderly, safe and robust lifestyle, the narrator read out details that helped the viewer understand the surroundings better. The last scene in the film, with the children playing with white pigeons in a lush garden, is rather lyrically described thus:

> What follows is a delightfully idyllic spot in the backyard of one of the great country houses that one finds in such great numbers beyond Master Cornelis: a lovely garden with sugar and coconut palms, a veritable paradise for children to play in.

[38] Toelichting: op de Kinematografische opname van, *Het Leven der Europeanen in Indië*, Colonial Institute Amsterdam.

> So a few children pick up a tampa (bamboo dish) that they keep. Pigeons are obviously very familiar with this feeding method and eat the food. A few moments later is a sweet scene of children taking turns running through the garden on a horse. The animal is anything but tame. They attempt to take off a few times, but all efforts are in vain for these young riders.
>
> This is how a few children allow food to be picked from a tampa (bamboo dish) they hold on their heads. The pigeons are obviously familiar and pleased with this feeding method. A few moments later, a sweet scene of children who take turns riding a little horse through the garden. The animal is anything but tame: while its young rider mounts it unsuccessfully tries to hit her a few times.[39]

Lamster's film is shot and ordered in a way that gives the impression that Batavia was a safe place to live and work for the Dutch population. It had large homes, ample servants, good schools and others from the Dutch community to mingle with. The European men in the film are energetic and efficient, and the women are shown as attractive, relaxed and at home. The East is not exoticized; it is made pleasant; it conforms to Dutch expectations. The dank locations found in much of the colonial literature are left out, and the races are clearly separated. Two additional layers, the intertitles and the 'illustrations', accompany the films. Much of Lamster's work was re-edited constantly; and new scenes, intertitles, stills and stock footage from Pathé were added to give his films the level of straightforward comprehensibility that the Colonial Institute insisted upon.[40]

Although the records mostly indicate that the first screenings of Lamster's films were held in April 1915 in The Hague, there seems to have been at least one screening in 1914. On 23 March of that year, the *Bataviaasch Nieuwsblad* carried an article about a four-part lecture series that J.C. Weatherhead, the director of the department of ethnology, gave at the Colonial Institute for a series titled *Omgang met Inlanders* [Dealing with the Natives]. In keeping with the new thrust of friendliness and winning over the trust of people in the colony, a key sentiment

[39] Ibid.

[40] In 1918 W.J. Geil undertook the task of re-editing Lamster's films to make them more appropriate for educational use, including the addition of 1,000 metres of stock footage from Pathé. The collection then expanded from 55 to 76 films.

highlighted in the article is 'mutual appreciation'. This is because all groups of Europeans, 'merchants, planters, and industrialists and all branches of the colonial machinery need the cooperation of the native more and more'.[41] It is reiterated that the natives are diverse and thus need to be understood in ways that address their specific cultures. The 'moral elevation of the natives in the colony' in the spheres of 'justice, mission and education' is a key duty of the Dutch. A strong link is advocated, which pushes for less domination and a stronger connection. The article reports that at the end of the first lecture a film is screened on the life of natives in the villages. This film, based on descriptions, was most likely *Het Leven van den Inlander in de Desa*, which Lamster made as a companion piece to *Het Leven der Europeanen in Indië*.

The former is similar in structure to the latter. Following one or two medium-duration shots, intertitles explaining the scenes appear onscreen. The intertitles reveal the content of the film (Figure 11). They give the impression that the audience had very little knowledge of what they were looking at.

In Lamster's celluloid world, Europeans and natives in Batavia have discrete existences. And these existences are by and large peaceful. In the films described above, the European world is centred on the ease of expatriate family life while the native world has a strong riverine theme. Neither scenario is developed very well. While the 'illustrations' were required to smooth out what was essentially a rather random sequence—from horse to buffalo to children to the chief to goat satay—they add little to a set of simple, staid images. It must, however, be noted that the apparent lack of plot and storyline in these films is not entirely indicative of Lamster's abilities as a film director.

While Lamster may have desired to project more complex impressions of the East Indies in these early ventures, he was handicapped by the very limited possibilities of cinematographic equipment at the time. He had to be outdoors in clear light, with a limited amount of time for each shot and without the option to film wide vistas (it was a fixed-angle lens). Film was dear, and the short films were supplemented by intertitles that lasted almost as long as the scenes. It is also possible that several scenes perished due to incorrect exposures or mistakes in the

[41] *Bataviaasch Nieuwsblad*, 'Omgang met Inlanders' [Dealing with the Natives], 23 Mar. 1914.

INTERTITLE I

De eenige reiniging der paarden bestaat in afboening in de river

The only way the horses are washed is a scrub in the river.

INTERTITLE II

ook is de rivier de algemeene waschplaats voor het voedsel (rijst, ketella enz.)

The river is also the general washing place for food (rice, cassava, etc.).

INTERTITLE III

De karbouwen kunnenniet buiten hun dagelijksch bad, maar gaan toch slechts schoorvoetend in snel stroomen water

The water buffalo must have a daily bath, yet they enter the fast-streaming water only reluctantly.

INTERTITLE IV

In het bad voelen zij zich zeer op hun gemak

The bath makes them feel very comfortable.

INTERTITLE V

De logge dieren worden de rivier uitgedreven

The ponderous animals are being driven from the river.

INTERTITLE VI

Onder waterstralen (pantjoerans), die uit de bergen stroomen, legt men waschplaatsen aan

Under jets of water (panchurans), that come from the mountain, washing facilities are constructed.

INTERTITLE VII

De heel kleine kinderen worden ook meedoogenloos in het koude water gedompeld

The very little ones, too, are mercilessly dipped into the cold water.

INTERTITLE VIII

Het dorpshoofd gaat naar de districts vergadering; men lette er op, dat de inlander aan de rechterzijde van zijn paard op en afstijgt

The village chief on his way to a district meeting; notice that the native mounts and dismounts his horse on the right side.

INTERTITLE IX

De inlander is zeer verzot op geroostert geitenvleesch (sesaté-kambing)

Natives are very fond of roasted goat meat (sate kambing).

Figure 11. Intertitles for *Het Leven van den Inlander in de Desa* [The Way Natives Live in the Countryside], J.C. Lamster, 1912–13

irregular on-site developing process. This seemingly slapdash filmmaking was actually common around the world during this period. Peterson, writing about non-fiction film in the 1910s, has queried this disjointed style: 'Most of these films remain reliant on the single-shot unit, their editing simply joining a group of disparate shots together. Rarely does the editing construct a unified space or narrative progression ... often the complete product does not add up to the sum of its parts.'[42] We can only surmise that the novelty of actually seeing the colony come alive on screen was enough to keep viewers interested in the images.

While it is difficult to establish from the records the order in which the films were made, the degree of sophistication of the productions may determine some sequencing. The two films discussed above are very possibly from an early set, as evidenced by their simpler construction. And while they indicate the general thrust of the propaganda style the Colonial Institute desired, they do not really add much to our knowledge of the East Indies. There were several films, however, which presumably came later, that highlight the new projects in health and social development that were beginning to be implemented. *Inlandsche Huisnijverheid* [Native Cottage Industry], for example, features women spinning cotton on a very basic spinning wheel, first in Bali and then in Java. Men are seen working on handmade sculptures. In *Meisjesschool te Bandoeng* we are taken through a day in the life of a school for teenage girls. In the second scene of the film, after the girls enter school, they are seen to *Groet aan de Onderwijzeres*, or 'Greet their teachers'. They do this in the traditional Javanese way—on their haunches and crawling. The school clearly does not exclusively follow the Dutch system—the crawling of the girls is not seen as demonstrative of a local tradition that needs to be 'Europeanized'. The girls then take lessons in cooking, washing and drying laundry followed by sewing, knitting and embroidery. At the end of the day they are seen leaving the school, presumably to go home. All the teachers in this school are native. But in some schools, where the skills taught are considered to be European, we see Dutch instructors. In the film *Inlandsche Veeartsenschool te Buitenzorg*, the teachers conducting anatomy lessons are Dutch. In subsequent scenes native students are shown helping Dutch veterinarians examine animals

---

[42] Peterson, 'Truth Is Stranger than Fiction', p. 77.

in a clinic. The animals on screen are a pedigree dog and what appear to be thoroughbred horses. The clinic does not seem to be for agricultural or farm animals.

If a school teaching local young women how to do laundry and a clinic healing European horses do not seem to be particularly helpful in providing new skills and services for natives, *Blindeninstituut en Ooglijdersgasthuis te Bandoeng* [Institute for the Blind and Eye Hospital in Bandung] documents a more serious effort at 'uplifting' natives. The short film documents blind residents of the school making brooms and straw hats, and a girl studying Braille. We are shown a surgical wing and an actual ongoing eye surgery in close-up. In *Strafgevangenis Te Batavia* [Prison in Batavia] we see how inmates are put to useful work by being organized in groups, almost factory style, and shown weaving and sewing. A prominent scene features the Dutch prison warden tasting the food that is prepared for prisoners. In *Koepokinenting in de Desa* [Cowpox Vaccination in the Countryside] a native man in Dutch uniform arrives and inoculates children against smallpox. Lamster had quickly improved in his ability to cover short episodes by filming in angles that captured the different stages of the sequence and editing them in a style that had temporal as well as spatial consistency.[43] While these films are propagandistic, they are actual records of schools and clinics. It would be hard to refute that there is clear evidence of at least some modicum of effort on the part of the colonial authorities to support the vision of the Ethical Policy and its welfare programmes.[44]

A series of films covering the remarkably detailed processes of the production of sugar, rubber, coffee and pepper was also produced. *Suikerrietcultuur op Java* [Sugarcane Cultivation in Java], *Rubbercultuur op Java*, *Koffiecultuur op Java* [Cultivation of Coffee in Java] and *De Pepercultuur* [Cultivation of Pepper] are part of a general series on cash crops in the Indies. The production of such a series is hardly surprising, considering that a number of commercial donors funded the Colonial Institute. What is interesting, though, is that Lamster's filming of these

[43] It is not possible to factually determine the sequence in which these films were made, nor how and by whom they were edited.

[44] Taylor (2015) also explores the extension of the Ethical Policy as represented in Lamster's films.

projects is actually better than when he has to present generally on European life or scenes from a native village. The 'process' film, a staple of the early non-fiction era, was perhaps easier to make as the sequences are in fixed order.

In 1914 W.F.G. Derk, an agronomist from the Colonial Institute, presented a lecture titled 'The Present and Future of Tillage of the Java Sugar' after a screening of *Suikerrietcultuur op Java* in Rotterdam. In his talk, Derk contended that the lack of a strong workforce had caused the price of sugar to rise. He then went on to describe the advantage of mechanically tilling the sugarcane fields: it would dramatically increase sugar output.[45] The film is remarkably well made considering the limitations of technology in the early 1910s. We see the entire production cycle—the digging of trenches, the cutting and planting of seedlings, manual fertilization, inspection, the cutting of grown cane, the transport of cane to the factories, the production of sugar, and the eventual transport of the finished good. What is striking is Lamster's documentation of children involved in several stages of production. In 1912–13, even for European audiences, this was not particularly shocking. Unsurprisingly, this is not mentioned in the newspaper article reporting on the lecture.[46]

It is difficult to categorize definitively Lamster's filming style. His oeuvre contains *actualités*, propaganda, travelogues and, arguably, proto-ethnographies: various subgenres of non-fiction that have been described closely in chapter 2. The camera is rarely close to the subject. The films do not provide nuance or interpersonal insight. Generally they are wide scenes, filmed in daylight with several intertitles that create a narrative when there may be one lacking via the images. The natives are mostly from the working class; they appear in the films either performing their duties or engaging in cultural performances. The films are short in duration, mostly under ten minutes, and on several occasions longer performances are collapsed in time to make them viewable as shorts.

---

[45] *Bataviaasch Nieuwsblad*, 2 Mar. 1909, p. 5.

[46] This is one of many films later edited by W.J. Geil, who introduced several still images to make the film ideal for lecture. It is thus difficult to ascertain exactly which version was seen at this early screening. However, most of the footage would have been shot at the same time and does not seem to have been re-edited or added to later.

The collection can be broadly demarcated along the lines of 'process' and 'non-process' films. When covering a general theme such as a location, a non-process film such as *Het Leven van den Inlander in de Desa*, while visually interesting, does not have enough of a thematic grounding to merit deeper analysis. It falls into that trope of early postcard travelogue film. Lamster is at his best when making films that follow some kind of process, a start and an end with several nodes in between. I compare two films from this collection, both touching upon aspects of how the Dutch presence in the East Indies interfaced with royalty, as further examples to illustrate this division.

In Djocjacarta [In Yogyakarta] has the somewhat wandering structure of a Lamster locational, non-process film. It opens with wide shots of the populous city of Djocjacarta (Yogyakarta). Streams of people walk on broad roads flanked with telegraph poles. There are fewer vehicles than in the scenes from Batavia, and horse carts pull passengers. The intertitle guides us to views of 'The Resident's house in the centre of the city'. This is a big, modern administrative building with a lawn. Statues and trees surround it. Next, Lamster starts following the afternoon adventures of two Dutch couples. They enter a building called The Society, a club for Europeans. Following this is a seemingly random scene from a native market, perhaps to create a contrast. Then there is a shot of the outside of a large white arch that is identified as the Kraton (palace) entrance. The scene then shifts rather surprisingly as, rather than enter the walls of the Yogyakarta Kraton, the group of four drive off to a location a little farther away to the west of the premises. The car stops, the group alights, and the intertitle reads 'The Water Palace, a dilapidated pleasure garden of the late Sultan Hamenkoe Boewana I'.[47]

The group then proceeds on a walking tour of this remarkably run-down palace built in the mid-18th century. Entire walls are covered with wild foliage. The men help the women through the overgrown gardens. The contrast with the well-painted, sturdy, white Dutch Resident's house shown earlier is striking. The four Europeans in their dazzlingly white clothes, carrying parasols, excitedly continue adventuring around

[47] Sultan Hamengkubuwono I built the Water Palace in the mid-18th century, when Yogyakarta became the new capital of his sultanate.

the Water Palace and seem to have travelled into the past. Was the film a statement of the contrast of the newly arriving modernity to the East Indies—with the smart buildings, telegraph poles and European clubs—with the decrepit ruin that the Sultan's palace had become? A viewer in Holland would not perhaps have had enough information to understand that the dingy collapsing palace—with stagnant water in the pools—was not actually where the royalty lived. If the rest of Java was shown as an industrious, efficient, rural community, on the cusp of modernizing, then why would a trip to the city of the royal family showcase such bleakness? It is impossible to ascertain whether this was deliberate. It is plausible that Lamster's subjects wished to visit the Water Palace that day and he merely accompanied them. It is also possible that there were other scenes filmed with them in the Kraton that were unusable later for technical reasons. Nonetheless, watching the film with little comprehension of the land would undoubtedly make viewers wonder whether the local royalty was a dysfunctional relic of the past. Furthermore, it cannot be denied that the location certainly provided a dimension of exoticism, a trope common in travelogue films of that period.

In her article on travel films from the 1910s, Peterson gives several examples of colonial films made in Southeast Asia—in Bangkok, Kuala Lumpur and Malacca—around the same time that Lamster was operating in the East Indies. She discusses the 'native types'—asserting that exoticism has a certain convention which fuelled the travelogue film's tension between the 'different' and the 'normal'. This binary cognition is based on Edward Said's general observations on Orientalism: the East is different in that childlike, depraved, fallen way that anti-Orientalists are quick to point out. Peterson adds that the goal of most colonial filmmakers creating travelogues had an identifiable style: 'the place must be (constructed as) exotic, yet in this presentation there is at the same time a certain disavowal of that exoticism, a desire to mark what is Other and then contain it, keep it at arm's length.'[48] But Lamster's general objective evidently was not to keep natives at arm's length. While it would have been difficult for him to create an intimate portrayal of Javanese life given the social and technological limitations of the period, he does not seem to strategically distance himself from his

[48] Peterson, 'Truth Is Stranger than Fiction', p. 81.

subjects. In a sense Europeans are as exotic as natives in his films—odd transplants in a tropical environment, moving around with exaggerated vigour and almost comical whiteness of attire. There is little exoticism of the Javanese in these films describing various welfare programmes. Instead, we are invited to look at their problems and the solutions that have been offered. Whether or not these solutions were effective, or whether the methods of problem solving were ethical, was outside Lamster's purview.

All colonial propaganda films contain some properties of being a travelogue. Lamster certainly straddled the two. There were traits in Lamster's work that treaded on yet another category of non-fiction: the cinematic observation of rituals and society with an eye for detail and precision—the form that film theorists would eventually call the ethnographic film.

Early Ethnographic Film

In the 17-minute film *Viering van den Gerebeg Moeloed te Solo* [Celebration of Garebeg Mulud in Solo], Lamster focuses on the process of an annual ritual, the Garebeg Mulud—a celebration of the Prophet Muhammad's birthday. Made in the royal court of Surakarta on 17 February 1913, the film chronicles the event in remarkable detail. The celebration of Mulud, a week of festivities leading up to a royal solemnizing attended by members of rank, followed by a procession of mountains of rice to the mosque, is still celebrated in many parts of the former East Indies. There have been numerous academic mentions of this ceremony, and amateur videos abound online.[49]

John Pemberton's book *On the Subject of 'Java'* describes this ritual in detail, especially with an eye for its unchanging execution.[50] Drawing on three primary sources to analyze the sociopolitical implications of this generations-long observation, Pemberton makes the case that the precision of the event, unaltered over two centuries, was indicative of a

[49] See J. Kathirithamby-Wells, 'The Islamic City: Melaka to Yogyakarta, c. 1500–1800', *Modern Asian Studies* 20, 2 (1986): 333–51; Margaret J. Kartomi, 'Music in Nineteenth Century Java: A Precursor to the Twentieth Century', *Journal of Southeast Asian Studies* 20, 1 (1990): 1–34.

[50] John Pemberton, *On the Subject of 'Java'* (Ithaca: Cornell University Press, 1994).

significant Dutch-native dynamic. The main source consulted is a manuscript believed to be from the late 1840s titled 'An Explication (Pratelan) of the Appearance of His Majesty His Highness the Susuhunan Pakubawana VII for Garebeg Mulud in the Year 1847'.[51] This manuscript breaks down every aspect of the event into specific items numbered chronologically. Pemberton observes that the thorough descriptions in this 'Explication' have a quality akin to an instruction manual. It is impossible to tell whether they were written as the event occurred, just after it, or even before it—as a sort of guide. Pemberton writes, 'At no point is a ceremonial mishap recorded—a tell-tale sneeze for example—which might historically situate the document.'[52] The document, according to Pemberton, matches with records from even older Surakarta documents—he uses the phrase 'chilling accuracy' when comparing it to the version by the Dutch colonial translator J.W. Winter from 1824.[53] He is again full of wonder comparing it with a version as late as 1940 from a Garebeg Mulud programme written for Pakubuwana XI. This time he uses the phrase 'eerily perceptive'.[54]

Pemberton's salient observation is that this unaltered event and the precision of the charade it involved were deeply indicative of the relationship between the Kraton's historical power over Java and how Dutch rule, represented by the arrival of the Resident, came to fit into it. Routine Kraton ceremonies typically did not include the Dutch Resident. For the Garebeg Mulud, however, the rules had changed. Unlike the normal protocol where the reigning Pakubuwana would enter only after everyone else was present, he now waited for the Resident, an act of acquiescence creating a 'virtual suspension of sovereignty'. The highlight of the encounter was manifest when, 'After a brief handshake, the pair walked at a gentle pace, arm in arm, back to the pavilion interior ...

[51] Reksadipura, *Pratelan Miyos Dalem Ingkang Sinuhun Kangjeng Susuhunan Pakubuwana VII Kaprabon Garebeg Mulud ing Dal 1775* (composed and inscribed Surakarta, 1847/8). Ms. RP H42; SMP MN 271C, as cited in Pemberton, *On The Subject of 'Java'*, p. 97.

[52] Pemberton, *On the Subject of 'Java'*, p. 98.

[53] J.W. Winter, 'Beknopte Beschrijving van het Hof Soerakarta in 1824', *Bijdragen tot de Taal-, en Volkenkunde* 54 (1902): 61–4, as cited in Pemberton, *On the Subject of 'Java'*, p. 97.

[54] Soeloeh Sekaten (compiled by 'Chronos, Free-lance journalist Indonesier') (Solo: B.T. Tijoe, 1940), p. 15, as cited in Pemberton, *On the Subject of 'Java'*, p. 99.

the ritual encounter on the Central Pavilion's threshold implicitly altered His Majesty, transforming him into a colonial bride, a veiled match for the Mister Resident.'[55] Pemberton posits that a power dynamic was put on display; the hierarchy of it is apparent.

Another account of this ritual can be gleaned from the prolific work of an anonymous Javanese poet-historian whose manuscript Nancy Florida stumbled upon, 'tucked away in a volume of royal correspondence whose home is now the library of the Surakarta Palace'.[56] The poem is 'The Prophet's Nativity' (in *Babad Jaka Tingkir* XVIII), which Florida translated in its entirety. Her accompanying notes mention that the poem is written as though it occurs in 19th-century Surakarta, although it situates the reader in the 'Grand Mosque of Demak', where the king began a tradition reportedly to 'Islamize' Java in the 16th century. In yet another testament to the insistence of the uniformity of the event, like the 'Explication' that Pemberton refers to, the *babad* stanzas too are precise and descriptive. The scene of the procession of people arriving at the Kraton for the ceremony (stanzas 19 and 20) is observed as follows:

> On the morn the procession
> Garebegan proceeded in parade
> Teeming in the subjects great and low
> Were arrayed: a crowded sea
> Filling the Alun-alun brim full
> Over the spilled to the by-ways
> Thronging in unbroken streams.
>
> Like a leafy forest lush
> The grand parade of subjects from
> All of Java's land
> Loomed like a long lolling darkening cloud
> Pressed in crowded crush
> In swarming teeming mass
> Like a thunderhead on high
> With darkness, covering all the sky[57]

---

[55] Pemberton, *On the Subject of 'Java'*, p. 100.

[56] Nancy Florida, *Writing the Past, Inscribing the Future: History as Prophesy in Colonial Java* (Durham: Duke University Press, 1995), p. 9.

[57] Florida, *Writing the Past*, p. 184.

Figure 12. Pakubuwana X enters the Central Pavilion with the Resident in 1913.

Figure 13. In 1923 Tassilo Adam filmed a close shot of the Resident and the 'colonial bride'.

Lamster covers this scene in the Garebeg Mulud well. Following an intertitle that reads 'On Pasar Gedeh and all the roads leading to the Kraton, comes in an extraordinary crowd', Lamster has about two and a half minutes of footage spread over nine different shots of men and women from all strata of society arriving at the gates of the Kraton. While not quite a 'darkening cloud' of people, it is certainly a very large congregation. The following stanza onwards describes the seating configuration of the Susuhunan in relation to his subjects:

> The Lord Sultan, holding audience
> In the Canopied Pavilion on the
> Elevated Earth, sat
> Upon his sapphire throne
> With the foremost of the wali
> Seated on thrones one and all
> On one level with his Majesty
> To the right and left of the king.[58]

The *babad* goes on to describe the ceremony till the very end, when food is distributed. Accordingly, in Lamster's film we do see the 'Canopied Pavilion' with the long-reigning Pakubuwana X seated on his throne and many others around him very carefully distributed according to rank and importance. Once again, the film footage matches the poet's description; the *babad* stanzas could almost be a shot list for Lamster.

I have two observations from these comparisons of Lamster's filming of the ritual of the Garebeg Mulud with the written sources cited above. First, the film is a reasonably accurate illustration of the different texts—Pemberton's descriptions of the 'Explications' from the late 1840s, as well as Florida's close translations of the *Babad Jaka Tingkir* XVIII. If Pemberton was struck by the 'chilling accuracy' and the 'eerily perceptive' aspects of written sources placed so far apart in time, he would possibly have been equally taken by Lamster's film footage. It corroborates his notion that the ritual had been very been carefully orchestrated for centuries. And if he was unsure at any point whether his written source was a live-observational piece (that 'tell-tale sneeze' he wishes for) or an edited piece of writing meant to project what the actual Garebeg Mulud ought to be like, he now undoubtedly has a live film record.

---

[58] Ibid.

The processions were too important and populated for Lamster to have creatively tampered with any aspect of them. Second, there is one fundamental difference between 'The Prophet's Nativity' and Lamster's film: The Dutch regent is not present in the *babad.* Between stanzas 20 and 21 of the *babad* is when the regent appears in Lamster's film. He is brought in with a tremendous amount of ceremony, 'with an air of authority so serious that it at least equaled if not surpassed the celebrated solemnity of the occasion itself'.[59] According to Pemberton, this sets the dynamic for the relationship between the Surakartan ruler and the Dutch Resident. After we see a long procession of people, parasols, buggies and cars, the Resident appears. A title card reads 'The Susuhunan moves on to the arm of the Resident and is followed by the carriers of the national jewelry'. And then Pakubuwana X is shown walking with his arm linked inside the Resident's, making him the 'colonial bride'. The shot unfortunately has a break in it, but it is clear enough. A decade later, cameraman Tassilo Adam would get a close-up of the same scene.

To give us a perspective of where the development of non-fiction film was during the period that Lamster made *Viering van den Gerebeg Moeloed te Solo,* I quote film historian Catherine Russell, who explores outliers in the genre of ethnographic film in her book *Experimental Ethnography*:

> Nonfiction films of the second decade of the twentieth century are in many ways a caesura in film history. Neither *actualités* within the aesthetic framework of the cinema of attraction, nor 'documentaries' in the style initiated by Flaherty in 1922, they constitute a wealth of cultural documentation that has only recently begun to be recognized by scholars and archivists.[60]

In these early days of non-fiction, several genres overlapped. As mentioned before, most of Lamster's films have aspects of propaganda, travelogue, *actualités,* ethnography and documentary. It is futile to try to tease out a predominant style. It is important, however, to recognize Lamster's pioneering efforts in some of these categories. The term 'documentary', as we know, did not enter the English lexicon until its

[59] Pemberton, *On the Subject of 'Java',* p. 97.
[60] Catherine Russell, *Experimental Ethnography* (Durham: Duke University Press, 1999), p. 99.

use as a noun (borrowing from the French) by Grierson in his 1926 review of Flaherty's *Moana*. Non-fiction film theorists claim that the documentary, or the art of 'cooking' a narrative from *actualités*-based footage, was born out of propaganda during the coverage of World War I. Ethnography, however, is not independent of documentary; it is not a separate category of cinema with different rules. As Heider observed, the ethnographic evaluation of a film is like considering the height of a building. All buildings have height; all films have some ethnographic content. But we consider a film to be 'ethnographic' when it has a high ratio of such content.[61]

The annals of cinema history, though, have not credited Lamster with any such distinction. His coverage of the Garebeg Mulud is remarkably accurate with no embellishment or major omission. The film has little subjective dimension—it was not easy in an era of filming with bulky equipment, especially as one was not allowed to get close to royalty. Perhaps the film can be compared with a well-made newsreel or reportage of an important event. While Lamster's films have been studied somewhat by a handful of academics—Jean Gelman Taylor, De Klerk and Strangio among them—considering the cultural significance of the events and their accuracy of coverage, social scientists could probably benefit from viewing them as ethnographic accounts.

What is somewhat surprising about Lamster's prodigious output is one notable exception: there is no clear reference to his original designation in the East Indies military. There is a film, however, that reflects Lamster's years in Aceh serving under Van Heutz. It is in remarkable exception to Lamster's style—it has re-enactments, almost a feeling of fictional production. *Het Nederlandsch-Indische Leger; De Infanterie* [The Netherlands Indies Army; Infantry] is a 25-minute film in two parts. The first part shows routine military drill, sports activities and barrack maintenance by natives, many of them concubines (per colonial army practice in that era) doing daily chores such as cooking and washing. The second part of the film stages a robbery plot by a group of Islamists that is pre-empted by the KNIL.

The story is simple and guided along with intertitles. The plot is titled 'Fight Mode of the Native Enemy'. We see a group of men with swords in scabbards secured at their waists greeting each other and then

[61] Heider, *Ethnographic Film*, p. 2.

Figure 14. Acehnese militants in prayer, *Het Nederlandsch-Indische Leger; De Infanterie* [The Netherlands Indies Army; Infantry], 1912–13

seated around for prayer (Figure 14). An elderly ulama figure leads the congregation in an open space in the backyard of a house. The group then tread through a wooded area, crouching down, holding up their spears, swords and guns, preparing for ambush. They stealthily creep up on an outdoor camp of the KNIL. Their attack is unsuccessful, however, as the Dutch troops appear to be expecting them. The KNIL opens fire, and the natives run away after putting up a brief resistance. Several of them fall to the ground.

The battle scenes involve possibly up to 100 people and in some sections are quite realistic. This is the only hint we have in Lamster's films about a Dutch fear of Islamic militants attacking, no doubt based on the guerrilla warfare that the Acehnese waged against the Dutch for decades—a situation Lamster himself had experienced when in the army.

Lamster was especially proud of this film. In the minutes of the meetings at the Colonial Institute, Wijsman, who was a constant critic of Lamster's work, elaborated:

> He had on his list amongst other things army and fleet, preferably while in action, and informed me as if it concerned a glorious piece that pleased him greatly, that he had arranged the robbery and encampment involving a group of soldiers dressed up like the native enemy with spies arriving, to finalize with the stabbing to death of the attackers, in such a natural way that it even fooled a friend from the military.[62]

[62] Brief, H.P. Wijsman (Secretary) to J.T. Cremer (Chair), Sukabumi, 14 Dec. 1912 (KIT 4314).

Wijsman found the premise for the film to be too controversial for the banner of the Colonial Institute and recommended the material be sold immediately should anyone be interested in purchasing it. Almost a century later, when Lamster was resurrected in a publication by the Tropenmuseum, a DVD carrying 15 of his short films was included in the biographical sketch.[63] *De Infanterie* was one of them. Lamster may well have made the first film in cinema history based on a religious terrorist attack.

In the Introduction to this book, I bemoan that while there have been substantial studies on still images produced in the Netherlands East Indies during the late colonial period, researchers, with rare exception, have yet to scour the significant film archives at Beeld en Geluid and the Eye Filmmuseum. Does Lamster have a legacy beyond being a cinematic pioneer to merit in-depth study? Is there promise of useful, dynamic history trapped in his image making that would make it worth a researcher's time to patiently view his substantial corpus? Arguably, Lamster's film are somewhat static; they cover from a respectable distance various towns and cities, cultural exhibitions, and benevolent colonial programmes. There is scant reference to any political tension or emerging nationalist movements. One especially cannot overlook the timing of his films—1912 and 1913, just when Sarekat Islam, a political group that would eventually promote a modern Islamic political awareness in the colony, was taking root in Java. It was especially in the areas around central Java where Lamster lived and travelled that influential chapters of the new nationalist group were emerging. The Dutch ruling machinery under Governor General Idenburg installed considerable surveillance mechanisms to monitor the group's growing influence.[64] Yet there is no reference to these significant developments.

Lamster clearly did not see fit to create for the Colonial Institute (nor was he instructed to do so) any film programmes that would give the people of the Netherlands even an inkling of what their ruling nation was up against politically. In the years to come, and in the hundreds of documentaries that were made, this theme seems to be startlingly absent from the concerns of many artists involved. The new 'lights' that

[63] Dijk et al., *J.C. Lamster*.

[64] Takashi Shiraishi, *An Age in Motion: Popular Radicalism in Java, 1912–1926* (Ithaca: Cornell University Press, 1990), p. 68.

Mrazek mentions, referring to Kartini's set of poems that championed an indigenous awareness of modernity appearing at the turn of the century, challenging the colonial status quo, are never projected directly onscreen.[65] It can be argued, however, as we observe the films in retrospect, that there is a subtle presence of this new direction.

Taylor suggests that these films provide us with a new vantage point for viewing this period. According to her, still images from the 1910s, and there are thousands of them easily available for perusal, typically represented the elite class—both Dutch and Indonesian—and created unbalanced social perceptions. Henk Schulte Nordholt underscores this observation: 'colonial photography was more interested in documenting official cultural heritage like temples, dances and things labeled *adat*.... There are limited numbers of photos taken in offices, where we see the middle-class employees at work.'[66] But Lamster's films did enter workforce vistas, so elusive in still images from that period. Complimenting this ability to capture with a motion picture camera a more dynamic sense of how the labour force operated, Taylor writes:

> Close-ups of foremen in action organizing, commanding and checking, with the white boss unseen, remind us who ran the colony at the ground level. The absence of royals in the colony's commercial centers, factories and on plantations perhaps prepared the workforce of the colonized for a republican society. The endless photos of royals and aristocrats in the image archives ... suggest to us, probably quite misleadingly, a society still in thrall to its hereditary chiefs. Lamster's films are a valuable corrective.[67]

Taylor brings to our attention that Lamster's films depict a lack of servility on the part of Indonesians towards the European class. She directs us to two sites in his films where this seems apparent: in the work environment, and in the street scenes where Lamster mounted the camera on a moving car. Indeed, in the many films where we see a young, dynamic Indonesian workforce engaged in varied tasks—building locomotives, inoculating children in the *desa*, or processing cash crops—

---

[65] R.A. Kartini, *Letters of a Javanese Princess* (New York: W.W. Norton, 1964).

[66] Henk Schulte Nordholt, 'Modernity and Middle Class in the Netherlands Indies', in *Photography, Modernity and the Governed in Late-Colonial Indonesia*, ed. Susie Protschky (Amsterdam: Amsterdam University Press, 2015), p. 246.

[67] Taylor, 'Ethical Policies in Moving Pictures', p. 65.

they seem to be confident and self-reliant. Though there are frequent shots of Dutch men in a managerial role, they seem neither overbearing nor haughty. Struck by the indifference of natives towards the odd Dutch person walking or cycling around, Taylor comments that the scenes from Lamster's car ride 'captures an unrehearsed fact of colonial life, meaningful *to us* because of its challenges to our received ideas of social relations, within colonies [emphasis in original]'. Many, especially those in urban offices, would perhaps fit into the category observed by Schulte Nordholt as the 'indigenous cultural citizen'—a middle-class group aspiring to modernity, who, by their co-option into the workforce, actually ended up sustaining the colonial regime.

It is difficult to tease out with any confidence those aspects in a large corpus of work that were deliberate from what was unintended. While we may only guess as to what Lamster's driving motivation was for each film or scene, we can discuss what it is that Lamster's films mean to us today—now that we know what happened. I agree with Taylor when she writes, 'Lamster was right to train his camera on the "new" young men and women. His paramedic and veterinary students joined the nationalist parties and filled the leadership circle of the republican movement.... Their descendants today run Indonesia, not the Dutch and not the royals.'[68]

If Lamster was true to his recording of the Ethical Policy, his highly selective depiction of Indonesian society notwithstanding, his vision can be corroborated by the fact that we now know it was ultimately this class of Indonesians who contributed to wresting power away from the Dutch in a drive to become self-sufficient—an effort to steer themselves away from the legacies of both feudalism and colonialism. Yet Lamster remarked that Indonesians would 'feel happy and contented under the shadow of the Dutch flag'. He seemed to be sure that the Dutch presence and stewardship would remain indispensable to the Netherlands East Indies. The very people whom he was suggesting that young Dutch nationals come and manage would ultimately take advantage of this turn in modernity and claim a nation for themselves. This contradiction is not surprising: after all, the dreamers of the Ethical Policy did not foresee it to be a force that would eventually derail its very architects. To be fair, no one in the early 1930s could have imagined that the

[68] Ibid., p. 68.

centuries-long colonial strangling of Asia would be over in most places in less than two decades. Taylor suggests, 'Historians gain information from images their creators did not know they were imparting.'[69] Indeed, while much of what we gain today from Lamster's oeuvre may have been inadvertent, his artistic instincts and considerable efforts are worth scrutiny for the narratives they could reveal about a class of people rarely ever captured on film. However flawed and limited the Ethical Policy was in scope and implementation, there might be a seedling of an argument that the policy, whose manifestations Lamster so diligently tried to capture on film, did contribute something to the intellectual and social empowerment of a class of Indonesians.

There seemed to have been a mandate in the early days of the Colonial Institute film enterprise to cover a multiplicity of themes: culture, labour, modernity, agriculture—the list goes on, as evidenced by Lamster's wide range of films. For its next filmmaker, however, the Colonial Institute decided to hone in mostly on one aspect and location—labour in the Deli plantations of Sumatra. Still mindful of the Ethical Policy, this next set of films would bring Dutch audiences into the world of labour, migration and cash crops being harvested at the edge of the colony—businesses valued at huge amounts of money. While the films were initially produced under the banner of the Colonial Institute, there was a gradual influence by the commercial patrons who held important positions on the institute's board. This was the start of corporate-driven propaganda in the Netherlands East Indies.

---

[69] Ibid., p. 63.

CHAPTER 4

Corporate Films (1917-27)

> A Dutchman without a pipe is a national impossibility.
>
> – Schotel[1]

In 1916, details of a meeting at the Colonial Institute about an upcoming filmmaking venture were printed in the *Sumatra Post*:

> The Committee was inclined to bestow the assistance requested and the Board of AVROS was willing to share the cost of an operator, provided that the cost assumed was not too great.... The Committee is of the opinion that the films made for the Colonial Institute should be exhibited in the villages of Java ... and thereby promote emigration to this region.[2]

L.Ph. de Bussy, a biologist in Sumatra, soon received a request from the Colonial Institute to film the cultivation of tobacco, tea and rubber in Sumatra. He was given the camera that Lamster had used before departing in 1913. De Bussy, like Lamster, was not a professional filmmaker; he had been serving as the director of an agricultural research station in Deli, Sumatra, where he developed insecticides. The films, assisted financially by Algemene Vereniging van de Rubber Planters ter Oostkust van Sumatra (AVROS), a research institute funded by corporate interests in Sumatra, were to encourage transmigration from Java.

[1] Iain Gately, *A Cultural History of How an Exotic Plant Seduced Civilization* (New York: Grove Press, 2001), p. 82.

[2] 'Opnamen van kinematografische films' [Recording Cinematographic Films], *De Sumatra Post*, 22 May 1916.

That the Colonial Institute chose this region of Sumatra as its next region of focus for making informational films was unsurprising given the area's large and hugely profitable plantations. While Lamster had documented the early outreach efforts of the Ethical Policy that were being implemented mostly in Java, the new policy affected the larger archipelago as well. Transmigration to the Outer Islands was a core tenet of the Ethical Policy.[3] It was important to film the shift of colonial economic enterprises from Java to the Outer Islands.

While Java remained the political epicentre of the East Indies, its commercial importance had diluted with the rapid development of mines and plantations in the Outer Islands by the late 19th century. As the late Indonesian historian Onghokham noted in his monograph *The Thugs, the Curtain Thief, and the Sugar Lord*, more than half the total revenue of cash crops was generated from outside Java by 1930.[4] In particular, labourers travelled in large numbers to Sumatra as the tobacco industry boomed. Although Deli and other parts of East Sumatra had introduced tobacco planting as late as the 1860s, the crop's yield grew swiftly, requiring an influx of labour. Additionally, the area diversified to large estates of rubber and palm oil. Deli was quickly transforming into the colony's new cash bowl, drawing much attention and scrutiny. Filming this process of large-scale commercial agriculture and multiracial migration was adjudged a priority.

There also was a need for film to help humanize the landscape of Deli and its new inhabitants. In the late 19th century, Deli had a reputation for being an isolated and distant place where it was difficult to assimilate. As one Dutch historian of the region aptly described it:

> Deli was an island; some said a society within a society, a particular form of European society, wholly different from that in Java. 'Java' and 'Deli' were entirely different ideas; the planter in Deli was an entirely different being. Deli was white, Java was mixed. In Deli everything had to be imported, the employees as well as the coolies. The staff came

[3] Jeffrey Burke Kingston, 'The Manipulation of Tradition in Java's Shadow: Transmigration, Decentralization and the Ethical Policy in Colonial Lampung' (PhD dissertation, Columbia University, 1987).

[4] The breakdown is 53.3 per cent from the Outer Islands and 44.3 per cent from Java, in Onghokham, *The Thugs, the Curtain Thief, and the Sugar Lord: Power, Politics, and Culture in Colonial Java* (Jakarta: Metafor Publishing, 2003), p. 244.

> directly from Europe, the coolies from Java. Deli was a conglomerate of white settlements with Chinese and Javanese colonies encircling it. But they were all foreigners, no one had roots.[5]

Deli harboured a dark past that needed a corrective public relations campaign. Since the 1870s, investors had made the most of colonial protections under a scheme of deregulated, liberal economics. But by the turn of the century, tales of wretched conditions of the labourers were reaching Holland, raising alarm and invoking anger. Dubbed 'The Dollar Land of Deli', this fertile area and the surrounding tobacco plantations were a constant source of concern for colonial officials as there were sporadic revolts from indentured labourers. Despite the harsh punishments received for any form of protest, the area became a maelstrom of oppositional activities, labour movements and riots. While the situation vastly improved by the second decade of the 20th century, the Dutch colonial government still needed to alter its image of plantation labour management. It also wished to showcase a system of humane, efficient cash-crop productivity.

Portraying the Plantation

The subject matter of De Bussy's films—documenting a burgeoning cosmopolitan contracted force, with labourers arriving from Java, China and India—was significantly different from Lamster's. And unlike Lamster, who worked for the Colonial Institute, De Bussy actually had two interest groups to satisfy with his productions: the Colonial Institute and the corporations that funded its productions. While De Bussy was supposed to showcase the new colonial approach towards a more humane treatment of native labourers vis-à-vis the Ethical Policy, his financial backers were the tobacco companies that wished to display their efficient management to their investors. That process involved depicting how cash crops could be cultivated in a rigid and economically advantageous system. The coolies working on the plantations needed to be shown as part of a labour system where they could be kept under strict subjugation. There was an inherent contradiction in attempting to portray a benevolent government making up for its past excesses and

[5] Rob Nieuwenhuys, *Oost-Indische Spiegel* (London: Fontana, 1978), pp. 346–7.

yet championing the operations of huge corporations that wished to show that their workforce was regimented. This tension comes across in many of the De Bussy films from 1917 onwards. It is this duality that makes for a more candid exposé of plantation life and its lingering, oppressive systems.

Because the issue of representation and authorship is important in our study of these visual archives, it is significant to note that several of these films credit an elusive cameraman named 'Mr. J. John', who seems to have been a freelance operator working with the Colonial Institute. De Bussy, a scientist and laboratory researcher, is on record expressing his satisfaction at having procured the technical services of Mr. John right at the commencement of his assignment: 'One of the hospital assistants in Senemba introduced me to Mr. John, a professional photographer familiar with developing film. This is a happy circumstance that will greatly benefit the work.'[6] While Mr. John's identity remains a footnote in the archives, his contribution may have been important in forming the look and style of this next wave of films and thus merits attention. There are several newspaper reports that specifically enquire about his work and presence in Sumatra. In 1918 the *Sumatra Post* reported speculatively, 'We hear Mr. John is currently working with different companies ... and on the behalf of the Colonial Institute, possibly for making necessary advertising in the United States.'[7] By 1919 another article in the *Sumatra Post,* titled 'Medan Filmed', glowingly covered the innovative work of Mr. John as he filmed life in the large city and then returned to the United States with a lot of footage. The *Sumatra Post* goes on to inform readers that even though the Colonial Institute had been filming in the East Indies in order that people in the Netherlands could learn more about their colony, the organization should bear in mind that 'every evening thousands and thousands of Javanese visit hundreds of cinemas. The cinema screen is an advertising medium.' In keeping with the transmigration initiative of the Ethical Policy, the reporter argues that such films are 'a practical tool of choice for the Javanese colonization of the East Coast'. He reminds readers

[6] Handwritten letter from Buitenzorg, Java, from L.P. Debussy to Director of Handel Museum, at the Colonial Institute, 8 June 1917. KIT 4829 Correspondentie reizen/verslagen: L.P. de Bussy, Indie, 1917.

[7] 'De Oostkust in Film' [The East Coast on Film], *De Sumatra Post,* 3 Nov. 1918.

that 'Film should appeal to the imagination, and so propaganda film should not only have a shot here or there, in this or that moment, but cover daily life on the East Coast—the labor, the relaxations, typical displays.'[8] In 1920 yet another newspaper article reported that Mr. John had filmed a few thousand feet and covered plantations as well as cultural aspects of the lives of the Batak people. In a subsequent interview he told the newspaper he had requested the Colonial Institute for more raw film stock.[9] The press was clearly interested in the films produced by the Colonial Institute and had opinions about their content and scope, and had some discussion with the filmmakers working on these projects.

These films by De Bussy and Mr. John (I have not been able to establish who he was) did indeed get closer to subjects than Lamster's films. There was more revealed of the life in the plantations than expected of a cursory informational effort. De Bussy, in fact, was noted for 'spending too much attention on the living and housing conditions of the coolies'.[10] If the literature and corporate reports lacked a vivid description of life and work in Deli, scenes from films such as *Immigratie in Deli* [Immigration to Deli], *Kolonisatie van Javanen op eene Delische tabaksonderneming* [Settling Javanese Workers on a Deli Tobacco Plantation], *Rubber Film* and *Sumatra Theecultuur* [Sumatra Tea Cultivation], produced in the ensuing years, provide visually vivid primary source material for our insight into plantation life and systems. Brief descriptions follow. But first we need to understand why a fair portrayal of labour in Sumatra was important to the Dutch colonial government.

As these films cover the arrival and activities of groups that were not native to Sumatra, a brief background on the debates surrounding the problems faced in the Deli plantations at the turn of the century would be useful. While there is little doubt that workers in Deli were exploited, the difference of opinion as to how perverse and exploitative the colonial plantation system was, has been a major point of contention. Labour historian Jan Breman and anthropologist Ann Laura Stoler have written extensively about society and politics on tobacco plantations in Sumatra. In an extended study of the very large plantation area of Deli, Stoler describes a historic tale of exploitation and resistance and

[8] 'Medan gefilmd' [Medan Filmed], *De Sumatra Post*, 17 Nov. 1919.
[9] 'Oostkust Films' [East Coast Films], *De Sumatra Post*, 28 Feb. 1920.
[10] Dijk et al., *J.C. Lamster*, p. 26.

a heightened awareness of colonial methods of exploitation, starting as early as 1870, when the area attracted a multinational business consortium with British, American, French, Swiss, Japanese, German and, of course, Dutch investments.[11]

Unlike the many sordid tales from Java revolving around the fallen Dutchman in novels from the period, as mentioned in chapter 3, there were few novels written about Sumatra at the turn of the 20th century that would have revealed embarrassing situations. There were, however, key investigative documents akin to what we would consider embedded journalistic reporting today. The stories of oppression in Deli eventually got out rather dramatically, and far more factually, due to the motivation of a lawyer in Medan who wished to expose the sordidness of plantations.

The Rhemrev Report

In 1902 Johannes van den Brand, a lawyer in Medan, published a slim volume titled *The Millions from Deli*, which sensationally detailed the exploitative situation of workers on the estates.[12] The book, advertised in the newspapers for sale at the price of one guilder, was read widely. It caused significant consternation; people took polar views.[13] In a series of essays with titles such as 'Mistreatment and Cruelty' and 'Insensitivity and Thirst for Money', Van den Brand attacked not only the employers of the coolies but the colonial government that was complicit in the system. In 1903 Van den Brand published a follow-up report, *Again: The Millions from Deli*. His persistence did not go unnoticed at the highest levels of the Dutch government. Some insisted that the accounts of exploitation were exaggerated, while others chastised the colonial government for being complicit in a brutal system of perpetuating cheap labour. Nonetheless, a new level of awareness about the region grew among the public in the Netherlands. In 1904 public prosecutor J.L.T. Rhemrev prepared a document, commonly known as the Rhemrev

[11] Ann Laura Stoler, *Capitalism and Confrontation in Sumatra's Plantation Belt, 1870–1979* (New Haven: Yale University Press, 1985).

[12] Johannes van den Brand, *De millioenen uit Deli* (Amsterdam: Pretoria, 1902).

[13] *Bataviaasch Nieuwsblad*, 8 Jan. 1903. Small advertisements appeared in the 'For Sale' section of popular newspapers.

Figure 15. Van den Brand's *The Millions from Deli*, 1902

Ontvangen:
Stratz, De schoonheid der vrouw bij verschillende rassen geb . . . . f 7.25
7423 G. KOLFF & Co., Noordwijk.

Verschenen:
De Millioenen uit Deli
door
Mr. J. van den Brand.
Prijs f 1.—
G. KOLFF & Co.

Figure 16. *The Millions from Deli*, for sale at one guilder in the *Bataviaasch Nieuwsblad*, 1903

Report, which brought under scrutiny the conditions of coolies on the plantations of Sumatra. The report, though leading to some administrative change, was suppressed and never officially published until 1987, when Breman located it in the National Archives at The Hague.[14] The convoluted history of the document reflects the concerns that the colonial government had with regard to its image in Deli. The region needed to remain attractive for foreign investors, and yet it had to adhere to higher standards of labour management practice. The desire to create films as a propaganda tool becomes apparent as we understand this history.

According to Breman, the initial expository writings of Van den Brand sent 'a chill of horror' through the Netherlands—resonating half a century after Multatuli published *Max Havelaar*, the well-known devastating novelized critique of Dutch colonial order in the East Indies.[15] Rhemrev's report, following on the heels of Van den Brand's book, was 'in some ways worse than what had been previously established or conjectured. The successful concealment of large-scale malpractice from the outside world was found to be even more reprehensible than the revelation of the systematic use of violence.'[16]

It is along these lines that academics Vincent Houben and J. Thomas Lindblad differ from Breman. They consider Breman's position, that the colonial government was complicit in sustaining 'reprehensible' slave-like conditions on the plantations, to be an extreme one: 'What we do not support is the kind of generalization Breman proposes, namely that the colonial state was evil, its officials being mere tools in the hands of capitalist enterprise and therefore causing the misery to which the coolies were subjected.'[17] Accusing Breman of perpetuating a 'simple black and white portrayal of the past', Houben and Lindblad have suggested that

---

[14] Jan Breman, *Koelies, Planters en Koloniale Politiek* (Dordrecht: Foris, 1987). Note that both the Rhemrev Report and the booklet by Van den Brand are included in Breman's 1987 publication. The English-language edition, *Taming the Coolie Beast*, from two years later, does not contain these documents. They can both now be downloaded from the library holdings of the Royal Tropical Institute.

[15] Jan Breman, *Taming the Coolie Beast: Plantation Society and the Colonial Order in Southeast Asia* (Oxford: Oxford University Press, 1989), p. 3.

[16] Ibid., p. 8.

[17] Vincent Houben and J. Thomas Lindblad, 'Correspondence', *Journal of Southeast Asian Studies* 33, 3 (2002): 559–60.

'colonial states were complex entities with several agencies working side-by-side but not necessarily in the same direction, although the ultimate outcome of the colonial policies may suggest so'.[18]

While we cannot be certain of either claim—whether the Dutch authorities knowingly played a dark, instrumental role in subjecting workers to a hand-to-mouth existence, or whether it was the result of a systemic failure of policy—it is clear that conditions were quite appalling, and the film footage actually does show us some of this.

Labour on Film

Given the historical context, De Bussy must have been aware of the consequences of what he was filming—after all, he had been hired to provide a positive image of plantation management. Documents indicate, however, that De Bussy filmed 'without any cover up', subsequently exposing the grittier aspects of life on the plantations.[19] While the film record does not show the plantations operating under inhumane conditions, it does provide us with a less sanitized understanding of that period. There may be several interpretations of why the films did show the rough treatment of workers, despite the fact that they were propaganda supported by the government.

De Bussy may have had a journalistic bent in that even though he had been hired to produce films to promote the tobacco industry, he may have felt compelled to reveal some of the truths about the basic nature of indentured plantation coolie life. Or, we could consider that in 1917, basic humanitarian standards were significantly different. Going by this, the scenes of bonded labour and child exploitation were simply representative of the norm at that time.[20] By this reasoning, the difficult

---

[18] For further elaboration on their position, see Vincent J.H. Houben, J. Thomas Lindblad et al., *Coolie Labour in Colonial Indonesia: A Study of Labour Relations in the Outer Islands, c. 1900–1940* (Wiesbaden: Harrassowitz, 1999).

[19] Dijk et al., *J.C. Lamster*, p. 22.

[20] Nico de Klerk is of the latter opinion: 'In the physical examination, the coolies may seem to us as if they are being treated as cattle (measuring, inspection of teeth, inoculation), but to people then this may rather have seemed harmless and necessary. Their living conditions are not in any way filmed as being dirty or neglected. Even though such scenes are—at least in the film collection of EYE—unique, one should remember that a critical way of filming was simply out of the question' (personal communication, 19 Apr. 2012).

living conditions and rough treatment we see of coolie workers were captured as part of the usual coverage, and only much later did they become an inadvertent exposé of a seamier side of colonialism. Indeed, child labour was discussed in a very matter-of-fact manner. An entire generation was born on the estates around 1900 and was co-opted into the labour force. As Breman writes: 'The planters were delighted with the quality of these *anak Deli* [children of Deli]. They had become accustomed at a very early age to earn a few cents by picking tobacco leaves and thus look after their own requirements. It was not unusual for children to start working at the age of seven.'[21]

Additionally, the producers of the films, those with direct corporate interest, may have wanted to show shareholders that the 'coolie beast' was indeed tamed and subservient to the plantation managers. A large, well-disciplined workforce would have conveyed to stockholders that their investments were being put to good use. Accordingly, a depiction of how large-scale systems of bonded and transported human labour operated was documented closely.

De Bussy's 1917 film *Immigratie in Deli* provides us with a powerful primary source of the transmigration project. Produced with financial support from the Deli Planters Association (DPV), a commercial conglomerate, the collaboration was indicative of the Colonial Institute's growing relationship with the private sector. The film is divided into two sections: the arrival of Chinese coolies and the arrival of Javanese coolies in Sumatra. Like other productions from that period, it is a silent film with several intertitles in Dutch. *Immigratie in Deli* is remarkably clear in its documentation. In the first section, migrants from China arrive on large ships in Belawan, the main port of entry in Sumatra. They disembark, appearing to be quite discombobulated from the long journey, thrust suddenly into their new surroundings.

The East Indies colonial government operated under the laws of a special Coolie Ordinance for the Outer Islands. The ordinance provided for a three-year contract for the arriving coolie in which desertion was punishable as a serious offence. There was considerable debate about the ethics of this form of labour contract as it placed great limitations on the physical and mental health of the workers. Women were almost never recruited for working on the plantations; Chinese women rarely

[21] Breman, *Taming the Coolie Beast.*

Figure 17. Women and children disembark. Still from *Immigratie in Deli* [Immigration to Deli], 1917

made the long journey.[22] *Immigratie in Deli*, however, makes it very clear that Chinese women and children were beginning to arrive at the plantations by 1917. This is the only filmed record of the actual arrival in Deli of Chinese workers who were recruited under the penal code contracts. Bold intertitles in the silent film set up these key moments, the first being 'Women and children, too, come along from China' (Figure 17).

Women, men and children are inoculated on arrival. They are then transferred to separate rooms. Naked men are filmed showering, after which they squat around; they eat bowls of rice they are given. Subsequently they are taken to an area cordoned off by wire mesh, where a series of booths are set up. Here they are pushed around and measured for height, and they exchange the money they have brought with them. At times the officers look as though they are about to strike the workers (Figure 18). The workers are inoculated again.

In the second part of the film, Javanese passengers disembark from a train in Medan. Unlike the migrants brought in directly from China, they do not undergo medical tests. Their treatment overall seems far more humane. Once again, the arrival of women and children is highlighted. They are taken to their quarters and fed a meal. The last part of the film shows a shelter that appears clean and orderly.

22 Wim F. Wertheim, 'Conditions on Sugar Estates in Colonial Java: Comparisons with Deli', *Journal of Southeast Asian Studies* 24, 2 (1993): 268–9.

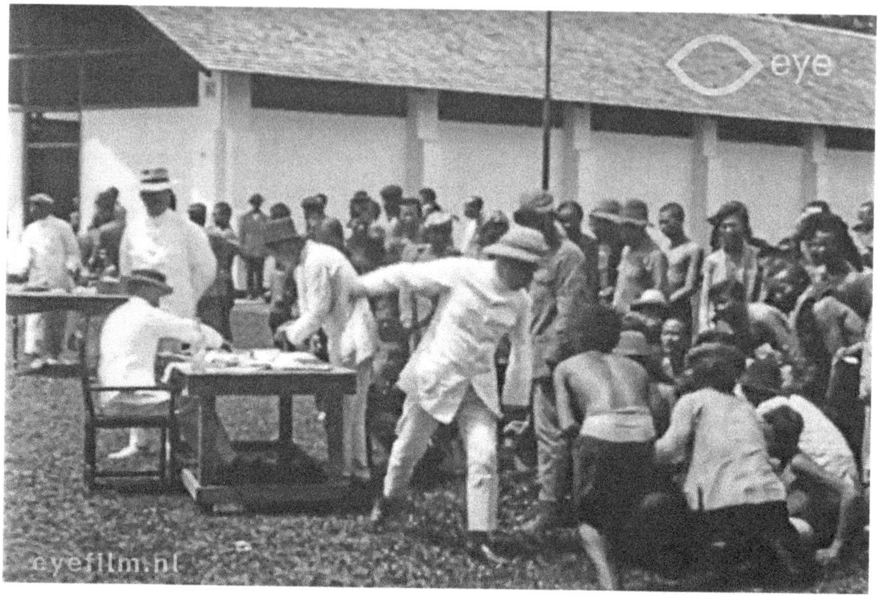

Figure 18. Chinese coolies being checked in. Still from *Immigratie in Deli* [Immigration to Deli], 1917

Despite the rough treatment, footage of generally orderly conditions, medical check-ups, sanitary arrangements, adequate nutrition and especially the creation of the shelter is indicative of the desire of a colonial government to portray itself as one that cared for the well-being of migrants, with particular emphasis on women and children.

Lamster produced a series of films depicting inoculation, surgery, clinics and hospitals in Java that are related to this focus on improving care of the natives. In Deli, too, given prior accounts of the horrific conditions created by the penal code indentured system, this would have been perceived as a move in a significantly humane direction. A newspaper report from Deli during that period corroborates what we see in De Bussy's film: 'In this beautiful setting is also the immigrants' shelter, where disabled and elderly coolies are housed. They often express the wish to return to their country of origin. But indeed they are nursed at the expense of the Deli planters.'[23] Though the report is not entirely

[23] 'De heer Eekhout over Deli' [Mr. Eekhout about Deli], *De Sumatra Post*, 8 Apr. 1923.

positive, chiding the government for its lack of care of those who are mentally challenged, the very consideration of elderly and mentally handicapped people requiring help was an improvement—possibly a trickle-down effect of the Ethical Policy. In the 1917 film *Kolonisatie van Javanen op eene Delische Tabaksonderneming* [Settling Javanese Workers on a Deli Plantation] this theme continues. De Bussy depicts the new, tranquil residential setting of Javanese transplanted families, once again with an added emphasis on scenes of women and children. A house for a headman or village chief is identified, and efforts are made to create a spatial sense of the re-fabricated community. We see the construction of several houses that are similar in style to the architecture typically found in Java.

These films allowed for Deli to be presented in a better light to the Dutch public, upholding the promises of the Ethical Policy. As Medan had a processing lab, the film stock may have been developed soon after shooting. De Bussy's films, however, were not screened in the Netherlands until as late as 1920 due to transportation difficulties during the war. W.J. Geil, the editor in the Netherlands who had worked on the reassembly of much of Lamster's films, was responsible for editing this new material as well. When the films were ready for screening in the Netherlands, the following announcement appeared in *De Filmwereld*:

> The Colonial Institute is finally able to give its due to those who have played such a large role in the making of these films. They will have the opportunity to have three film screenings. The first is Thursday, November 11, at noon and exactly half past two in the large auditorium of the Laboratory for Health Education, Mauritskade 57:
>
> I. Immigration in Deli. 1. Immigration of the Chinese 2. Immigration of the Javanese. Immigrants in shelter
> II. Hygiene measures on the East Coast of Sumatra
> III. Tobacco Culture of the East Coast (3 parts)
> IV. Rubber Culture of the East Coast
> V. Tea Culture of the East Coast
> VI. The Corps Volunteers on the East Coast[24]

[24] 'Binnenland. Filmvertooningen van het koloniaal instituut' [Inland. Film Screenings of the Colonial Institute], *Het nieuws van den dag voor Nederlandsch-Indië*, 27 Dec. 1920.

The films were screened in other parts of Europe as well. One of the goals of the propagandistic efforts of the late 1910s and early 1920s was to demonstrate to audiences across Europe (not just in Holland) that the Dutch colonial government was conducting fair business in its colony, balancing lucre with social development.[25] The impetus for this may have come from the creation of the League of Nations in 1919, when in a desperate scramble to normalize global relations after the horrors of World War I, several countries opened doors of communication. According to Hendriks, this led the Netherlands to defend its position as a humane colonial power and ushered in a new era of accelerated propaganda.[26]

The foreign screenings of these films were arranged so other Europeans could view the East Indies as well as young Dutchmen living abroad. A Dutch reporter living in Germany in 1921 describes a crowded lecture about the colony, which the ambassador to Berlin and Baroness Gevers attended along with several hundred Dutch living in Berlin. There were screenings of four Colonial Institute films. The article quotes the speaker, Max Blokzijl, beseeching the Dutch audience to 'proudly send your children to the Indies, rather than they be paid badly in Holland or Europe in menial work, to toil without any future relations. The Indies can always use good Dutch forces.' He added that the retired governor general, Count of Limburg-Stirum, had recently opined that 'To his regret young Dutchmen still lack desire to go to that beautiful country, where many a splendid job beckons. For life in the Indies in recent years has become much more attractive in every way, and there the Dutchman could be proud of what his ancestors and his contemporaries have achieved.'[27]

---

[25] Hendriks' research indicates that the proposal to create a government film company in 1921 (different from the Colonial Institute) was not accepted, as the enthusiasm from the Ministry of Colonies had abated. The Ministry of Foreign Business, however, expressed a need for colonial films that showed healthy business practice. The Catholic Church followed in this trend, and gradually propaganda filmmaking took off in a large way, mostly managed by commercial production companies. Hendriks, 'Een voorbeeldige kolonie', p. 25.

[26] Ibid.

[27] 'Buitenland Brieven Uit Berlijn' [Foreign Letters from Berlin], *Bataviaasch Nieuwsblad*, 24 Dec. 1921.

'Please,' added Blokzijl, 'Tropical Netherlands and European Netherlands can possibly be back together in the future, as they were in the heyday of the East India Company—but a healthier, more independent relationship of power is of the first importance.'[28]

Produced a few years apart, the films of Lamster and De Bussy had both similarities and differences. Like Lamster, De Bussy filmed in hospitals and healthcare facilities to give visual credence to the Dutch government's growing mandate to take better care of its subjects. If Lamster, however, captured, purposefully or inadvertently, the growing irrelevance of a certain class of white colonials, in De Bussy's films they seemed very much active. The plantations had a low ratio of Dutch colonials to coolies, and it seemed important to establish the latter's subservience. If some emancipation from white overlordship is evidenced in numerous Lamster films, where we see a native class running institutions, factories and educational facilities, it is not seen in the De Bussy material.[29] A paternal, parochial, class- and race-based system seems to drive the plantation economy. The Dutch managers here are aggressive and command a striking presence amidst meek coolies, many of them immigrants, further lowering the latter's entitlement and status. Thus, the burgeoning, modern, more empowered class in Batavia that Taylor observes in Lamster's footage is in strong contrast with the subservient labour force in De Bussy's films. An ongoing, inherited system of indentured life in Sumatra is in evidence. To be sure, the Deli region had come a long way since the days of the Liberal Policy economics as corrections were made after the Rhemrev Report's release in the wake of the Ethical Policy. Yet, unlike in Lamster's footage, which carries a prescience of the end of Dutch rule, this material does not give one the impression that colonialism was on its last legs. Or perhaps, to remove a class barrier, it does not convey that the indentured groups of people were going to have their lives improved any time soon, even in what was to become modern Indonesia.

De Bussy, industrious as he was, was not a motion picture professional. He was fortunate to have a competent collaborator in Mr. John, which resulted in several original films. Like Lamster, he was recruited

[28] Ibid.

[29] This is one of the salient observations about Lamster's films by Taylor (2015).

by the Colonial Institute, provided with minimal training, and handed a camera. They produced several dozen films between them and add an important visual dimension to our historiography of the 1910s in the Netherlands East Indies. With these titles, however, the Colonial Institute concluded its active participation in the production of films. It continued to perform a curatorial role, showing 'educational' films to a certain demographic—continuing to stay away from screenings in cinema halls and mainstream venues. In the years to come, commercial film production entities would take over the motion picture enterprise in the colony. Their focus remained mostly on showcasing plantations, mines and the large labour forces that drove the colonial economy.

Mullens, King of News

The next director to embark on filmmaking in the colony had a profile that was very different from Lamster's or De Bussy's. Willy Mullens was the most famous documentary filmmaker in the Netherlands in the 1920s. Along with his brother Bernardus Albert, Mullens had founded one of the earliest Dutch film production companies—Alberts Freres—in 1899. In 1914 he went on to start a second company, Haghefilm, which eventually surpassed the original family company in reach and reputation. With the decline of Colonial Institute productions, Mullens saw an opportunity in the Netherlands East Indies and arrived in 1924, several years after De Bussy had completed his films about Deli and the plantation system.

Given his reputation and standing, it was not difficult for Mullens to raise substantial sums of money for his new venture. A consortium of oil companies funded his first project in 1924—it was simply titled *Oil Film*. The film proved to be an excellent public relations asset for Bataafsche Petroleum Maatschappij, the reigning petroleum company.[30] Encouraged by his early success, Mullens eagerly wished to return to the

[30] The goals of the film were reflected in the welcome speech by the company's director, A. Philips: 'Our men are there in the East to earn money for our shareholders. But in doing this, they spread much wealth and prosperity far beyond the circle of shareholders.... I am convinced that what you see will not give the impression that we impoverish the Indies, but we enrich it; that we do not depress the native, but he benefits.' *Nieuwe Rotterdamsche Courant*, 19 June 1924.

East Indies and began lobbying for a return expedition. Film historian Bert Hogenkamp notes:

> Although Haghefilm received more than enough jobs, the Netherlands did not hold enough of a challenge for Mullens. However, there was a part of the Kingdom of the Netherlands that the King of News was waiting for: the Dutch Indies. Among the wider public, there was great interest in movies on the archipelago. The Colonial Institute systematically collected films about the Dutch Indies, organized regular movie nights and had copies sent off to cinemas in schools.[31]

Mullens was a maverick, a self-promoting showman who once blasted himself as a human cannonball in a fair. But, just as important, he was politically astute and highly regarded in the Dutch media. In 1917 he made a 2.5-hour documentary called *Holland Neutraal: Leger en Vlootfilm* [Holland Neutral: The Army and Fleet] espousing Dutch neutrality (while subtly indicating a strong army reserve), which attracted a mass audience and won him a coveted reputation with the royal family. Dubbed the 'King of News' at a young age, he dramatically expressed his opinions on the importance of documenting Dutch involvement in the East Indies in the newspaper *Het Vaderland*:

> A polemical work is always effective. Uncle Tom put an end to Negro slavery. For us Max Havelaar put an end to the abuses in the Indies. Both took action against wrong attitudes.... To me it seems a duty of the government to inform its population in the most illustrative way about what essentially is the survival of its people.[32]

With his professional reputation and subtle posturing as a modern, cinematic Max Havelaar, Mullens received several more contracts to film in the East Indies. On the eve of his second departure, in 1926, he announced on radio an astounding number of enterprises that were backing his work—the Department of Colonial Affairs and Education, Koninklijke Paketvaart-Maatschappij, Baron Baud's companies, Senembah,

---

[31] Bert Hogenkamp, *De Nederlandse documentaire film 1920–1940* (Amsterdam and Utrecht: Stichting Film en Wetenschap, 1988), p. 19.

[32] Cited in 'Mullens over z'n reis' [Mullens about His Journey], *Nieuw Weekblad voor de Cinematografie*, 25 July 1921.

the Deli Batavia, the Tobacco Bureau, the Association for Rubber Cultivation, Dordtsche, the South-Preanger and the Indies Rubber Society. By the time he returned to The Hague in 1927, Mullens had filmed a staggering 34 kilometres of footage.[33]

Despite his personal clout, Mullens was not entirely free in his choice of what subjects or topics to film. He was accompanied by G.C. Janssen, the inspector of education, who played a supervisory role. But Janssen's report, as located in the Eye Filmmuseum archives by Hendriks, indicates a less stringent outcome of the filming style: 'When one starts filming, coincidence often plays a big role. We believe in that respect we have been lucky to "grab" some issues that were offered up only by chance.' Janssen had a list of topics from the ministry but took the freedom to modify it: 'As some subjects were no longer existing or were in special circumstances, they were impossible to film.'[34] Effectively, Mullens made the best of the situation. But perhaps there was no real necessity for such censorship and control, as his vision of the machinations of a 'just' colony dovetailed with what the colonial government and its corporate allies wished to see on film: a simulacrum of an ethically administered archipelago that continued to prosper under Dutch tutelage.

Elaborately produced pamphlets accompanied the films' screenings. They often listed in detail every scene in the documentaries screened. By now it was clear that the Dutch government was fully open to collaborations with the private sector to promote the cash crop industry. The introduction of the document *Rubber Film*, a text accompanying a film produced primarily in the Deli region by Mullens, indicates this clearly: 'The Netherlands Government and various important Cultivation Companies and Industrial Concerns, they had at the same time the privilege of taking, for the—Industrial Association for the cultivation of Rubber and other Cultivations in the Netherlands a great film, viz the RUBBER FILM which they have the pleasure of displaying to you' (original in English).[35]

---

[33] Hogenkamp, *De Nederlandse documentaire film 1920*–1940, p. 21.

[34] EYE archive, Willy Mullens, inv. No. 27 Letter Ministry to Mullens, 16 June 1926. As noted in Hendriks, 'Een voorbeeldige kolonie', p. 64.

[35] *Rubber Film*, International Association for Rubber and Other Cultivations in the Netherlands East Indies, c. 1927.

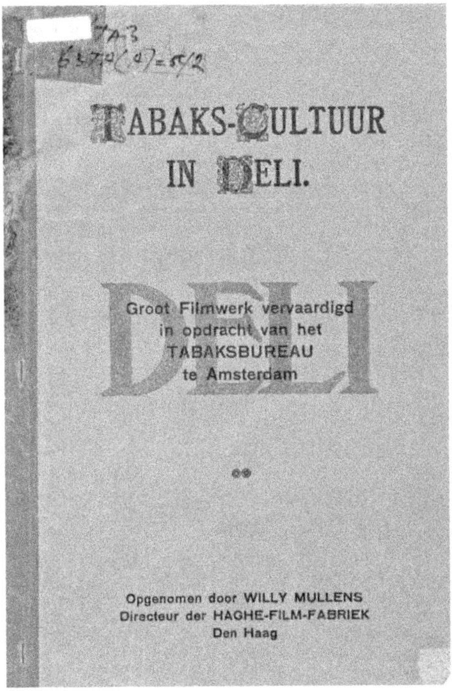

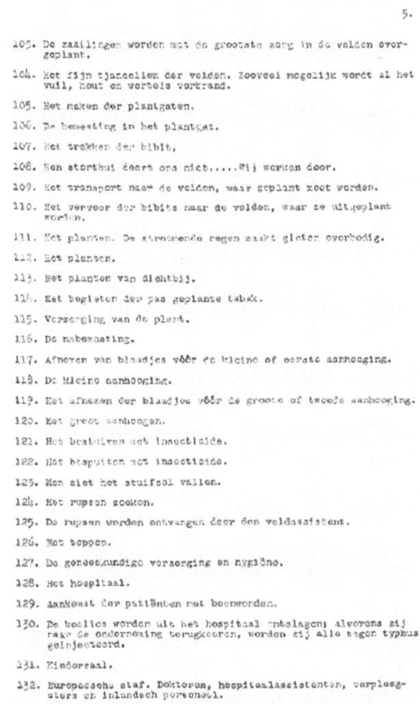

5.

103. De zaailingen worden met de grootste zorg in de velden overgeplant.

104. Het fijn tjangkoelen der velden. Zooveel mogelijk wordt al het vuil, hout en wortels verbrand.

105. Het maken der plantgaten.

106. De bemesting in het plantgat.

107. Het trekken der bibit.

108. Een stortbui deert ons niet.....Wij werken door.

109. Het transport naar de velden, waar geplant moet worden.

110. Het vervoer der bibits naar de velden, waar ze uitgeplant worden.

111. Het planten. De stroomende regen maakt gieten overbodig.

112. Het planten.

113. Het planten van dichtbij.

114. Het begieten der pas geplante tabak.

115. Verzorging van de plant.

116. De nabemesting.

117. Afnemen van blaadjes vóór de kleine of eerste aanhooging.

118. De kleine aanhooging.

119. Het afnemen der blaadjes vóór de groote of tweede aanhooging.

120. Het groot aanhoogen.

121. Het bestuiven met insecticide.

122. Het bespuiten met insecticide.

123. Men ziet het stuifsel vallen.

124. Het rupsen zoeken.

125. De rupsen worden ontvangen door den veldassistent.

126. Het toppen.

127. De geneeskundige verzorging en hygiëne.

128. Het hospitaal.

129. Aankomst der patiënten met beenwonden.

130. De koelies worden uit het hospitaal ontslagen; alvorens zij naar de onderneming terugkeeren, worden zij alle tegen typhus geïnjecteerd.

131. Kinderzaal.

132. Europeesche staf. Doktoren, hospitaalassistenten, verpleegsters en inlandsch personeel.

Figures 19, 20. Pamphlet for the film *Tabakscultuur in Deli* [Tobacco Cultivation in Deli] listing scenes

The films that Mullens meticulously produced were showcased for investors and recruiters. They provided detailed coverage of the complex processes involved in both agricultural production and plantation management. In addition, there was substantial coverage of the social lives of the workers, including amenities provided for them by their parent company. In the pamphlet released with the film *Tabakscultuur in Deli* [Tobacco Cultivation in Deli], a stunning 375 scenes are meticulously described (Figures 19, 20).[36]

In the document, we can clearly see the inclusion of some non-commercial aspects—more in line with the expectations of the Ethical Policy. For instance, descriptions of medical facilities are entered as follows:

[36] Willy Mullens, *Tabakscultuur in Deli: groot filmwerk vervaardigd in opdracht van het Tabaksbureau te Amsterdam* (Den Haag: Haghe-film-fabriek, 1927).

127.	'Medical care and hygiene'.
128.	The hospital.
129.	Arrival of patients with leg wounds.
130.	Coolies are discharged from the hospital. Before they return to the company, they are all inoculated against typhoid.
131.	[Undecipherable]
132.	European staff. Doctors, nurses and Indian staff.
133.	The physicians regularly visit the companies where the workmen are inspected.

Figures 21.1–6 show a selection of corresponding stills representing the above entries.

Entry #127

Entry #128

Entry #129

Entry #130

Entry #132

Entry #133

Figures 21.1–6. Stills from *Tabakscultuur in Deli* [Tobacco Cultivation in Deli], 1927

The film presented improved labour conditions as generally upheld by the new direction of the administration. It was important for Mullens to include shots of relatively content workers, in compliance with larger governmental and societal goals. The message was clear: The colonial government had turned a corner; the accusations of inhumane treatment and pure maximization of profit that had led to the Rhemrev inquiry in 1903 were no longer valid. The visual depictions by Mullens are indeed in great contrast to descriptions of plantation bondage from the early 20th century. Consider the following portrait of life in Deli:

> But for the great majority and especially for the less thrifty Javanese, most of whom had been plain peasants in their *desa* (village), there was after the expiry of the three years' contract no alternative but to sign on for another term. The management did everything in its power to prevent the coolie from quitting: he was seduced into playing hazard, which was a much-used method of getting an old-timer whose contract had nearly expired into debt. For most of the labourers, many of whom had been cheated into signing a contract, working on a Deli plantation meant lifelong bondage made even harsher by the nearly exclusively male composition of the frontier society.[37]

Directly addressing the concerns of coerced, indefinite servitude to the plantation, Mullens added a section on the expiration of the contract. Towards the end of the film, an effort is made to show that the penal code was fair and that workers, both Chinese and Javanese, did return home after serving their three-year contracts.

288.	The Javanese, who go back to Java ... wait for the arrival of the train.
289.	Packed and loaded they go back to Java.
290.	Also for the Chinese it is time to leave.
291.	Cheerful and boisterous they go back to their family and friends back in their country after years in Deli.

Entry #288

Entry #290

Entry #291

Figures 22.1–3. Stills from *Tabaksculture in Deli* [Tobacco Cultivation in Deli], 1927

To further counter allegations against depictions of inhumane plantation and industrial life in Sumatra, Mullens released a thick, glossy,

[37] Wertheim, 'Conditions on Sugar Estates in Colonial Java', p. 269.

self-promoting coffee-table-size 'golden' book based on his numerous films in the East Indies. It is important to note that he insisted on the importance of the participation of his government in a way that was not merely industrial and mercenary: 'We see that the petroleum industry was not just a money-making venture for shareholders; that they not only draw oil from the ground ... but that, where she comes, a prosperous colony is created and her beneficent influence is widely spread. Undoubtedly many will open their eyes, and this is good.'[38]

In 1928 the newspaper *Het Vaderland* carried a brief article, 'Oost en West Vertoont de Tabaksfilm' [East and West Exhibit Tobacco Films], which covered screenings at the Trianon Theater of Amsterdam of several promotional documentaries made in the East Indies that the Tobacco Agency had funded. The review glowed:

> The audience gave their full attention from beginning to end, followed by great praise. But we should not be surprised: after all, they are films by Willy Mullens, and that says everything. We saw mines, sowing of plants, fertilizers and the spraying of crops in some phases, transport of the harvest, drying, sorting ... we saw the homes of officials and coolies, immigrants from China and Java ... hospitals are shown on film as well as the medical control of the plantations.[39]

There is little doubt that superior films were beginning to be made under Mullens. They were of a more professional quality compared to De Bussy's efforts and could be screened in various venues in the Netherlands, both academic and commercial. They were also shown around the world at public events. Mullens was clearly a success, but his vision was stilted. What his films portrayed about the colony was limited. As Hendriks observes bluntly, 'The Dutch Indies was an area where it was not all peace and harmony, where Indonesian nationalism had became stronger and grew to resist the Dutch government. The films made by Mullens, commissioned by the Dutch government, are interesting because of what they do not show.'[40] It would appear that

---

[38] Willy Mullens, *Enkele Pagina's Uit Mijn Gulden Boek* (Den Haag: Staatsdrukkerij, 1929).

[39] 'Oost en West Vertoont de Tabaksfilm' [East and West Exhibit Tobacco Films], *Het Vaderland: staat- en letterkundig nieuwsblad*, 8 Dec. 1928.

[40] Hendriks, 'Een voorbeeldige kolonie', p. 69.

Mullens, while being renowned for his ability to bring news to the Dutch people (hence the moniker 'King of News'), had little or no interest in important events unfolding in the East Indies during his stay there. Consider the following gory newspaper segment in 1926 asking for an investigation into the murder of Soegono, an alleged Communist:

> Javanese who have seen the corpse have declared that on the forehead was a blue mark, those of the fingers; the upper and lower arms and the elbows bore similar marks, and the toes of the right foot were crushed. Around the neck was a stripe.... It is no doubt highly desirable that a minute investigation of the case be made ... the charges being of such a serious nature, and coming on top of the many complaints of ill treatment of political prisoners.[41]

Immediately below the report of the murder was the following announcement: 'The Dutch film operator Willy Mullens who is in the colony to take films of various scenes, etc., will attempt to film the eruption of the volcano Batoer in Bali.'

A reasonably good reporter might have attempted to cover the ill treatment and murder of political prisoners. Hendriks highlights a report from 1927 by Inspector of Education A. Vogel, indicating that Mullens was unable to film in Sumatra as a 'result of the communist turbulence'.[42] Indeed, unlike what we see in Mullens' films, by the late 1920s Dutch rule was facing a myriad of uprisings and was on its way to coming rapidly undone. Mullens was not interested.

There is yet, I contend, value in viewing and analyzing the footage of Mullens. While there is arguably nothing new or unusual in this material, it provides an insight into the Dutch colonial mentality. It is also an extraordinarily detailed record of every aspect of plantation production, more so than previous efforts by Lamster and De Bussy—especially the new direction that the government was taking by investing in larger agrarian systems. It indicates that in a turbulent political atmosphere, the necessity of showcasing a perfectly functioning agricultural export system, based on heightened scientific application, was a key

41 'The Week in Java: Grave Accusations over Prison Incident', *Straits Times*, 23 Aug. 1926.

42 EYE, archive Willy Mullens, inv. 29 Report of the Sumatra-trip, by the Inspector of Native Education, A. Vogel.

strategy. The backdrop to the philosophy and the aim of this new direction follows.

Science on Film

Historians generally agree that by the early 1920s, implementations of the Ethical Policy had begun to wane. World War I had taken its toll, and the global economy had suffered; justifying and maintaining the colony was proving complicated. The East Indies underwent significantly increased taxation to subsidize Holland's armed neutrality during World War I, and, accordingly, several welfare programmes were reduced or curtailed.[43] As support for the Ethical Policy crumbled across all quarters, the Dutch government paradoxically continued to aggressively pursue commercial interests in its colony during what is referred to as 'the heyday of the late colonial state'.[44] 'Pure science' became a singular and unique defensible strategy for continuing a Dutch presence; it transcended colonial occupation and administration.[45] The aim of large corporations to maximize revenue and the colonial government's push to solve problems by seeing through a 'scientific lens' appeared to have merged. While Suzanne Moon notes that the use of science as a tool of empire was already a deeply embedded direction that had originated along with the Ethical Policy, she also suggests that a modified technological implementation in the 1920s saw 'an unexpected vitality' in that original vision for ethical reform.[46] Indeed, the idea of a technically enhanced colony, functioning systematically and utilizing the most relevant scientific procedures, had remained the operating bedrock since

---

[43] Robert van Neil, 'The Legacy of the Cultivation System for Subsequent Economic Development', in *Indonesian Economic History in the Dutch Colonial Era*, ed. Anne Booth, W.J. O'Malley and Anna Weidemann (New Haven: Yale University Southeast Asia Studies, 1990), p. 42.

[44] Peter Boomgaard, 'The Making and Unmaking of Tropical Science: Dutch Research on Indonesia, 1600–2000', *Bijdragen tot de Taal-, Land- en Volkenkunde* 162, 2/3 (2006): 206.

[45] Andrew Goss, 'Decent Colonialism? Pure Science and Colonial Ideology in the Netherlands East Indies, 1910–1929', *Journal of Southeast Asian Studies* 40, 1 (2009): 188.

[46] Suzanne Moon, *Technology and Ethical Idealism: A History of Development in the Netherlands East Indies* (Leiden: CNWS Publications, 2010), p. 124.

ethical reforms were introduced at the turn of the century.[47] There were, however, significant alterations over the next two decades in how technology was to be adapted. Several Dutch filmmakers, especially Mullens, documented that transformation to a more 'scientifically based' large-scale production.

In the second decade of the century, a policy of 'close contact' with the people was developed. At this stage, the colony operated on the principle that aggregates of smaller, well-developed plantations would yield a higher volume of crops. It also contained the ethical dimension of transferring technology from the more privileged knowledge bases of scientific analyses to local farmers. Films by Lamster in 1912 and 1913 that focused on small-scale agriculture do actually capture some of this innovation. Instead of using just the special strains of crops that were developed in laboratories, farmers from all over were asked to participate in demonstrating how local strains fared. Based on the yield studied, a more heterogeneous set of rice strains that originated from the farmers was used. This system generally fared well.[48]

The colonial government, however, soon abandoned its approach of taking chances on experimenting with native knowledge. Lab-tested strains that worked well in European-style farms with huge resources became the new approach. The emphasis shifted to larger operation; an era of 'betting on the strong' was ushered in.[49] Andrew Goss writes:

> Even as challenges to the civilising mission multiplied in the 1920s, the colonial government's ideological support for 'science for science's sake' justified their continued presence in the colony. This new civilising mission was probably less relevant inside the colony, where political

---

[47] Boomgaard, 'Making and Unmaking of Tropical Science', p. 205. A compelling example is the development of the 'POJ 2878' variety of Javanese sugar that gave it an edge over its competitors.

[48] Moon, '*Technology and Ethical Idealism*', pp. 29–43.

[49] 'Betting on the strong' was a phrase coined by Suzanne Moon to describe the shift in emphasis from close interaction with small-scale agriculturists to larger farm owners. Her conclusion, however, is that despite this general change in policy in the 1920s, an undercurrent of technological use as applicable to the small-scale farmer lingered on, and eventually recycled back as the trend in a post-1930s East Indies. The early ideology of the Ethical Policy in promulgating a close contact model did see its benefits in the long term.

> conflicts overshadowed it, but it remained important in the international context ... it had long-lasting effects, certainly in the way the Dutch continued to understand their colonial past as decent.[50]

Science was now a face-saving avenue for the colonial government, which had abandoned much of the vague idealism of the Ethical Policy. Mullens would be the first to embrace the visual projection of these much larger 'scientific' operations. Gone were the patient films of Lamster that often showcased public projects and the arts and crafts. The new films were mostly about the booming large-scale plantation and mining industries. Mullens had received considerable backing from the conglomerates with investments in rubber, palm oil, petrol and tobacco. With the de-emphasis on the Ethical Policy and on small farmers, the smaller films on East Indies life reduced in number. These plantation movies, though not representative of the small-scale farming that still continued, were not devoid of historical value. They provide a window to observe swiftly changing colonial systems.

Perhaps the most innovative film Mullens made to showcase the application of science in the colony was the 1926 three-part *Pest op Java* [The Plague on Java]. It was intended to educate the Javanese and help them eradicate the plague that had decimated about 120,000 people in the previous decade. A very convincing and detailed film, *Pest op Java* utilizes early cell animation techniques, re-enactment of scenes, and documentary footage to tell the story of a village afflicted with the rat-borne disease (Figures 23.1–3). Mullens uses this amalgam of styles to build a narrative that is easy to follow, entertaining, and yet useful in its sequential, scientific approach to explain the causes and prevention of the plague. A newspaper article in the *Bataviaasch Nieuwsblad* about a special screening in Batavia in 1928 reported the following:

> We followed the scenes with great interest, how the disease began in 1911 in Java, and in a short time spread over a vast area, the cause of this expansion and the measures taken against it.... The vibrant images were particularly strong, to the smallest details, like the showing of microscopic germs, etc. The audience was fully engaged.[51]

---

[50] Goss, 'Decent Colonialism?', p. 192.

[51] 'De Pestfilm' [The Plague Film], *Bataviaasch Nieuwsblad*, 15 Dec. 1926.

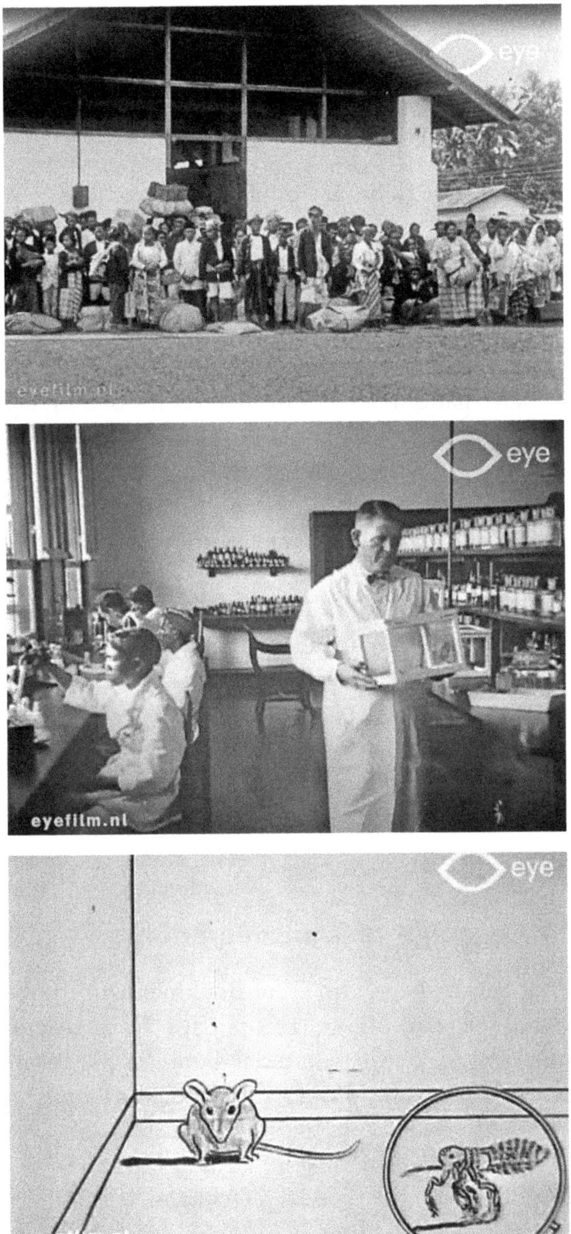

Figures 23.1–3. Science on film. Stills from *Pest op Java* [The Plague on Java], 1926

Despite the report in the newspaper about a captivated Javanese audience, films produced during this period were, surprisingly, rarely screened in the colony. *Pest op Java* was one of the very few films made for a native population. Two aspects make it stand out from the usual Mullens production on the East Indies—there is a re-enacted scene, and throughout the film there are dual Dutch and Indonesian intertitles onscreen. In the re-enacted sequence, a style rarely seen till now in this archive, a woman tries to lie still on a bed, evidently having lost her life to the dreaded disease, while she is mourned rather dramatically by her family.

After *Pest op Java* Mullens would leave the colony in 1927, never to return. He had made a large number of films and would continue to make his presence felt in documentary projects about the East Indies by re-editing much of this material well into the 1930s. While the new infusion of science, embraced by corporations and adapted to the crumbling architecture of the Ethical Policy, was compellingly captured on camera, the most valuable aspect of the filming in the 1920s, often a by-product of the increased scale of operations, is the tale of human transmigration. How did a group made up mainly of migrants and transplants arrive at their destinations? How did this alter the structural and societal landscapes of the outlier regions? I will next go into a more detailed analysis of the works of more filmmakers to come. 'Corporate films', in their attempt to closely document every aspect of plantation procedure, did capture a diverse and fascinating visual ethnography of the movement of labour.

Ethnographic Coverage of Transmigration

There were other filmmakers who were documenting the boom in large-scale operations. The collections at the Eye Filmmuseum and Beeld en Geluid, where most of this material is archived, list the makers of some films as *Onbekend* or 'Unknown'. The films mostly have similar coverage—life on the estates, the various processes through which crops grow, and an occasional social scene. Their credits indicate that they were mostly produced with financial help from the DPV and AVROS, both groups that subsidized productions for De Bussy and Mullens. Perhaps they saw less exposure because the directors lacked the institutional connections of De Bussy or the political and commercial clout of Mullens.

Sumatra Theecultuur, produced in 1921 by the lesser-known Nationale Filmfabriek Bloemendaal and having no director listed, is one film that stands out among the 'Unknowns'.[52] While there is scant trace of this film in newspaper records or Colonial Institute archives, it may have been used internally by tobacco companies for screenings at meetings and corporate events. There could be a couple of reasons for its omission from the general record. The opening scene of the film shows a woman standing on a plantation, smiling at the camera; her breasts are exposed in classic Orientalist portraiture. This was not the common form of dress for tea pluckers in Sumatra, and perhaps it was the gratuitous nudity of this shot that kept it out of the Colonial Institute's programmes. Screenings under the banner of the Colonial Institute assumed a modicum of modesty.

The film continues in a predictable manner—intertitles explain the various steps of the planting and harvesting process, and improvements in sanitation and housing for the workers. A few minutes in, another scene jars: in an open field two Dutchmen stand supervising a coolie. Although scenes of Dutch officers, almost always dressed in bright white and supervising workers, are common in these films, this particular scene is somewhat extreme in its representation of the master-coolie dynamic —the men smoke cigars and give directions by waving a walking cane. In the last scenes of the film we see the quarters for the planters and their families. Dutch women and infants are seen walking around, appearing content. It is important to note that barely a decade earlier neither Indonesians nor white planters were allowed to have wives and family on the plantations. Wim Wertheim notes that the marriage ban for white assistant managers was abolished around 1920. The arrival of Dutchwomen changed the atmosphere considerably, and 'a normalization occurred in the frontier society'.[53]

The end section of this film is, however, unusual in its deviation from the norm of filmmaking of that period. In this last sequence we

[52] H.W. Metman, a local-born Dutch, is listed as producer. Nico de Klerk, in the annotations for the Eye Filmmuseum archive, indicates that some scenes in the film were lifted from a similar film made by De Bussy in 1912. This would indicate some collaboration with the Colonial Institute—but neither director nor cameraman is listed.

[53] Wertheim, 'Conditions on Sugar Estates in Colonial Java', pp. 268–74.

see a large group of Dutch women, men and children at an outdoor festivity. They are dressed for the party, having drinks and in general making merry. This is followed by a long scrolling intertitle that reads as follows:

INTERTITLE

Hoewel de bewoners dezer tot voor korten tijd geheel woeste landstreken oorspronkelijk sterk gekant waren tegen de stichting van cultuurondernemingen in hun gebied, werden zij ten volle overtuigd van de voor hen zegenrijke resultaten met deze vestiging bereikt

Although until recently the people of these wild lands strongly opposed the establishment of agricultural enterprises in their areas, they were fully convinced of the results of the establishment of these companies.

This is a rare scene. As mentioned earlier, in the films of this period direct political references were almost never made. The underlying propagandistic agenda of the film is reinforced again in the very last frame, where we see the image of a handwritten letter signed by seven local chiefs who purportedly agreed to the construction of the estate (Figure 24). The letter states:

> The seven chiefs of Bah Biroeng Oeloe Estates, who have signed above, who had resisted the establishment of cultivation in their lands, visited today under the guidance of the undersigned the factory of the enterprises in order to get an impression of the benefits that the cultivation has brought to these lands. They were astonished by everything they saw.

J. Tideman, an Assistant Resident, provided the optimistic letter. The document is signed 21 March 1918.

The three-year delay in the release of the film, perhaps due to processing problems related to the war, led to an interesting contradiction. In 1919, a year after issuing this letter that ended the film on a positive note, Tideman wrote a rather pessimistic account of his impressions of the area. He argued that the poor health of the coolies and the resulting high mortality rates would render the estates unprofitable in the future. He added that plans to create individual homes for the transmigrants

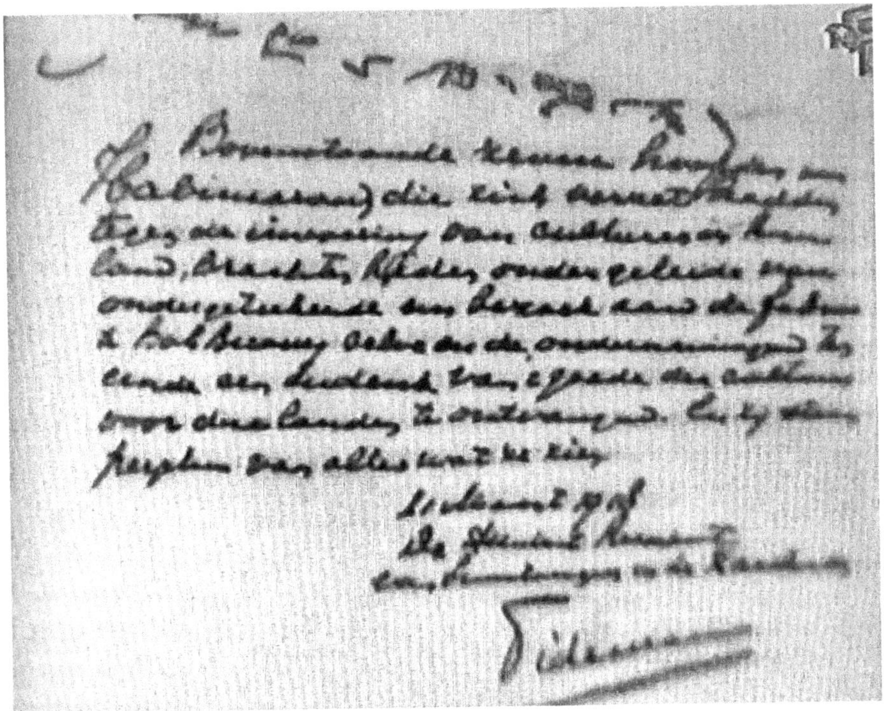

Figure 24. Still from *Sumatra Theecultuur* [Sumatra Tea Cultivation], 1921. Note the signatures of the seven chiefs above the letter, descending at an angle.

rather than the barrack system would spread them out even further, making it harder to administer health programmes.[54] Things were clearly not as well as the film would make them seem.

Sumatra Theecultuur was heavy-handed propaganda, possibly made for the purpose of recruiting Dutch officers to work in Deli and to indicate to potential investors that conditions in Sumatra were peaceful and productive. Few of the films made in the 1910s and 1920s, despite the original missive from the tobacco corporations to 'make Deli better known' to the Javanese population, seem to have been made for the purpose of convincing Javanese of the benefits of transmigrating to Sumatra. They were rarely shown to the local population. One salient

[54] J. Tideman, *De Huisvesting der contractkoelies ter Oostkust van Sumatra* (Weltevreden: Albrecht, 1919), pp. 126–7, quoted in Stoler, *Capitalism and Confrontation*.

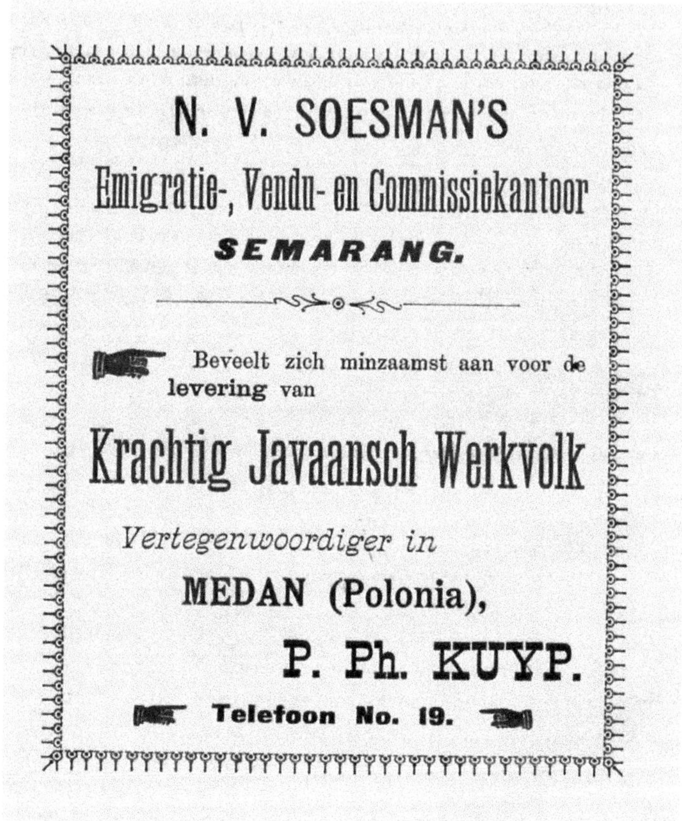

Figure 25. Newspaper advertisement for labour emigration services

exception is a film logged in the East Indies archives at Beeld en Geluid titled *VEDA*, the name for a system of emigration contracts. It is estimated that it was produced in 1925 and the original annotators of this material credit AVRO and DPV as the producers, but this information cannot be definitively corroborated. It was common at the time for companies that specialized in emigration services to advertise in newspapers (Figure 25).

This film, rather than following the more typical format of showing the production cycle of a cash crop, illustrates the entire journey Javanese villagers made from central Java to Sumatra (Figure 26). It begins with a labourer asking his village head for permission to leave for Sumatra. A Dutch sales manager then counts the number of people

Figure 26. Javanese coolies arrive in Belawan, *VEDA*, c. 1922

signed up as part of the contract. Payments are made, and the villagers leave in buses to arrive in Semarang, from where they take small vessels to Tanjong Priok in Batavia. From here they travel on a large ship to Singapore, where a new group joins them. The Javanese families finally arrive in Belawan and then are taken to Deli, where they are given meals upon arrival.

The film seems to have a minimal amount of re-enactment and consists mostly of documentary details of the journey from Java to the plantations of Sumatra. It is a rare and remarkable visual record of the phenomenon of transmigration, a significant cornerstone of the Ethical Policy. There are, however, no records located as yet to determine whether this film was shown in Java.[55] The films were beginning to have

[55] Chronicling the long journey that Javanese often made to the estates was rare. It would not be till almost a decade and a half later, in 1938, that Mannus Franken would direct the highly stylized and well-regarded film *Tanah Sabrang*, which utilized actors and puppet masters performing *wayang* scenes to inspire Javanese villagers to emigrate to Sumatra.

a more intimate and human component to them. The focus seemed to shift from merely looking at infrastructure and institutions to a closer visual documentation of the labour force.

Ochse and the Paradox of Intimate Coverage

Just as Mullens had come to the East Indies to make documentaries subsidized by corporations, other professional filmmakers too had sponsors for their projects in the Indies. Perhaps the most remarkable of these would be Isidor Arras Ochse, who came to the colony in 1925 as a cameraman for NIFM, an East Indies subsidiary of Polygoon, a Dutch news agency. NIFM had two principals: B.D. Ochse, who ran the business; and his brother I.A. Ochse, who was a well-regarded camera operator known for his newsreel coverage in Holland.

I.A. Ochse came to the region expressly to compete with Mullens and brought with him the best available equipment. The *Straits Times*, a Singaporean newspaper, heralded his arrival with much optimism. In the candid words of its correspondent, who had little regard for the quality of the prior Dutch propaganda films: 'It is hoped, however, that this time a little more attention will be given to the daily lives of the people, European as well as native, as all previous films of the Netherlands Indies are conspicuous by their lack of this, and are, accordingly, rather dull.'[56] Ochse would make a series of high-quality films—at least visually.[57] If Lamster's 'process' films outdid his ethnographies in terms of quality, that tradition did seem to linger. Vincent Monnikendam, who has perhaps reviewed the Dutch East Indies film archives more closely than any other individual, remarked, 'Without any doubt the best cameraman by that time (mid-twenties) was I.A. Ochse. He was the only one who moved with his tripod and camera near the people. He seemed the only one who had respect for the indigenous people.'[58]

---

[56] 'The Week in Java', *Straits Times*, 4 July 1925.

[57] Many of Ochse's films are related to evangelical efforts, such as the popular *Warta Sari*, which places a strong emphasis on depicting the improved health care and education brought by Christian missionaries. Ochse's best-known film project, the *Maha* series—often re-edited as *Mahakoeasa*, *Mahamoelia* or *Mahasoetji*—covers the breadth of the archipelago, including the lesser-known Outer Islands such as Celebes, Sumba and Papua.

[58] Monnikendam, 17 Dec. 2013.

Hendriks' comments are critical, though, finding I.A. Ochse's works lacking in any coverage of the ground realities of colonial politics:

> I.A. Ochse must have noticed or heard of the social unrest in Java and Sumatra during his stay in the archipelago, but as in the films of his competitor Willy Mullens, there is nothing about this unrest in his films. Poverty and exploitation are the big absentees in the *Maha*-cycle. In that respect, not much had changed since the first films. The social stratification of society was something better left out of the canvas.[59]

Hendriks' criticism of the Dutch film propagandists is valid: they showcased the colony and its purported efforts at incorporating aspects of the Ethical Policy and its subsequent transformations, but any serious investigation of politics or native dissonance with Dutch policies was overlooked. Yet, I will argue that there is some value in observing how I.A. Ochse covered plantations and, later, tin mines.

Included in I.A. Ochse's 23 films on the East Indies is an hour-long, four-part overview of the tobacco plantations in Java, *De Tabakscultuur op Midden Java* [Cultivation of Tobacco in Central Java], produced in 1927. Ochse was meticulous in detailing every aspect of the production of tobacco from the very first experiments in a laboratory (in keeping with the heightened 'scientific' direction) to isolate the perfect strain of tobacco, all the way to the finished product being traded in markets in Frascati, Holland. No technical information is spared in the intertitles as well as the visual coverage. The film begins in Klatten, Central Java, in a laboratory where a Dutch scientist and his assistant try to produce the best strain of tobacco, reminiscent of the efforts of noted Dutch botanist Melchior Treub in the early 1900s (Figure 27). The intertitle reads *In het Proefstation voor de Vorstenlandsche (Midden Java) Tabak, waar men voortdurend experimenteert ter verkrijging van de beste resultaten* [In the Research Institute for Forest Land (Central Java) Tobacco, where one is constantly experimenting to obtain the best results]. Women are then seen germinating the new strain in a nursery before it is distributed across the plantations.

The germinating, sowing, watering, sheltering, harvesting, irrigating, protecting, replanting and final harvesting processes are all depicted sequentially. Men, women and children toil in the fields. Women in

[59] Hendriks, 'Een voorbeeldige kolonie', p. 85.

Figure 27. Still from *De Tabakscultuur op Midden Java* [Cultivation of Tobacco in Central Java] showing laboratory research in Klatten, Central Java, 1927

indoor warehouses carefully separate tobacco leaves. The leaves are then compacted manually and transferred into huge crates by sinewy, sweaty men before being hoisted onto railcars and taken to the port.

While these unrelenting, labour-intensive tasks may have been orderly production modes a century ago, the workers appear to be undernourished. Perhaps the most revealing aspect of *De Tabakscultuur* is its unguarded depiction of child labour on the plantations. A group of about a dozen children are shown crouched over and moving slowly, supervised by an adult. The boys and girls seem to range in age from five to ten years. The children tread slowly through the tobacco plants and pick off the caterpillars they find on the large leaves (Figure 28). Then they carefully collect all the worms in one spot.[60] The intertitle reads *De verzamelde rupsen zoeker sorteren hun buit in afwachting van hun loon* [The finders collect the caterpillars and sort through their loot

[60] Using small children to trap insects and pests was common on the plantations. In another Polygoon film, *Bezoek aan een Indische Theeplantage* [Visiting an Indian Tea Plantation], we see small children trapping mosquitoes by hand. The intertitle explains that they are paid based on the number of insects killed.

Figure 28. Children looking for caterpillars among the tobacco leaves. Still from *De Tabakscultuur op Midden Java* [Cultivation of Tobacco in Central Java], 1927

and await their wages]. The children were presumably paid according to the number of caterpillars caught. In 1925, *Het volk: dagblad voor de arbeiderspartij* reported that 6,000 children between the ages of 12 and 16 were working on tobacco plantations.[61] The children in the film look significantly younger.

While there are references to nursery accommodations for infants during the time their parents worked, there are hardly any newspaper reports of the time covering the aspect of such small children toiling in the fields. Yet it did not seem inappropriate to show them on screen. I.A. Ochse, more than Mullens, seems to have been interested in documenting a grittier aspect of the colonial management of the plantations. While Mullens produced several films, his footage tended to be benign, focusing more on the technical specifics of the various stages of crop

[61] 'Indische Berichten. Kinderarbeid' [Indies Report. Child Labour], *Het volk: dagblad voor de arbeiderspartij*, 15 Sept. 1925.

cultivation and on the welfare programmes on the large plantations such as housing and schools for children. His camera rarely intruded or conveyed much more than was described in the intertitles. Ochse's footage however, with its close-ups, unusual vantage points and journalistic sensibility, shows us more. It is precisely when this happens that the material is useful as it helps us visualize living in these conditions a century ago.

Perhaps it was Ochse's superior camerawork, or his inherent interest in the human detail, that led to some of the intimate scenes. Noted British film historian Laura Mulvey, discussing *Mother Dao*, wrote the following in reference to footage from the plantations:

> Colonization opens a space for the industrialization of agricultural production and the people are transformed into a labour force and subjected to the inexorable logic of capitalist exploitation.... Tobacco (an imported crop) plantations transform the land; small children wade along water-filled ditches to care for the plants. Workers are measured, weighed and their fingerprints recorded before they are collected into large processing camps.... This material was, of course, filmed with the complacency, celebration and self-congratulation of the masters.[62]

Even though the origin of the footage is not identified, the description seems to be of Ochse's coverage of the tobacco plantations. Mulvey's observation on the intimacy of the material is disturbing—that it was filmed with grit and detail because of a sense of pride and accomplishment. If this is true, then we must accept the disturbing corollary—that even if the footage is indicative of colonial complacency, and especially *because* it is so, the material is valuable. The disregard for censoring the grimness of coolie life has left us in this case with a more honest account of colonialism than the prior sanitized versions depicting the Ethical Policy. Mulvey goes on to comment, 'The colonial ideology is displaced by the startlingly raw reality of the events taking place before the camera. The passing of time itself... has transformed celebration into a disturbing reflection on colonial power.' The value of the Ochse

[62] Laura Mulvey, 'Compilation Film as "Deferred Action": Vincent Monnikendam's *Mother Dao, the Turtle-like*', in *Projected Shadows: Psychoanalytic Reflections on the Representation of Loss in European Cinema*, ed. Andrea Sabbadini (New York: Routledge, 2007), pp. 112–3.

footage is that it lies on the fault line of propaganda and ethnography. I will continue to argue, with examples, that such visual records, in conjunction with the historical analysis made via other existing primary sources, might provide scholars with a better understanding of indentured life in the East Indies. Nowhere is this more evident than in a film commissioned by the behemoth mining company Billiton, on the island of Belitung in the Java Sea.

The islands of Bangka and Belitung, rich in tin ore, are in the Java Sea, off the eastern edge of Sumatra. Scholars have studied in depth the history of these two mineral-rich islands, especially in the way they contributed to the booming Outer Islands' economic output in the late 19th and early 20th centuries. What distinguished these islands from the rest of the colony was that the migrant labour working on salvaging the tin was predominantly Chinese. Of the two, Belitung, larger and more to the east, developed a reputation for an atmosphere that was less exploitative. Mary Somers Heidhues has written extensively about this island, drawing information from records of the Billiton tin company and Dutch labour inspectors.[63] She describes a large mining island run almost entirely by the new Chinese labour brought in by the colonial system, in contrast to Bangka, where many had migrated long before. Developed long after Bangka, Belitung was reputed to allow for a better life. Heidhues quotes a labour inspector's observation on a visit in 1929:

> For someone with sympathy for Chinese, a visit to the Billiton tin company is genuinely refreshing. Whereas elsewhere, Chinese coolies are often pictured as bestialized, as animals, scum and refuse, here not only are their strength and diligence valued, but their other good qualities are not overlooked.... The distance between masters and servants is not so great as elsewhere; coolies are not looked down on but met with kindness. I left Billiton with the impression that nowhere could a Chinese miner have it more to his liking.[64]

The description above is in contrast to the scenes from the 1917 film *Immigratie in Deli* by De Bussy on the Deli plantations, where thousands of coolies arrived by ship from China and were rather roughly

[63] Mary F. Somers Heidhues, *Bangka Tin and Mentok Pepper: Chinese Settlement on an Indonesian Island* (Singapore: Institute of Southeast Asian Studies, 1992).
[64] Ibid., p. 125, referenced as 'Arbeidsinspectie XIV (1929), p. 24.

treated as they entered the colonial estates. The Rhemrev Report and Breman's extrapolation of other information available about the Deli plantations painted an even grimmer atmosphere. So, was Belitung an exception? Jurrien van den Berg corroborates Heidhues' research in an essay about the relatively humanistic way of coolie life on Belitung, especially when compared with its neighbour, Bangka. He posits that the main reason why Belitung fared better was that its workers had a different contract system. They were freed from their contracts sooner and had the option of working in smaller teams of *numpangs* that were managed by the Chinese themselves, requiring less Dutch intervention. Other factors such as housing, facilities and salaries were comparable.[65] Heidhues, while certainly not painting an equitable picture of mining life in Belitung, concedes that research indicates Chinese labourers were somewhat better off here than in other regions, with far lower rates of desertion and hardly any attacks on the Dutch.[66] The majority of research on these mining towns comes from the economic and statistical analysis of data sets that were a remnant from various official records. What is missing is an actual sense of being a coolie in Belitung. In reading these accounts, the reworking of statistics refracted through the cultural distance of a century, it is difficult to develop a tangible sense of life there.

In 1927 the Billiton tin company celebrated its 75th anniversary. There are several newspaper accounts of the pomp and ceremony of the celebrations in the Netherlands. There were dance parties, the publication of a commemorative book, lectures, and a four-part film made by Ochse. Prince Hendrik, husband of Queen Wilhelmina, attended one of the events. One newspaper, the *Algemeen Handelsblad*, carried a long article on Billiton, its history and technological innovations to assist in the very hard task of extracting tin ore, its financial successes and future prospects. In particular it singled out the role of the Chinese:

> The increase of machinery does not make the industrious Chinese workers redundant ... for the working of lands that is not suitable for

---

[65] Jurrien van den Berg, 'Tin Island: Labour Conditions of Coolies in the Billiton Mines in the Nineteenth and Early Twentieth Centuries', in Houben, Lindblad et al., *Coolie Labour in Colonial Indonesia*.

[66] Heidhues, *Bangka Tin and Mentok Pepper*, p. 126.

> moving large amounts of earth, thousands of miners are still needed. These Chinese are worth all the attention. They come from the farm centres of south China and are therefore not the scum of the densely populated large cities. On the contrary, they are quiet farm boys, mostly married and unable in their country to earn livelihoods.... The company never has trouble with the addition of workers who voluntarily and deliberately come to Billiton via clan emigration.... Immediately after arrival the *singkehs* [new arrivals] are protected with typhus cholera vaccinations.[67]

In Ochse's documentary *Tin Film*, we experience this mining island. Against a backdrop of stunning oceanic beauty, with sailboats trawling slowly and local fishermen working freely in the seas, we are privy to the luxuries of Dutch management. We see enormous bungalows with native servants running around, tennis courts, men drinking their sundowners, and women sitting around with the languid demeanour of being on a tropical vacation. We then observe operations of the extractions—small trains carrying miners to their destinations and an enormous factory where the ore is separated. The scale of production is colossal and mechanized—the phrase 'betting on the strong' is illustrated well. As Billiton operated on a part mechanical, part manual system of dredging, there are also several scenes that show the hard, manual work of the Chinese coolies that are in sharp contrast to the mammoth-sized dredge. The film seemed to have been well received, barring a minor criticism in the *Bataviaasch Nieuwsblad*: 'The last part of the film is dedicated to the life and work, the care and treatment of Chinese coolies. This is perhaps a little too long.'[68]

In the archives of Beeld en Geluid, where much of the material researched for this study is located, there are at times, in addition to the complete films, some outtakes or *restmateriaal*. There is quite a bit of this for Ochse's film on Billiton. One reel of particular value is an extended coverage of the arrival of Chinese coolies on the island (Figure 29). The footage is reminiscent of some of the material filmed by De Bussy in Belawan in 1917, when coolies arrived on ships to work in Deli.

---

[67] 'De Tinwinning op Billiton: Geschreven bij gelegenheid van haar 75-Jarig jubileum op 16 Mei 1927', *Algemeen Handelsblad*, 5 Dec. 1927.
[68] 'De Billiton-Film' [The Billiton Movie], *Bataviaasch Nieuwsblad*, 16 Jan. 1921.

Figure 29. New arrivals from China get off the boats at the Billiton mines. Unedited material from Isidor Ochse's filming in 1926

There can be several reasons for why these outtakes did not make it into the final cut—the film might have become too long, a single aspect could have been overemphasized, or perhaps some parts were censored. While some of the scenes seem to be near duplicates of what we see in the film, there are notable differences. In the sequence of events in the reel marked *Billiton Tin Restmateriaal #5* [Belitung Tin Outtakes #5], we see the coolies being taken to their living quarters. They are marched along by men in uniform and entered into a compound that is enclosed by a barbed wire fence. In addition, there are about five to six feet of barbed wire at an acute angle from the fence to the ground preventing anyone from coming close to the fence.

The new coolies are then taken for a health check-up and inoculation. While one coolie is standing stiffly to have his height measured, his feet are kicked in. The coolies are then given haircuts—the term 'shorn' seems befitting. A group of officers take thumbprints on several documents. Later the coolies are returned their papers and photographs

Figures 30.1–3. Labourers in Billiton are 'prepared' and await their identity cards. Unedited material from Isidor Ochse's filming in 1926

through the wire mesh. In their eagerness or fear of missing their documents when their names are called, they stand on the barbed wire with bare feet and lean in on the fence (Figures 30.1–3).

While these scenes do not resemble the acute slave-like conditions in the earlier days of colonialism on plantations, they do not exactly make us feel that an equitable sense of human dignity was operating in Billiton. What we do know about Billiton is from econometric data and quotations from officers in charge and the company's minutes. On record, the coolies here did earn more, had relatively better freedoms, and seemed to resent their employers less. However, the scenes where new arrivals are manhandled and anxious men reach through barbed-wire fences to receive their documents do affect our impression of Billiton. Could it be that the film record shows us a new perspective, a visceral on-the-ground engagement that was not possible to glean from the written records and analyses? I contend that the films do give us a glimpse of the life of miners beyond what we have gleaned from written records to date.

Mullens and Ochse both filmed a staggering amount of material in the 1920s. In addition to plantation life, they also filmed other aspects of the East Indies, and several compilation series were distributed by both Haghefilm and NIFM Polygoon for consumption in the Netherlands and other parts of Europe. Of the two, Ochse was clearly the better artist. In the late 1920s he produced the *Maha* series, a stunning body of original work from locations all over the archipelago. Adhie Gesit Pambudi, an Indonesian scholar researching aspects of these propaganda films at Leiden University, wrote about that collection:

> His [Ochse's] capability as a documentary filmmaker was undeniable. His most notable work was a documentary film entitled *Maha-Cyclus* that was produced in 1928–29. It was a film that illustrated the panorama and people in Java, Bali, and Papua. This film consisted of three scenes, which were *Mahasoetji*, *Mahamoelia*, and *Mahakoeasa*. *Maha-Cyclus* achieved a positive response from the public. Many cinemas in the Netherlands and Dutch East Indies used this film to attract audiences. Also, the Dutch government considered Ochse's films to be a decent tool for educating people in the Netherlands and showed his films at Dutch universities and schools.[69]

In the large combined repository of films on plantations there seems to have been one broad category that was left out: unlike Lamster, neither

---

[69] Adhie Gesit Pambudi, 'The Audiovisual Battlefield: The Use of Dutch Documentary Films about the Issues of Indonesia, 1945–1949' (MA thesis, Leiden University, 2012).

De Bussy, Ochse nor Mullens seemed to be interested in filming the work of small-scale Indonesian producers, a primary tenet of the Ethical Policy that had endured. Although large plantations were depicted in the films from the 1920s, by the end of that decade significant agricultural contribution actually came from the smaller producers, which dominated coconut, pepper and kapok production. This significant phenomenon is missing from the propaganda films bankrolled by large private and government conglomerates. The explanation might simply be one of resources—the backers of these companies had the funds for their films to be produced.

In 1989, when he published *Taming the Coolie Beast*, Breman did not have access to De Bussy's or Ochse's material. It appears, though, that he would have benefited from the records when he wrote, 'Photographs can be a great help in clarifying social relations, but they can also distort reality. What is needed is a special photo album that will depict the structure and culture of work and labour control on the colonial planation.'[70] De Bussy's filmed material of the Deli plantations and Ochse's depictions of the tin mines may have provided Breman with the 'special photo album' that he sought in order to portray a more compelling sense of what the bonded, regimented labour environment was like. While the film material is propagandistic, it could not, in spite of itself, hide a certain stark reality of the difficult conditions. While the material was certainly not depictive of the accusations in the Rhemrev Report, it would not be difficult to conceive of an environment that could just as easily turn unjust. The differential in power between the arriving migrants and the authorities overseeing them is palpable. If coolies are pushed and manhandled on film, we can only imagine what happened off camera. Unsurprisingly, there were no newspaper reports to my knowledge that criticized the heavy-handedness of the managers seen in the films. The film record, perhaps unwittingly, shows this in a form that print records could not.

The economic imbalance between plantation workers and their masters has been studied assiduously by scholars of 19th-century labour; this was the period when the situation was at its most exploitative. I argue that the lives of cash crop labourers once conditions improved have not been as closely scrutinized. Documentation of this phase in

---

[70] Breman, *Taming the Coolie Beast*, p. 11.

labour history, the 1910s and 1920s, however, has been done meticulously by those hired by corporations to further their goals of showcasing the scope and scale of operations. If De Bussy pioneered the first views of early plantation emigration and operations, Mullens added professional polish and detail, especially in the way he integrated the thrust of a new science-based agenda in the colony. Unknown directors in the early 1920s take us through immaculate details of the transmigrant experience, while Ochse trained his camera on the colossal scale of production as well as close, detailed observations of coolie servitude, providing us with an ethnographic texture of bonded labour. These films fill a lacuna in existing primary sources with visual evidence that could help historians further explore labour conditions in the late colonial era.

By the 1920s the Netherlands East Indies propaganda films moved away from the Colonial Institute's initial thrust of capturing a greater diversity of life in the colony; they became about showcasing capitalist power. The makers were talented cameramen working under commission from large corporations with specific mandates. What would happen, however, if a very different set of image-makers were to start filming? How would evangelists conceive of and film local lives? Would they provide us with anything valuable in the way of historical or ethnographic records? The next chapter looks at such an enterprise.

CHAPTER 5

Films with a Mission (1923–30)

In 1927 the *Eindhovensch Dagblad*, a daily serving the province of Limburg in the south of the Netherlands, ran an advertisement for a movie called *Flores Film*. Comparing it to *Ben-Hur*, the most expensive film of the silent era, it billed the film as 'the *Ben-Hur* of reality, a most delightful piece of authentic life among an uncivilized people'.[1]

Figure 31. The '*Ben-Hur* of reality'. Advertisement in the *Eindhovensch Dagblad* in 1927

The producers of *Flores Film*, members of the Societas Verbi Divini (SVD), had created a two-hour documentary in the east of the archipelago that followed the adventures of their own priests. They were successful in their campaign to have the film viewed widely. It did

[1] Advertisement, *Eindhovensch Dagblad*, 1927.

well commercially, selling 2,000 tickets a week in Utrecht, with three screenings per day.[2] There is a long, enterprising history behind how the unexpectedly popular film got made; it involves a combination of evangelical ambition and the pursuit of ethnography. While the corporation-backed films discussed in chapter 4 were being made primarily in Sumatra and Java, remote Flores, far to the east of the archipelago, was beginning to fall under a different lens. This chapter will narrate how media played a significant role in the effort to bring missionary activism to Flores. It will also detail the ethnographic value of the innovative material filmed during the period of Dutch propagandistic filmmaking—some of the finest to emerge from Dutch colonial filmmaking. It re-establishes the main argument of this book that valuable primary sources, available via the medium of archival film, have to be resurrected and contextualized within the discourse of colonial study of the Netherlands East Indies.

The SVD was a Catholic group founded in 1875 in Steyl, in the south of the Netherlands, by Arnold Janssen during the Kulturkampf—a rising wave of secularism that greatly reduced the power of the Roman Catholic Church in Prussia. In exile but still influential, it comprised many German and Dutch priests and had a penchant for the close study of diverse cultures. During the early 1920s, Johannes Giessen, an SVD priest from the Netherlands also known as Father Berchmans, was impressed with evangelical films his mission had commissioned in the Congo and Uganda. Supported by his diocese to further his ambition to produce more films, Berchmans approached the German filmmaker Willy Rach to create non-fictional works in China. When the enterprise proved to be politically risky, Rach lobbied instead for permission to film in the East Indies. Arnold Verstraelen, the bishop in charge in Flores, gave his consent. In 1924 Rach travelled to Flores and filmed 15,000 feet that he brought back to the Dutch seminary in Steyl. Back at the seminary another SVD priest, Father Buis, a former superintendent of schools in Flores, became fascinated with the material Rach had brought back and took on the responsibility to develop the project further. He envisioned a new strategy for promoting the evangelical cause in Flores.

[2] Eddy Appels, 'Faraway Places and Exotic Cultures in a Movie Mission', Cultuur Wijzer, https://static.kunstelo.nl/ckv2/cultuurwijzer/cultuurwijzer/www/cultuurwijzer.nl/cultuurwijzer.nl/i000741.html, accessed 11 Nov. 2020.

Several years before coming across this material in Steyl, Father Buis had been sent to Flores as superintendent of schools and spent three full years devoted to the development of education in the region. In 1922 he left for the United States to study at the Techny seminary, near Chicago. Upon his return to the Netherlands in 1925, he viewed the footage that Rach had brought back from Flores. The material had hit a creative hurdle; it had several disjointed scenes and was proving difficult to edit into a viewable narrative. Father Buis started collaborating actively on the footage, eventually wresting the project away from Berchmans. Utilizing his personal knowledge and experiences from Flores to shape and promote the documentary. Father Buis transformed what he considered slow visual ethnography into a faster-paced film with a clear plot line.[3] He organized the footage into a narrative about Catholic priests leaving the Netherlands on an epic, arduous journey through Flores while observing the latter's 'primitive' culture. Though Father Buis himself would not return to Flores for another five years, he edited the footage in the Netherlands to produce a two-hour-long film. Self-taught, he also filmed several scenes on a ship docked in the port in Amsterdam to illustrate the long journey to the East. The creation of a narrative plot in an ethnographic film, with re-enacted scenes blended into documentary footage, was the new trend in international documentary cinema. Father Buis would develop this hybrid form soon after, when he moved from travelogues to fictional 'story' movies in 1930. His new collaborator, Father Piet Beltjens, admiringly observed, 'His rich imagination flourished as he found new methods and his sentimental romanticism could express itself.'[4]

[3] Marie-Antoinette Willemsen, 'De *fictive* kracht: De missiefilms van de missionarissen van Steyl (SVD)', in *Bewogen missie: het gebruik van het medium film door Nederlandse kloostergemeenschappen*, ed. J.P.A. van Vugt and Marie-Antoinette Willemsen (Hilversum: Stichting Echo, 2012), pp. 62–3. Original source: Henk de Beer, SVD, 'Pater Simon Buis en zijn inzet voor de Missiefilms van de paters van het Goddelijk Woord- s.v.d. Achtergrond en totstandkoming' (Teteringen: Archivist of the Provincial Archive, 1992), p. 2.

[4] Eddy Appels, 'Mission to Flores: Father Simon Buis and His Flores Films, 1925–1934', Film and Science Foundation, Audiovisual Archive, Amsterdam, 1997, pp. 13–4. Original Source: Piet Beltjens, SVD, 'Herinneringen aan pater Simon Buis' (Teteringen: Archivist of the Provincial Archive, 1992), p. 2.

Father Buis was a consummate film promoter and evangelist; he made Flores a recognizable name in the Catholic churches of the Netherlands. But before describing the ethnography in Father Buis' footage, and his tremendous efforts at outreach, it is important to establish the power struggle that emerged in Flores during the early 20th century, as this constitutes the geopolitical backdrop to his films.

The War of Pacification

At the turn of the 20th century, the Dutch colonial government scoured the Outer Islands of the East Indies for areas that could provide new tax bases. Although Flores had not been considered particularly lucrative in this respect, it now came under scrutiny. Central and western Flores remained predominantly Muslim along the coasts, with many autochthonous groups residing in the highlands. The powerful Islamic sultan of Bima, just across the waters to the west, controlled the western region of Manggarai.[5] But there was a Catholic presence on the east of the island, a remnant of the long Portuguese rule from 1613 to approximately the mid-1800s. In 1907, emboldened by the mandate of expansion by the new Dutch Controleur A. Couvreur, Captain Hans Christoffel carried out what noted historian Karel Steenbrink describes as a 'blitzkrieg' in the central and western parts of Flores. The mass murder, characteristically dubbed as Perang Pasifikasi/War of Pacification, was barbaric. In one incident, 52 men, women and children who had sought refuge in a cave were killed as Christoffel had evidently promised his soldiers the equivalent of 2.5 guilders for each head. Couvreur began writing letters in secrecy to the Catholic mission in Larantuka. He beseeched them to populate the area with their missions as a matter of urgency:

> If we do not act fast, Islam will occupy the interior and we will have lost this cause forever.... If we act fast, Flores, with the exception of a few coastal places, can be secured for the Catholic Church.... If we

[5] Karel Steenbrink (2007), *Catholics in Indonesia, 1808–1942: A Documented History*, Vol. 2: *The Spectacular Growth of a Self-confident Minority, 1903–1942* (Leiden: KITLV Press, 2007), p. 89.

> succeed in inducing them to say *saya orang serani* [I am a Christian], we still have thousands of years to make them true *serani* [Christians].[6]

While there was a clear tussle for political influence over the native non-Islamic community, the colonial administration, in principle, was not permitted to favour particular faiths. As they were not allowed any direct form of evangelism, Jesuits proselytized through the education system. The island soon began to fill with young native recruits hired to start schools and spread Catholicism. In addition, European priests started arriving in the 1920s as the end of World War I caused a departure of SVD priests from former colonies in Africa. It was around this time that Father Buis arrived and became superintendent of these new schools.

The dynamic Father Buis bore the dual evangelical and colonial cudgel quite fervently. His writings in *Katholieke Missiën*, a religious magazine in Holland, reveal a priest dedicated to denouncing Islam and championing a greater influence for Catholicism. In the article 'Pas Op Voor De Scholen' [Beware of the Schools], he writes that one must be very suspicious of Islamic 'fanatical opposition to Christianity'.[7] He complains that because schooling was not compulsory in Flores, the Muslim opposition could not be countered properly. In a subsequent article titled 'Beleedigende Taal' [Insulting Language], he states dramatically that 'one of the heaviest crosses' that a missionary in the Lesser Sunda Islands has to bear is the daily insults from Muslims, who typically saw Catholics as intruders and referred to them as 'dogs and boars' and 'enemies of Muhammad'.[8]

Urgently wanting schools and missionaries to encourage conversions across Flores, Father Buis was eager to engage in alternate forms of propaganda in addition to his writing. Making films, he decided, could serve the purpose of depicting inappropriate, 'uncivilized' behaviour and help his proselytizing cause. The attempt eventually became the very records that provide us with a unique historical source of the region.

[6] Letter from Couvreur to Jesuit priest Jos Hoeberechts dated 12 Feb. 1908, in Steenbrink, *Catholics in Indonesia*, pp. 458–9, quoted in Karel Steenbrink, 'Dutch Colonial Containment of Islam in Manggarai, West Flores, in Favor of Catholicism, 1909–1942', *Bijdragen tot de Taal-, Land- en Volkenkunde* 169 (2013): 108.

[7] Simon Buis, 'Pas Op Voor De Scholen', *Het Mahomedanisme op Flores* 1 (1925).

[8] Simon Buis, 'Beleedigende Taal', *Het Mahomedanisme op Flores* 3 (1926).

Despite his evangelical bias, Father Buis was a competent ethnographer. Missionaries like himself were thoroughly trained in ethnology and linguistics in their home countries. Susanne Schroeter reminds us that 'the SVD was distinguished by a certain anthropological openness, and has brought forth a number of prominent ethnologists, an anthropological school of thought, as well as several ethnological institutions that are still influential today'.[9] Indeed, Father Wilhelm Schmidt, a member of the order, had founded the reputed anthropology journal *Anthropos* in 1906 and taught the discipline in Vienna. Schroeter also lists several priests practising ethnography in the East Indies—Paul Arndt, Herrmann Bader, Wilem van Bekkum and Jilis Verheijlen, noted scholars whose articles and books are still considered to be foundational texts for the study of Flores. The very approach of SVD missionaries, according to Schroeter, was one that compelled them to 'discover evidence of the supposedly primordial monotheism among those to be proselytized'.[10] The belief was that these primitive, older, animist systems were essentially not in contradiction with Christianity—the locals were just not aware of the similarities.

While the SVD took a paternal approach to highlanders in Flores, towards the coastal Muslims they demonstrated intolerance. The vitriol that Father Buis demonstrated towards Islam is not surprising. In years to come the SVD would join with the colonial government to foist a stratagem of ridding Flores as much as possible of the theological and political influences of Islam. Despite the heavy anti-Islamic bias, if we consider writings on the history and ethnography of Flores by SVD priests, it would behoove us to look at their cinema as well.

Flores Film and Evangelical Publicity

In 1926, after working with Rach's original footage for almost a year, Father Buis released *Flores Film*, a long non-fiction film, in the Netherlands (Figure 32). As mentioned earlier, it was commercially successful. It was also lauded for its ethnographic and evangelistic content. *De Tijd* gave it a glowing review:

[9] Susanne Schroeter, 'The Indigenization of Catholicism in Flores', in *Christianity in Indonesia: Perspectives of Power*, ed. Susanne Schroeter (Berlin: Lit Verlag, 2010), p. 144.

[10] Ibid., p. 145.

Figure 32. Booklet accompanying screenings of *Flores Film* (courtesy of Provincial Archives SVD, Teteringen)

The simple viewer admires *Flores Film* for its beautiful pictures and pleasant variety of performances. The scholar, the connoisseur of the Indies, sees even more: he sees the beautiful presentation of tropical opulence ... the grace of our Indies brothers and sisters. This the botanist, ethnologist, geologist, psychologist and especially sociologist enjoys. It is a singular fact that the film captivates everyone, but each according to his own knowledge of the East. This is the greatest merit of *Flores Film*.[11]

[11] *Een kostbaar ordeel over de Flores-film* [A Precious Opinion on the Flores Movie], *De Tijd*, 15 Dec. 1926.

Father Buis would capitalize tremendously on the popularity of the ensuing screenings, beseeching audiences for their support:

> Dear little friends, you have surely not forgotten the friendship that we have concluded, when thou art come to see the Mission Movies? All together there are nearly twenty thousand children who have been to see the film in Utrecht, Amsterdam, Den Hague and Tilburg. [...] What fun we had.... Do you think that the Mission no longer needs your help? Well, as long as a thousand million pagans are not converted (and that will take a while), we have hard work to continue for the Mission. And so we must keep the fire in it.[12]

In his 1997 essay 'Mission to Flores', Eddy Appels, a Dutch visual anthropologist, attested that the genre of the mission film, after some initial opposition on account of its 'entertainment' aspect, had found a niche in the world of evangelical fundraising and advertising in 1920s Netherlands:

> In 1925 Father Simon Buis of the SVD assembled film material shot in 1923 by the German filmmaker Willy Rach on Flores in the Dutch East Indies. *Flores Film* was thus the pioneer of the Dutch mission movie. The Dutch mission films focused on the ordinary church people, especially the farmers in the Catholic Brabant and Limburg. From those circles finally emerged the missionaries, and to a lesser extent the money for the missions. For many people the screening formed an excellent opportunity to know about foreign nations and see exotic regions (it was also the only option for boys to see half-naked women). For the generally poor peasantry, the screenings in the parish house were often the only contact with the medium of film.[13]

Flores Film had done very well. The reason for this may have been the exciting narrative that Father Buis crafted, which created a vicarious sense of adventure for those imagining themselves as missionaries going to a wild, faraway land. The first 20 minutes of the film show various scenes of student life at the seminary in Steyl. The mission cross is then handed to a group who board a ship stopping at several destinations on its way to the East Indies. We fleetingly visit Italy, Gibraltar, Cairo and Colombo before the missionaries arrive in Batavia. Some of this

---

[12] Willemsen, 'De *fictive* kracht', p. 63.
[13] Appels, 'Mission to Flores', p. 11.

Figure 33. Father Simon Buis in staged contemplation. Still from *Flores Film*, 1926

footage was filmed after Rach had handed over the material to the SVD. Father Buis appears a couple of times, inserting himself into the reconstructed narrative (Figure 33).

After the missionaries arrive in the colony, they make cursory halts at the large Roman Catholic cathedral in Batavia and the Buddhist temple of Borobudur. A celebratory reception in Flores occurs only 50 minutes into the film, when the local parish in Ndona receives the travellers with a brass band. The missionaries continue on their long, arduous journey on horseback, travelling along the river valley to the north of Ende. They are seen drinking from streams, asking for directions and, on one occasion, falling clumsily into the water. The scenes appear staged but are effective (Figures 34.1–2).

Figures 34.1–2. Missionaries braving the mountainous and riverine terrain of highland Flores. Stills from *Flores Film*, 1926

Figure 35. Killing a Komodo dragon. Still from *Flores Film,* 1926

The first significant, long sequence in the film is the tracking and killing of a Komodo dragon (Figure 35). This appears to be the first time the large, prehistoric lizard is captured on film. In addition to the thrill of the hunt, this sequence references a complex political story. Attempting to restrict the hunting of the exotic lizard that had become a zoological fascination around the world, the Dutch colonial government issued a series of bureaucratic measures in the early 1910s requiring permits to be procured for hunting. The Sultan of Bima, however, controlled much of the hunting activity from adjacent Sumba as many groups stopped there to gather coolies. In response, the Dutch colonial authorities strategically placed the island of Komodo under the jurisdiction of Manggarai in western Flores, effectively wresting authority away from the Sultan. The stubborn Sultan, however, continued to act autonomously, creating consternation within the colonial authority. Flores thereafter became a political battleground, with both the SVD and local Muslims straining to win influence over the native, autochthonous dwellers.[14] In 1930, in keeping with the efforts to control political power in the region, the Dutch colonial government resorted to a desperate move and brokered the appointment of a young man—Alexander Baroek—to undermine the Islamic authority of Bima.

[14] For details on this power struggle and to read more on Dutch attempts to manage the environment and ecology of their colony, see Timothy P. Barnard, 'Protecting the Dragon: Dutch Attempts at Limiting Access to Komodo Lizards in the 1920s and 1930s', *Indonesia* 92 (2011): 97–123.

The following scenes are replete with close-ups of native inhabitants, the flora and fauna, and several short sequences of dance and fairground-type festivities, including gambling. These segments are disjointed. One unusual intertitle reads *Wacht u voor de leer der blanken* [Be careful not to accept the doctrine of the white people]. It shows a few elderly men who seem to be angry at the presence of the camera. But there is neither further contextualization of this scene, nor other evidence of resistance against the missionaries. A large local place of prayer is filmed being built, preceded by an intertitle that reads *Dieper in 't heidendom* [Deeper into paganism]. Again, there does not seem to be any judgement of the activity. Steenbrink is of the opinion that there would have been professional *explicateurs* (lecturers) accompanying the screenings of *Flores Film* who may not have been guarded about their opinions on non-native 'heathens' in Flores.[15] We do know from SVD mission records archived in Teteringen that in addition to the booklets handed out about each film, there would be an *explicateur* present to speak over the projected images. Based on the intertitles and the visuals, however, it cannot be said that *Flores Film* embellishes conditions in Flores or encourages anti-autochthonous sentiment.

The last section of the film is dedicated to showing up close the efforts of the mission workers. Steenbrink makes the observation that it depicts Catholic missions as a modernizing movement rather than bringing a new and powerful religion. The intertitle at the start of this end section reads *De Missionaries Brenger der beschaving* [The missionary: bringer of civilization]. We see a quick montage of missionary activity. The montage covers events where the native population is trained or assisted: furniture making, livestock and poultry farming, planting seeds in large gardens. A section of tree planting supervised by a missionary is preceded by the intertitle *Om meer gebedel te voorkomen Plant de Broeder kokosboomen* [To do away with begging, the brother plants coconut trees]. A mission nurse is shown at an outdoor blackboard teaching what appears to be fairly complex algebra to a large class of teenage girls. In other classrooms the language of instruction is Jawi (Arabic script

[15] I sent a digital link of *Flores Film* to Steenbrink for his insights. He published these in an online blog. See 'Sandeep Ray and Colonial Movies', Relindonesia, http://relindonesia.blogspot.nl/2014/05/sandeep-ray-and-colonial-movies.html, accessed 11 Nov. 2020.

Figures 36.1–2. Administering holy rites; Bishop Verstraelen blesses new converts. Stills from *Flores Film*, 1926

form), as Malay was still being taught in the Arabic script in the early 1920s. This conforms with Steenbrink's observation on the containment of Islam—that it was the classrooms where the Dutch evangelists tried their best to secure and convert native non-Muslims to Christianity.[16]

Direct examples of proselytizing are also shown in this film. A robed priest gives an elderly native man a photograph of himself, which is viewed with much conviviality. The intertitle reads *Van vriend tot leeraar* [From friend to teacher]. The ensuing scene resembles a large congregation of people at a Sunday outdoor church session. A priest narrates what appears to be a sermon from the Bible and then demonstrates how to make the sign of the cross. The moment is powerful. We finally arrive at a very instrumental instance in this epic sojourn from the Netherlands, when non-Muslim natives are converted. Right after this is an intertitle stating *Offervaardige en ijverige christenen* [Sacrificial and zealous Christians], and we are shown hordes of locals—boys, men, and even women carrying infants—bringing in rocks and beginning the construction of a church. In the penultimate sequence, a large congregation attends a marriage ceremony, but the priest is soon pulled away to pray over a recently deceased man. In the last scene we see a service led by Bishop Verstraelen, who had originally green-lighted the Flores film project (Figure 36.2). The contrast between the smaller-statured,

[16] Steenbrink ('Dutch Colonial Containment', pp. 113–4) discusses how from 1909 Jesuits sent Malay-speaking teachers to the area and by 1925 they were already teaching in 25 schools. During these years visiting priests would baptize children who were prepared for the conversion by their teachers.

hesitant, recently converted local residents and the physically larger missionaries resplendent in official church regalia is very telling of the ensuing power dynamics. It comes as no surprise that it was just a matter of time before Catholicism swept the island.

There was yet another film made during this period with a shared theme: *Bali-Floti* follows the same SVD priests through roughly similar terrain. The archival logs for *Bali-Floti* credit Rach as cameraman and Father H. Limbrock as director. It is unclear who edited the material, but there is little overlap in the visuals of the two films. Rach, originally hired by Brother Berchmans to film in Flores, had provided enough footage for two long documentaries. Both films are impeccably restored and preserved at the Eye Filmmuseum in Amsterdam. It was *Flores Film*, however, that became famous as it was released with considerable outreach efforts by the indefatigable Father Buis, who took it upon himself to promote it.

It is surprising, perhaps, that a devoted evangelistic priest is also remembered for being a competent filmmaker. It is the central tenet of this study that there were many useful ethnographic and historical records that came out of these early cinematic propaganda efforts. To hastily classify them as evangelistic or biased Church reportage would be dismissive. The SVD's aim was to show people in the Netherlands that Flores needed mass conversions and induction into the Church. And to that end the SVD displayed natives, mostly from the remote highlands, emphasizing their primitiveness and their othering heathenness. In the process, however, it captured that very important moment of the colonial contact and established a visual essay of how exactly evangelism, buttressed with the colonial military and administrative apparatus, entered a remote, non-Christian area and took over the local faith. Considering that there are few early visual records of life in Flores (as compared to Java, Sumatra and Bali), this aspect of the mission's propagandistic work makes the footage both rich and unique.

Father Buis, as already mentioned, filmed neither *Flores Film* nor *Bali-Floti*; nor was he present during filming. It was Rach who travelled extensively to capture the footage. While we do not have a clear record of how Rach's footage was initially assembled, it is evident that the SVD credits Father Buis with being the creative force behind the project. It is often overlooked in the records and newspaper articles that it was Rach who filmed every frame of the footage in Flores along with Father Limbrock, the SVD priest who had accompanied him. While newspapers often mention Rach limited to being a crew member, only one article in the *Tilburgsche Courant*, titled 'Willy Rach', gives Rach credit as a principal and yet unknown maker of *Flores Film*:

> A matter of justice ... More than a hundred thousand people, in cities and villages of our land, have seen and admired his work since last winter; and yet they do not know his name! Let us introduce him to you; he deserves it. Willy Rach, German-American by birth, is the maker of *Flores Film*.... For months he crossed Flores and several other of the small Sunda Islands—especially Bali. There could be a separate book written about the incredible difficulties, adventures, calculations, plan and manoeuvres involved in Rach's journeys that conclude with a fine film![17]

Surprisingly, after many screenings and critical discussions of the film in the newspapers, the idea of its potential as a historical document did not surface much. Father Simon Buis was not identified as a pioneering ethnographer until the 1990s, when Appels resurrected his contributions

Figure 37. Simon Buis seated in his Ford Model T publicity vehicle for *Flores Film* (courtesy of Provincial Archives SVD, Teteringen)

[17] 'Willy Rach', *Tilburgsche Courant*, 4 Nov. 1927.

to early ethnographic filmmaking. While *Flores Film* has been understudied, there has been some academic effort to recognize it as an important film. I contend, however, that it is *Bali-Floti* that is the more valuable film of the two and yet has remained completely unresearched. It contains several extraordinarily filmed sequences of life in Flores. Accordingly, that film is discussed in some detail below.

Willy Rach and the Under-exposed *Bali-Floti*

Like many of the films produced during the period of Dutch propagandistic filmmaking, *Bali-Floti* had an accompanying booklet containing background information and photographs that explained the events depicted in its six reels (Figure 38).[18] The first logs in this booklet describe a temple dance in Denpasar. The film shows a *legong* performance in the temple's courtyard. Rach's filming is meticulous and intimate. For the first time we see nuanced, artistic camerawork such as rack focusing and slow, gracious, close-up pans of body movements. However, as several filmmakers, including Lamster, Mullens and even Charlie Chaplin, had filmed this dance, the scenes are less unique as visual documents.

Rach and director Father Limbrock next take us to Flores. They travel far through rough terrain to meet the natives. The initial filmic encounter is awkward. People stare at the camera. Rach takes a series of facial close-ups with little action. In one sequence titled *Man of Vrouw?* [Man or Woman?], he films elderly people with wizened skin and long hair; their genders are perhaps not immediately obvious. He seems to be moving around the island, filming in pieces, unsure of his direction. The sequences are abrupt. As in Lamster's earlier works, however, it is when he starts to concentrate on the 'process' type sequences that Rach's work becomes valuable. The subplots within the films, scenes where we are actually taken through a ritual or activity, start coming alive.

The first long sequence is 35 minutes in. It follows the labour-intensive manufacturing of cloth in the distinctive *ikat* style of Flores. We are swiftly taken through the various steps—plucking cotton, processing the harvest, producing thread utilizing a hand-cranked spinning wheel, dyeing the thread, and then weaving large, rectangular swaths

[18] The booklet was titled 'Bali-Floti, Cultureel-Ethnologische Film Over De Kliene Soenda-Eilanden, N.O.I.'.

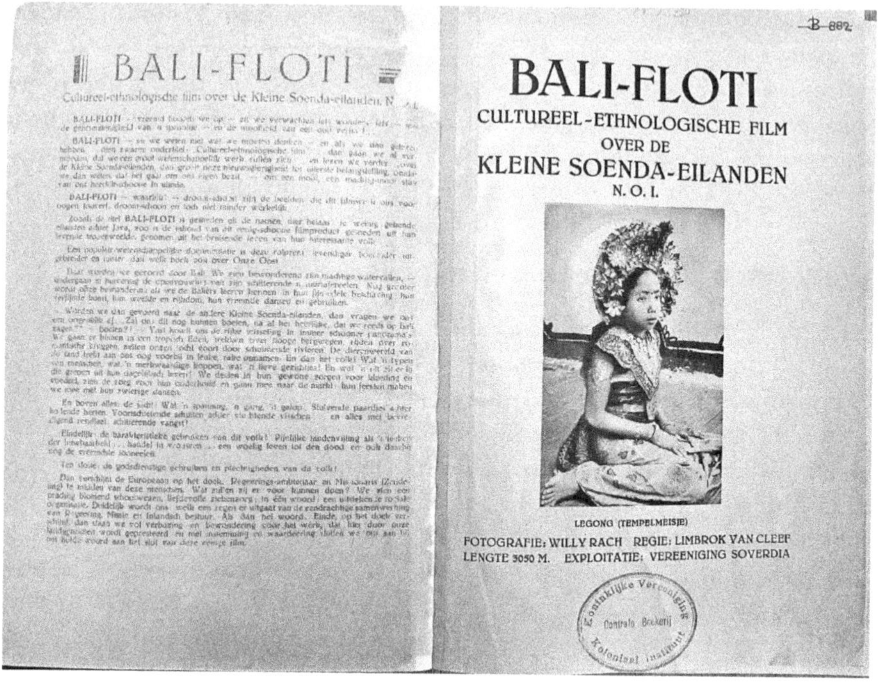

Figure 38. Booklet for *Bali-Floti* archived in the Tropenmuseum, Amsterdam (It credits Willy Rach and Father Limbrock with being the makers of the film.)

of cloth. The method is filmed from a variety of angles, revealing its mechanical details as well as taking us through the spatial environment of production.

In her article 'Without Cloth We Cannot Marry', Ruth Barnes details several reasons why such woven cloth was significant.[19] Unfortunately, as the film is in black and white, we cannot ascertain Barnes' important observation that a brownish red tone is a must for bridal cloth in most parts of eastern Flores, where this footage is taken. Observing the film closely, however, one can corroborate other properties. Barnes points out that a particularity of the cloth in a marriage context is that

[19] Ruth Barnes, 'Without Cloth We Cannot Marry: The Textiles of the Lamaholot in Transition. Papers from "The Walrus Said", the MEG Meeting on Materials and Techniques Held at the Pitt Rivers Museum on 2 October 1987 and Papers from the MEG Meetings at Brighton and Durham in 1988', *Journal of Museum Ethnography* 2 (1991): 95–112.

Figure 39. The unsewn edge of *ikat*, also called the 'hair', is a primary gift in marriages. Still from *Bali-Floti*, 1926

the wrap is left open as it comes off the handloom. Also referred to as 'hair', this natural, unsewn state at the edges represents 'the threads of kinship and descent'. Upon close inspection of Rach's footage we do see that some of the gift cloths are in this somewhat raw state at the edges. We can see this in Figure 39, where the marriage cloth is accepted by the bride's family. Note the lower edge of the sheaf on the left being taken by the woman (face obstructed).

The details in these scenes make it evident how useful it is to have a step-by-step filmic guide to the complex *ikat* process. These are some of the oldest images available, and this is certainly the first film of this precious, distinctive commodity.

Noted textile curator Roy W. Hamilton points out that while the peoples of Flores are not homogenous in their customs, 'hand woven textiles play a central role across the various groups, serving not only as clothing, but also as key ingredients in a web of social and economic transactions'.[20] He adds, 'It is in the context of bridewealth exchange that textiles offer their richest realm of meaning on Flores.'[21] In addition to the manufacturing process, Rach filmed the social-cultural relevance of the cloth. In a subsequent section in the film titled *Een koningsdochter verkocht* [A King's Daughter Sold], he contextualizes the

[20] Roy W. Hamilton, 'Behind the Cloth', in *Gift of the Cotton Maiden: Textiles of Flores and the Solor Islands*, ed. Roy W. Hamilton (Los Angeles: University of California Press, 1994), p. 21.
[21] Ibid., p. 44.

ritual aspect of this material production. While the characterization of 'sold' is inaccurate, as gifts are traditionally exchanged from both sides, the film does document events closely.

The sequence begins with a number of buffalo being brought in as bridewealth. Several elderly women, presumably from the groom's family, bring baskets laden with jewellery. We see the groom's helpers arriving followed by several villagers, and then a woman counts and inspects the finely filigreed gold ornaments that are filmed in close-up. In the next scene, about a dozen people bring in stacks of cloth and deposit them with an elderly couple. The couple accept and inspect the gifts. What is not made clear in the sequence is that while the buffalo and gold are gifts from the groom's side, the gift of the cloth traditionally comes from the bride's side. Thus, a daughter may have been 'sold', but a return gift of valuable cloth is made from the 'king' in this account. These two sequences show the steps in the manufacture of the cloth and its cultural currency, both of which are markedly representative of ritual life in 1920s Flores. Per the ethnographic research cited above, they appear to be accurate and unstaged.

The SVD filmmakers were on a mission to capture the 'unusual' lives of people in Flores—to showcase tantalizing otherness, possibly judged as lacking in moral direction. Their ways strongly contrasted with European lifestyles and social mores. The SVD perhaps wished to expose areas that needed missionary interjection, highlighting a people that needed to be 'saved'. Their films were shown in hundreds of missionary outreach programmes in the Catholic parts of the Netherlands. At the end of the screening, monies were raised for the mission cause. Many were inspired to join. The question that arises then is, What would these scenes reveal other than particular rituals of production and ceremony? After all, the cloth was seemingly well made and the exchange not particularly one sided or unjust. Why would the SVD have produced an ethnography without an obvious propagandistic aspect? Was there an underlying perspective here that helped bolster its missionary cause? The answer stares us in the face. It was the opulence of it that was critically perceived. For a society that had so little, a people who seemed undernourished and dressed in cloth and bark, a marriage ritual with gifts of dozens of buffalo, trays of gold earrings and several folded lengths of precious cloth was perceived in the Netherlands to be irresponsible. By way of explanation, Schroeter refers to German anthropologist

Karl Heinz-Kohl's research on the 'wife-taker' and 'wife-giver' phenomenon in eastern Flores. Groups that could 'give' a wife to another community had a higher value, making marriage alliances most important, ranked right below blood relations. In order to stay ahead in the prestige hierarchy, an impractical amount of money and resources would be spent on marriages. The sheer exchange of commodities and livestock for one marriage and the ensuing feast, as shown in the *Bali-Floti* footage, would wipe out vast resources. It was this excessiveness, according to Schroeter, that the missionaries discouraged. In contrast with the evident penury, it was an immodest, unsustainable way to live.[22]

While the cloth-making and marriage gift rituals were documented well, perhaps the most comprehensively covered sequence or mini 'event' in *Bali-Floti* is a whale hunt filmed in the village of Lamalera, in the east of Flores, in a region called Lembata.[23] The visuals of this classic man-versus-nature ethnographic drama are riveting.

Lamalera, an enclave without much agrarian land, has been historically dependent on the sea for most of its nutrition and bartering power. It maintained a small Catholic population following an initial Jesuit contact in the 1880s. It thus stands to reason that the SVD-backed filmmakers would arrive in this small, somewhat remote area. In 1920 Bernardus Bode, a priest formerly on mission in Togo, arrived at the end of the War of Pacification and began an efficient 'cleaning up' and conversion operation. Five years later, he claimed that only a single heathen remained in the village.[24] It is perhaps not surprising that he was glad to receive Limbrock and Rach to film in this area where Catholics had a stronghold. There are, however, no accounts of their meeting.

Of the several changes that Bode ordered in Lamalera, a significant one was the permanent burial of ancestral skulls. Skull worship was considered to be depraved animist behaviour and strictly forbidden by the Catholic Church even though the Church was at times accepting

---

[22] Schroeter, *Christianity in Indonesia*, p. 141. She refers to Karl-Heinz Kohl, *Der Tod der Reisjungfrau: Mythen, Kulte und Allianzen in einer ostindonesischen Lokalkultar*, Vol. 1 (Stuttgart: Kohlammer, Religionsethnologische Studien des Frobenuis-Instituts Frankfurt am Main, 1998), p. 177.

[23] Lamalera is often spelled 'Lamalerap' in earlier articles.

[24] R.H. Barnes, *Sea Hunters of Indonesia: Fishers and Weavers of Lamalera* (Oxford: Clarendon Press, 1996), p. 52.

of other milder forms of the ritual. Bode also forbade any ceremony that utilized blood. Remarkably, Rach may have arrived right before these restrictions were enforced, because we see both of these strong non-Christian symbols in the filmed footage.

In *Sea Hunters of Indonesia*, anthropologist R.H. Barnes draws on decades of his own research in the region, including interviews with older members of the community who remembered the era before Bode. When Barnes describes hunts and the rituals that accompanied them, two of his most frequently cited sources are Father Bode's entries and those of ethnographer Ernst Vatter, who was there in the late 1920s—the only academic in Flores prior to Barnes' arrival. Considering that Lamalera had not drastically changed in the decades since Barnes began his fieldwork in 1970, many of his details of this small community and its activities resonate with the earlier writings. Barnes was fascinated with whale hunting, an arduous, exciting activity that lingers in Lamalera to this day:

> Yet the opportunity to observe this industry with its traditions intact still exists, despite many changes in the cultures, though with the threatened extinction of many species of whale, this opportunity may not last much longer. No comprehensive accounts have been made, nor can be produced on the basis of the few scanty published reports of Lamakera and Lamalerap.[25]

Despite stating that the traditions are intact, Barnes is careful to observe changes in the rituals that occurred with the swift advent of Catholicism. It is these close descriptions that make Rach's footage impressive, because when compared with ethnographic reconstructions of a few years prior they actually show us the period right *before* Bode's changes were enacted. Interestingly, Barnes itemizes important film footage that was taken in Lamalera by various film crews—German, British and Japanese; the earliest listed is from 1963. Barnes was unaware of Rach's 1922 film expedition.[26]

---

[25] R.H. Barnes, 'Lamalerap: A Whaling Village in Eastern Indonesia', *Indonesia* 17 (1974): 137.

[26] Indeed, in communication with R.H. Barnes it was clarified that he had not seen this film material. In a personal email on 4 August 2014, he made valuable comments on much of this footage after viewing it for the first time.

The 14-minute sequence of whale hunting in *Bali-Floti* begins with carpentry and construction. About a dozen men and some children saw, hammer and assemble a medium-sized fishing boat. The coverage is detailed and interspersed with title cards describing the actions. The ritual aspects start soon after the completion of the task. As in Bode's descriptions, there is an offering made to the large rocks in the sea and also to a shed where ancestral skulls were kept. In 1993 Barnes wrote an article on the rituals of sacrifice:

> When Bode first arrived in Lamalera in 1920, some clans kept the skulls of their ancestors on a shelf at the back of boat sheds, from which they would take them from time to time at ceremonies. They made regular offerings to the skulls in connection with going to sea and returning from fishing. At the same time that Bode buried the skulls, he also buried the sacred stones, *nuba nara*, which he later placed in the foundations of the new church. This step was an act of overt appropriation of ritual capital of a familiar kind.[27]

Though long gone, these rituals are visible in *Bali-Floti*. Notice the skulls in the still frame in Figure 40 and the sacred stones in Figure 41.

These were no longer to be seen by the time Vatter had begun to write down his observations in 1929. A personal anecdote described to the author from Barnes reflects society's lingering and awkward relationship with this ritual:

> Pater Bode made them bury the human skulls, but some hid them in holes along the shore. I once was in Lewotala with Pater Dupont when he decided to visit a man unannounced. We found him polishing his skulls. We were all embarrassed. Dupont told him that he was not aware that he had skulls, and he replied 'I did not know that you were coming Pater.' In other words he would have hidden them.[28]

Though Vatter was not able to witness the killing of chickens to bless the boat, he transcribed oral accounts of it. Less than a decade prior to Vatter's arrival, however, Rach had been able to film it. The film record, among other things, verifies that Bode's accounts of pre-Catholic-era

27 R.H. Barnes, 'Construction Sacrifice, Kidnapping and Head-Hunting Rumors on Flores and Elsewhere in Indonesia', *Oceania* 64, 2 (1993): 149.

28 R.H. Barnes, personal email communication, 4 Aug. 2014.

Figure 40. Ancestor skulls. Still from *Bali-Floti*, 1926

Figure 41. Sacred stones. Still from *Bali-Floti*, 1926

practices were accurate and remarkably detail oriented. An appropriate example would be the description of exactly which parts of the boat the blood of the sacrificed chicken might be applied to in order to appease the spirits:

1. the mouth, *fefa*, of the bowsprit, *menula* (at the very top),
2. the base of the bowsprit,
3. the fore outrigger boom, right and then left,
4. the well, right and then left,
5. the aft outrigger boom, right and then left,
6. the triangular apex, *ora*, joining the two mast poles at the top,
7. the base of the decorated stern piece, madi, on the inside,
8. the fork of the blade of the harpoon, *kafe leo*, used for ray and porpoise.[29]

In Rach's footage, almost all of these points on the boat, and the accessories described, are sequentially accessed. The editing is not seamless, and there seem to have been two sequences intercut. Nonetheless, unless one watches the scenes with a peculiar intensity, the list by Barnes above seems to match well with the actions on screen.

The next sections in the film cover the actual hunt. In 1974 Barnes, not knowledgeable of the epic cinematographic journey that Rach had undertaken, wrote, 'I think I am the first European to witness the capture of whale; I am certainly the first to do so from the vantage point of one of the vessels involved, and the following account and the accompanying photographs are the first published results of such direct observations.'[30] Rach had also filmed from the vantage point of the vessels. He seems to have had the two critical angles—from the point of view of the harpooners and boatmen, and from beside the large boat by following it adjacently. Considering the unwieldy nature of film equipment during this time and the risky, jerky movements of the open sea, the cinematography is commendable. Very few documentary filmmakers in the 1920s were filming live action by varying close-ups and wide shots, and intercutting scenes filmed from different angles to immerse the audience in the activity. This style was to become the forte of *cinéma vérité* filmmakers many decades later. One very famous

[29] Barnes, *Sea Hunters of Indonesia*, p. 245. There are three more itemized accounts (9–11) having to do with the ropes and harpoons.
[30] Barnes, 'Lamalerap', p. 154.

celluloid whale hunt from this period inevitably comes to mind—the sequence in Flaherty's *Nanook of the North*. In contrast, Rach's coverage, where the hunters actually catch a whale (the scene in *Nanook* was staged), is presented with far more evolved technical and aesthetic skills.

In the three days prior to when the actual hunt begins with a new boat, there are a series of rituals, smaller excursions and feasts. Though he did not capture every aspect as documented by Barnes, Rach did demarcate the days, as evidenced by the intertitles and the ensuing scenes. It may have been impossible to film the festivities at night. The sequencing of the intertitles is as follows:

INTERTITLE

Eerst Dag. De boot voor het schuithuis. Het feest begint.

First day. Before the boathouse. The party starts.

INTERTITLE

Tweede Dag. De jongens leeren harpoeneeren.

Second day. The boys learn harpooning.

INTERTITLE

Derde Dag. Eerste tocht: Bezoek aan 'n naburig dorp

Third day. First trip: visit to a neighbouring village

On the first day rituals related to the sprinkling of blood, blessing the boat and getting strength from ancestors are conducted. A goat is slaughtered and cooked. The boat is tested in waters close to the shore. On the second day we see boys being trained to hunt. The older men pretend to be whales and swim close to the boat, while the boys are goaded to jump in with their spears. The third day begins with loading up the boat with livestock and rowing out to a neighbouring village. Per Barnes' description, this village was possibly Larantuka, a predominantly Muslim village on the coast. After the initial warm-up the hunt for whales begins in earnest. This portrayal of the downtime between the completion of boat construction and the onset of serious hunting corroborates the older records. Although some of the events have been omitted or collapsed, Rach considered it necessary to accurately and sequentially represent the progression of the days.

While the hunt is described with a series of intertitles, the visuals are also clear; Rach takes advantage of the repetitive nature of the activities in a whale hunt and films from various angles using just one camera. A sail is raised to take the dozen-odd men into deeper waters. The whale is spotted, and Rach films from the helm of the boat, focusing on the rowing men as the harpooner prepares his weapon. Rach then films from an adjacent boat as the harpooner prepares to jump. Right before that moment we are behind him again, looking at the sea from his vantage point. As he jumps in, we see him from in front of the boat. This short sequence takes place in a matter of seconds but is remarkably covered by editing shots from four different angles (see Figures 42.1–4).

1. Rowing towards the whale and preparing harpoons

2. Standing at the helm and taking aim

3. About to dive into the sea

4. Diving in and harpooning the whale

Figures 42.1–4. Stills from whale hunting filmed by Willy Rach in 1923

Figure 43. The captured whale about to be cut up and divided

Arguably it was the additional skill of the editor that contributed to this spectacular multi-angle sequence. Without the footage from all the different vantage points above, however, an editor would not have been able to piece together as thorough a sequence. Rach might not have been involved in the editing of the film, but he clearly knew how to cover a hunting sequence. The rest of the hunt continues in similarly close, multi-angled coverage. As soon as the whale has the first harpoon in it, the men loosen several lengths of rope and allow the large mammal to pull them along until it tires. They keep tugging at the rope, and once the whale is close to the boat again, the harpooner jumps for a second time and spears the whale. The men then all jump off the boat to tackle the whale collectively; the creature has lost most of the battle by this stage. The large mammal is dragged ashore and cut open.

There appears to be strict adherence to hierarchy and a distribution protocol as to who gets which portion of the whale. Boat owners and boat crew are the first in line. The portions vary depending on the type of creature caught—whales, turtles, porpoises, mantas and sharks are all distributed differently. Barnes explains, 'The master builder for the boat which captured the animal, or for the first boat to harpoon it when several boats share in the capture, carefully marks each section, before the men who have the relevant rights begin to cut into the animal.'[31] In the footage, it is difficult to discern between the members of the crew and the master builder. The men, all extremely tanned and sinewy without the aid of gratuitous close-ups, look similar. Perhaps had the hunt been filmed more along the lines of a Flaherty-esque 'documentary' we would have been able to identify the master builder. The lack of close identification of crew members creates a more egalitarian account of the whale hunt. Emphasis on one or two primary characters may have given the sequence unnecessary individual focus and detracted from our experience of how the community collectively worked on capturing whales. Why was this compelling sequence then overlooked? It would be appropriate to revisit an observation by Gunning quoted in chapter 1:

> The most frequently given reason for this neglect, the belief that this early material remained too raw, too close to reality and bereft of artistic and conceptual shaping (compared to the more 'cooked' documentary) does not take us very far.... The voyeurism implicit in the tourist, the colonialist, the filmmaker and the spectator is laid bare in these films, without the naturalization of dramatic structure or political argument.[32]

Indeed, while aesthetically brilliant in sections, *Bali-Floti* does not have a plot. It was this style that could well have disqualified it from being considered a documentary and subsequently not promoted as much as *Flores Film*.

All of *Bali-Floti*, however, is not filmed in this style. There is one section near the end of the film that appears to have been re-enacted, as the characters seem to play roles. The short segment is titled *Handel in Meisjes* [Trafficking in Girls] and shows a young native woman being sold to Muslim visitors. As there are no records indicating such activity, one can only speculate that there may have been two reasons for this unusual recreation. First, it may just have been difficult to film something as culturally sensitive. Second, it may not have been very prevalent

[31] Barnes, *Sea Hunters of Indonesia*, p. 188.
[32] Gunning, 'Before Documentary', p. 24.

Figure 44. The girl (left) unwilling to be sold. Still from *Bali-Floti*, 1926

and needed staging. It was, however, the kind of scene that a missionary film would require—there is perhaps no easier way to express the moral turpitude of a non-Christian society than documenting the forced sale of girls.

In the segment, a group of men arrive and offer money to an old man for the girl seated next to him. He readily accepts the coins and turns to her for approval. She makes it apparent that she does not wish to be part of the transaction (Figure 44). She is then symbolically shackled with a bamboo trap around her leg. She is forced to serve her buyers what appear to be betel leaves. Merriment ensues among the guests. The girl being sold remains sullen but seems to have surrendered to her fate. The next intertitle reads, *In Orde. Als de koopsom betaald is, wordt de bruid afgeleverd* [Per custom. The purchase price is paid, and the bride is handed over]. The girl mounts a horse, and the group of buyers take her away (Figure 45).

While the scene is compelling, its veracity is hard to corroborate as there is scant mention in the literature on Flores about such swift trading of a bride. There are, however, several ethnographic entries that describe related themes. To be sure, there are far more disagreeable accounts of bride capture—in those cases actual kidnappings take place,

Figure 45. The girl led away on horseback by her buyers. Still from *Bali-Floti*, 1926

and they eventually break into various degrees of clan warfare.[33] R.H. Barnes' 1999 article 'Marriage by Capture' describes a practice around this region in eastern Indonesia where a young man might capture a woman of his desire, only to be chased after by the family. Eventually a more formal negotiation is held, and the woman is 'paid' for. In the scene described above, the woman is still at her father's house; this eliminates the need for a forced heist. Barnes' main sources, Vatter and the missionary priest Arndt, have also commented on coerced marriages. Vatter mentions that he believes the practice occurred but it was impossible to get anyone to admit to it (filming it would be presumably even more difficult). Arndt explains situations in nearby Adonara where parents could be so devious that they would negotiate a certain deal for their daughter and then tell her to go to a certain location, where she

[33] R.H. Barnes, 'Marriage by Capture', *Journal of the Royal Anthropological Institute* 5, 1 (1999): 57–9.

would be ambushed and captured. In almost every situation there was a reconciliation with the parents, performed in a more or less socially agreeable way.

Barnes' assessment of the different sources contains variations of forced but socially accepted marriage. He comments, 'To this extent, therefore, it stands apart from rape, pillage, slave raiding, or the actual selling of wives and daughters. On the other hand, it is an activity which strongly brings these negative activities to mind, and there is historical evidence that these other activities also occurred within the Lamaholot region.'[34] Barnes does not, however, provide us with any of the actual sources on the selling of daughters as shown in this scene. There are accounts of slave trafficking of brides, but the process of capture and exchange is far more elaborate. In other instances, even when the bride is less agreeable—or disagreeable—to the alliance being made, there is a ceremonial delivery of gifts, more in line with the material marriage exchanges described earlier in this chapter. There is no record that would concur with such a rapid exchange. The possibility that it took place, however, cannot be categorically ruled out. What we can safely deduce is that a scene like this had a considerable impact on Christian communities viewing it in the Netherlands. That may explain the motivation for creating the innovative but somewhat far-fetched scene.

The end section of *Bali-Floti*, like in *Flores Film*, focuses on mission work. We saw missionaries travel to Flores early in the film. Now, in the last 20 minutes, they feature again. First a priest hands out tobacco to a group of men, who then go on to slaughter a large number of buffalo. After that we see missionaries in a variety of roles: tending to patients, training natives in carpentry, and teaching young women how to sew. The enormous church in Ende, where large ceremonial processions convene, looms before us. Following this, in a small rural church priests baptize a number of young men and women. The scenes are a bit haphazard with little sequencing, unlike the detailed coverage of rituals in Flores seen earlier in the film. While these scenes portray Church involvement in benign outreach efforts, the emphasis of the overall film seems to be on capturing ethnographic details of life and customs in Flores rather than highlighting the missionary cause. The much more

[34] Ibid., p. 59.

popular *Flores Film*, edited and promoted by Father Buis, however, had a stronger narrative that integrated the arduousness of the daily work of priests in the region.

I have described two films with mostly the same camera operator but different directors and very different outcomes in their place in film history. While *Flores Film* is the relatively more popular film, I have argued that *Bali-Floti*, avoiding re-enactments and 'cooking' the narrative, is richer in ethnographic content. This contrast between the two films, *Bali-Floti* and *Flores Film*, is not intended to discredit Father Buis' contribution to early ethnography in Flores. His pioneering efforts were considerable—it was Father Buis who founded Soverdi, which would give a banner and identity to these films created from the rolls of footage that Rach had brought back. If the Catholic community in the Netherlands, and in several other parts of Europe, heard about Flores and saw its peoples, it was to Father Buis' credit. Soverdi would go on to produce three long features—*Ria Rago*, *Amorira* and *Anak Woda*—all directed by Father Buis between 1930 and 1933. What is intended in this comparative analysis of the early Flores film material, in addition to rehabilitating its ethnographic strengths, is to recognize Rach's contribution to the process. In 1923 it was quite an achievement to travel to a remote area like the eastern Netherlands East Indies to shoot, expose and process film. The footage had a hybrid nature of travelogue, documentary, *actualités* and re-enactment. These are the only visuals that exist today of many aspects of life in Flores. Often, they complement and actually verify lone textual sources. It is also not too far-fetched a conjecture that it was Rach who may have inspired Father Buis to embark on his cinematic career. It was after being involved with this material that Father Buis vowed to return to Flores and make long fiction films. In order to train himself to become more adept at cinematography and directing, Father Buis went to the United States for a second time in 1929—this time to enroll at the New York Institute of Photography. Father Piet Beltjens, a colleague from the SVD, accompanied him. In 1930, feeling more technically capable and artistically confident, they headed back to Flores to make films.

Ethnographic Fiction: *Ria Rago*

The first fiction film Father Buis directed had an uncomplicated theme. He used locals to play the various roles, an innovative style for that period. A Christian girl, Ria, is forced to marry Dapo, a Muslim boy who has grown tired of his first wife. A Muslim broker encourages and arranges the deal. Ria's greedy pagan father, Ragho Dago, accepts the money readily and welcomes his prospective son-in-law. Ria, however, refuses to give in and seeks help from local Catholic priests. They intervene and warn her family against the forced marriage. Realizing she will eventually be married off to Dapo, she escapes to a nunnery. After being kidnapped by her family members and brought back, Ria is beaten and tied down. When Dapo tries to force himself on her, she outwits him and escapes again. This time, however, she falls ill. By the time her family finds her again, she is taking her last breath. She forgives her parents just before dying, clutching her cross.

While *Ria Rago* was fiction, it clearly strove to build a reputation of being based on actual, or at least plausible, facts. Appels has speculated that Father Buis may have been influenced by the film *Nanook of the North* during his stay in the United States. Did he incorporate Flaherty's style of blurring fact and fiction to provide an impression of authenticity? Both films certainly advertised the 'actual' aspect of the narratives. Appels writes:

> It seems plausible that Buis during his film studies in New York saw *Nanook of the North* by Robert Flaherty although nowhere does he mention this being his cinematic inspiration in his letters or diaries. Or maybe he saw *Nanook* on a mission exhibition, where it was played frequently. His method and approach to *Ria Rago* seem very much that of Flaherty.[35]

I hazard the speculation that Buis may have also been influenced by the sequence that Rach filmed of the forced sale of the girl in the section titled *Handel in Meisjes* discussed earlier. Being his contemporary, Flaherty is unlikely to have influenced Rach. Thus, the first re-enactment in Flores had already taken place long before Buis tried it. To his credit, though, Father Buis did it on an unprecedented and complex scale. It has an identical theme and is done in the manner of appropriating locals in a melodramatic retelling of a social ill. We do know that Father Buis had been obsessed with the theme of forced marriage since his days as school superintendent in Flores. If one looks at some of his

[35] Appels, 'Mission to Flores', p. 14.

Figure 46. Poster for *Ria Rago*, 'a film of actuality' (courtesy of University of Westminster Archives, Ref: RSP/6/6/17)

Figure 47. Poster for *Nanook of the North*, 'a story of life and love in the actual Arctic', Robert J. Flaherty/Pathé Pictures (Wikipedia Commons)

writings in the Catholic newspapers, this becomes evident. In an article section titled *Onvriendelijkheden* [Unfriendly Gift], written in 1926, he highlights incidents of coastal-area Muslims in Maumere who forcibly take away girls from the highlands. The backdrop is the ongoing tension between Christians and Muslims for control over the autochthonous groups in the mountains:

> Elizabeth, a young girl of marriageable age, was sold by her parents to a young Mohammedan. Although they are pagan, she led an exemplary virtuous life. The parents tried to force her and chastised her, but Elizabeth suffered patiently and remained steadfast. The parents gave up and finally returned the money to the young man.... Our new converts from the Islamic villages sometimes have much hardship to battle. Very often they come to the mission and show their bruises and tears in their clothes, when they have opposed the Moslems.[36]

In yet another entry, a hadji brokers the sale of a Catholic girl to a Muslim boy. Father de Lange, the local priest, was furious and went to the hadji and demanded the return of the girl to her parents. The hadji initially relented but then forced the parents to sell their daughter for marriage. The priest was powerless, and the girl led a Muslim life from then on.[37] Father Buis wrote these accounts after his return to Flores in 1926. They form the kernel of the plot for *Rio Rago*. It was not easy, however, to transform these ideas into a film made in such a remote location.

Lisabona Rahman, an Indonesian film restoration expert, has written an important account of the making of *Ria Rago* in the online film essay portal Film Indonesia.[38] With her specialist knowledge, she emphasizes the many technical challenges that Father Buis and Beltjens faced in Flores. Like Lamster, who processed films when the temperature was cooler, Beltjens, too, developed the rushes at midnight. It was especially challenging to chemically compensate for the warmer temperature:

[36] Ibid., p. 36.

[37] Ibid.

[38] Lisabona Rahman, 'Lembah Ndona di Dunia Maya: Roman Adat-Relijius ala Flores tahun 1930-an', Film Indonesia, Oct. 2013, http://filmindonesia.or.id/article/lembah-ndona-di-dunia-maya-roman-adat-relijius-ala-flores-tahun-1930-an#.U6W_so2SzCl, accessed 14 Jan. 2021.

22–24 degrees Celsius instead of the desirable 18 degrees. Beltjens, who was already having trouble processing the high volume of pure filtered water required, had to devise ways of 'cheating' on the wash time and yet being mindful of the contrast of the negatives. Given the restrictions, he produced a film with remarkable clarity. Filming was possible only between late morning and early afternoon or it would be too warm for the chemicals to properly react. When it was cooler, such as earlier in the morning or later in the evening, the light was inadequate for proper exposure.

There is more in Rahman's reading of the making of *Ria Rago*. Like Appels, she situates the film in the historical time frame of early cinema. As there are no film anthologies that detail any of this work, these references are precious. Rahman says that Soverdi collaborated with the native population, a strategy that was not unique. But it was among the initial efforts:

> This joint strategy was not merely for cost-saving purposes as commonly done by commercial film producers of exotic fantasy films such as *Tabu* (Murnau and Flaherty 1932) or *Goona-Goona, An Authentic Melodrama of the Island of Bali/Kris, the Sword of Death* (both by Armand Denis and Andre Roosevelt 1932). In the case of Soverdi, the involvement of local actors was essential to create an authentic description of local people's lives.[39]

Indeed, there is something tangibly genuine about the locations, costumes and props in the film. Whether the story would have appealed to an audience beyond a narrow, sympathetic and religious group is, of course, debatable—it is, after all, a rather straightforward, flat tale of unwavering allegiance to Jesus. If the storyline appears to be too simplistic, Rahman reminds us that this type of plot structure was actually rather common during that period. While the father and the villagers represent the collective interests of the greedy indigenous people, Ria represents an individual moral voice guided by the Christian mission. This form of Western-influenced individual conscience versus a native-based ideology conflict was typical of the Dutch-produced Indonesian *Balai Pustaka* (Bureau of Literature) stories popular in the 1920s and

[39] Ibid.

1930s. Published as novels, the stories typically featured intergenerational conflicts such as arranged marriages and cultural values.[40]

While the film is shot in natural locations, utilizes local participants, and is based on a plausible story, it contains little primary source value for historians when compared to *Bali-Floti* or *Flores Film*. The film does, however, provide us with detailed and vivid visuals of Flores. The costumes are authentic. Hamilton, in his book *Gift of the Cotton Maiden*, devotes a page with inset photographs to the costumes of *Ria Rago*. He notes that Ragho Dago, the father of the rebellious Ria, wears a sarong in a style seen only on the remote island of Palue, to the north of Flores.[41] Daniel Dhakidae, a political scientist from Flores, has remarked that some of the ceremonial aspects of the film—such as Ragho Dago's animist offerings and the hadji's ceremonies—are authentic.[42]

The impact that *Ria Rago* had at the time of its screening is noteworthy. On 11 December 1930, the day after the film's first press screening for journalists in Holland, several newspapers published long reviews about the film. They were mostly favourable. Some were complimentary of its innovative on-location filming:

> In judging a film like this, which is not acted by professionals and recorded in a studio with plaster backgrounds, paper scenarios and lights, but under the scorching heat of the tropical sun, it is necessary to consider the almost insurmountable difficulties that filming in such warm regions entails.[43]

Others remarked on its moral lessons:

> This new film work visualizes how Christian love triumphs over pagan cruelty. One sees a Christian girl in Flores oppose the pagan laws of marriage *adat*, which her ancestors and her immediate family still remained loyal to.... After undergoing very heavy persecution and ill treatment she dies, true to her Christian ideal, with a word of forgiveness on the lips and in full surrender after having received the HH Sacraments of the Dying.[44]

---

[40] Bakri Siregar, *Sejarah Sastera Indonesia Modern*, Vol. 1 (Jakarta: Akademi Sastera dan Bahasa Multatuli, 1964) pp. 33–49.
[41] Hamilton, 'Behind the Cloth', p. 39.
[42] Rahman, 'Lembah Ndona di Dunia Maya'. Interview with Daniel Dhakidae conducted by J.B. Kristanto and Lisabona Rahman, 8–9 Aug. 2013.
[43] *Algemeen Handelsblad*, 11 Dec. 1930.
[44] 'Werkzaamheden op Flores', *De Tijd*, 11 Dec. 1930.

A rare negative review, though, did comment on the bare-bones plot of the film:

> A failure in both cinematic and propagandistic respects.... It is no more than an insignificant story of abuse, which a converted native girl must undergo when she does not want to marry the groom her father has accepted. Despite that, assaults lead to her death ... the history remains totally uninteresting, because nowhere is psychological acceptability achieved or even sought.[45]

Even though Father Buis and Beltjens would go on to make *Amorira* and *Anak Woda* in quick succession, *Ria Rago* would prove to be the most successful mission film ever. An entire generation of Dutch schoolchildren, many of their parents, and church attendees would see the film in the 1930s. Appels has reported that all three films were thought to have been lost during the German occupation of the Netherlands until *Ria Rago* and *Amorira* were discovered by Father Hank de Beer in the SVD archive in Teteringen in 1990.[46] In 1992, the Dutch Filmmuseum restored them in their entirety.

But a month before *Ria Rago* opened in the Netherlands, Father Simon Buis had already made cinema history by projecting the film in Flores.

Two Films and a Coronation

Per *Katholieke Missiën*, on 13 November 1930 Father Buis had travelled to Flores to attend the coronation ceremony of Alexander Baroek. This was a monumental event: the 30-year-old would become the first Christian Raja of Manggarai, symbolically ending the long Islamic rule by the Sultan of Bima.[47] Baroek, who was the son of a chief and had been educated in a mission school, had, in an unanticipated sleight of hand by the Dutch governor general, replaced the previous nominee, an illiterate non-Catholic chief.[48] On the eve of the coronation, Father

---

[45] 'De Flores-klarikfilm Rio Rago. Propaganda voor de missie', *Kunst en Letteren*, 11 Dec. 1930.

[46] Appels, 'Mission to Flores', p. 8.

[47] Simon Buis, 'De Kroning van Koning Baroek van Manggarai', *Katholieke Missiën* 56 (1930): 104–9.

[48] Steenbrink, 'Dutch Colonial Containment', p. 117.

Figure 48. Father Simon Buis and the newly appointed Raja Alexander Baroek. Flores, 1930

Buis screened *Ria Rago* and *Flores Film* in the presence of 4,000 villagers and 38 district heads. This was possibly among the largest film audiences ever assembled in the Dutch East Indies. The newspapers would describe the screenings as quite extraordinary:

> It was lovely clear weather at 7 o'clock in the evening, and Father Buis showed the old film, well-known in the Netherlands, *Flores Film*, and the new film *Ria Rago*. All were astonished. Ancient pagans murmured: 'Toeanhitoe kanang Mori Kraeng' 'The pastor must be our Lord himself!' They saw new and strange things! A train in motion, Amsterdam, big boats and big cities, and Dutch ladies and gentlemen and children and so many other things. The first sliding images on the silver screen elicited cries of surprise ...

The report continued, describing the coronation:

> The full morning, the sun bathed all in gold. In the distance were the colossal mountains, resting in light clouds with golden edges. Down on the slopes were layers of deep green gardens with young corn, and on the plateau of the many villages, hidden among bamboo groves. The sun shone on the tin roof of the great Roman Church and shone on the metal crosses of the lofty towers.... The imposing figure of the Resident of Timor and Dependencies came forward and announced to the people the decision of the Dutch government: the appointment of Alexander Baroek as overlord of Manggarai. In Malay, he exhorted

> the young king to always remain true to Her Majesty Wilhelmina and serve faithfully the Dutch government in pristine honesty and dedication.[49]

Father Buis was embedded as an integral part of the ceremony, and the newspaper bore pictures of him and the new Raja. It must have been a tremendous occasion for him. Twelve years earlier he had arrived with the first wave of SVD priests and had set up schools all over Flores. He had returned to the Netherlands, then trained himself in the United States, started a film company, and tirelessly advocated for the missionary cause in Flores through evangelical work, his writings and his cinema.

The tussle for Flores had begun with the ghastly blitzkrieg by Captain Hans Christoffel about two decades earlier, ostensibly to rid the island of the slave-owning oppressive Bima rulers of Sumbawa. It had gradually transformed into a more benign assistance via education, medical help and community building through the work of missionaries. Now there was a new Catholic Raja. Father Buis, priest and filmmaker, stood by and watched him get sworn in.

If the core of this book rests on the accruing evidence that despite an obvious propagandistic slant to the films made by the Dutch colonial government—and its approved collaborators—there is historical value to this archive, the SVD material makes the strongest case for it. Noted academics working on various aspects of culture in Flores—handicrafts, religious and social anthropology—have not been privy to much of the film material detailed above that was shot by Rach, Father Buis and their crew. Perhaps during their era of research these films were not made available easily. Or, very possibly, the idea that film footage, especially overt propaganda material, could serve as unique evidence was one whose time had not yet come. I have teased out, often to the welcome surprise of these dedicated academics, several scenes that not only corroborate and augment their scholarship but also, on occasion, serve as sole surviving primary sources of events. Rach and Limbrock's brilliant filming of the whale hunt in Lamalera, their arduous journey through much of uncharted Flores, and the close observation of social rituals are unique documents that lead us to sites of memory that have

[49] 'Een Katholieke Koning in Manggarai: Zijn Eedsaflegging aan het Nederlandsch Gezag' [King in a Catholic Manggarai: His Oath to Dutch Rule], *De Tijd*, 1 May 1931.

Figure 49. Still from *Rawana*, dir. Henk Alsem, 1932. Alternate title: *The Demon of Opium*

long been vanquished by encroaching modernity and the march of time. I argue that this effort of locating overlooked primary sources cannot be at odds with the most fundamental approaches to studying histories and ethnographies of the colonial era. The pictorial turn has deep and rich resources that are still waiting to be tapped.

There would be more films made in the ensuing years along the lines of the fiction-ethnographic style that Father Buis had pioneered. Father Buis himself subsequently made *Amorira* and *Anak Woda*, both dealing with issues of morality and religion among the newly converted peoples of Flores, a region where he had spent much of his working life. Possibly taking a cue from these projects, more films featuring actors began to be produced by the Dutch in the 1930s to further their propagandistic needs. The narratives tended to expose social and moral ills. *Rawana* (Figure 49), made in 1932 by Henk Alsem, an early example of this emerging genre, is described in the Eye Filmmuseum catalogue as a 'Partially staged and acted ethnographic documentary on trafficking and use of opium with subsequent healing of addicts in the Immanuel

Mission hospital in Bandung'.[50] A 1.5-hour-long production with an entirely amateur cast filmed in Sri Lanka and Indonesia, the movie takes us through the process of ocean-borne drug trafficking culminating in the seedy underbelly of Batavia. The mission hospital is championed as a haven of mercy and recovery for addicts. For the first time we see the sophisticated use of lights, night locations and a large cast of characters in an urban environment.

The early thrust and feverish production of colonial propagandistic films came to a halt by the late 1920s. In keeping with political changes, the Dutch East Indies had begun to be referred to as 'Indonesia' in the newer films and their accompanying reviews in newspapers. I thus take 1930 as a less-than-arbitrary cut-off point to stop my investigation of the colonial non-fiction propaganda enterprise.

[50] Described in film logs maintained onsite at the Eye research database in Amsterdam. Access is granted only via an intranet system. The Eye external catalogue is accessible online and contains descriptions of films in the collection as well.

CHAPTER 6

Dismantling the Picturesque

> Film delivers an experiential access to the past far beyond the capacity of the written word, showing not just images of locations and characters, but also their dynamic interactions, relationships and contexts.... The eye and the ear receive and process information from montage, symmetries, juxtapositions and transitions, motifs, pace and changes in pace of editing, composition, tonality and the use of light and dark in ways unavailable in written text. Film, along with other visual media, needs to be considered as a vehicle for history in its own right, and not simply as an occasional supplement to the written word, illustrating statements established in the printed text.[1]

Through much of this book I have identified specific sections of film footage from the vast and seemingly inexhaustible repository that makes up the Dutch East Indies propaganda collection. These precious films have survived almost a century of atmospheric exposure, remained undamaged through two world wars, and been relocated several times. Most are from completed works, some from outtakes preserved in different archives over the decades. The excerpts selected were subsequently cross-referenced and verified with multiple text-based sources—newspapers, books, literary works and bureaucratic reports—to establish their historical place. I contend that they have ethnographic value and are rare primary sources of historical evidence. I have argued for their value in helping us to reimagine and better understand the colonial encounter.

[1] Landman and Ballard, 'Ocean of Images', p. 5.

A common criticism of colonial-era visual works is that they hinged on the picturesque—displaying an abstract, aestheticized world that never quite existed.[2] Romanticism triumphed over realism, content was subservient to form, and nostalgia and the yearning for an exotic cultural and geographic otherness were fully exploited. This reputation of a predominant style driven by Dutch painters may have impinged on the reputation of that other visual form depicting the colony, the medium we are inspecting in this book—the propaganda film. While this allegation may have been true of the very early Dutch Indies colonial films, I contend that the aesthetic of the films produced in the Netherlands East Indies gradually shifted.

The earliest propaganda films strived to showcase beauty and the promising future of the colony in ways often divorced from the reality of the immediate surroundings. Initially, film, like paintings, was an effective way of providing an impression of that aesthetically 'picturesque' state of the colony. It was a means to persuade civilians in the Netherlands to take pride in developing the colony, to improve its society and its vistas. A hybrid form of the prevalent *Mooi Indië* (Beautiful Indies) sensibility and its graceful entry into modernity was on display in these films. There were numerous images of steam trains chugging past well-ordered fields and in tunnels bored through mountains. Smooth asphalt streets lined with tall, taut, well-maintained trees were in contrast to the equally pleasing rustic rural landscapes of plantations and huts in the *desa* (village). Lamster devoted several films in 1912 and 1913 just to the arts and aesthetics of the time—graceful movements of dancers, close-ups of the reliefs on the sides of temples, and the architectural symmetry of modern constructions in the capital.

It is important, however, to look closely at the term 'picturesque', for it becomes something different when applied to the medium of cinema. To be sure, like a painting, the cinematic frame too can be composed through a picturesque aesthetic. Shots may be set up from vantage points that make the landscape appear especially inviting. The single

[2] The most eloquent of these criticisms came from Indonesian painter S. Sudjojono: '*Mooi Indië* is for the stranger, who has never seen coconut trees and paddy fields ... for the tourists who are tired of seeing skyscrapers and find the environment and new sights ... to blow away the contents of their minds ...' (*Keboedajaan dan Masjarakat*, Oct. 1939).

frame of a painting or a photograph can be made to look unnaturally attractive rather easily. Any landscape can be selectively modified in this manner, and there is a considerable tradition of such paintings in Indonesia classified by art historians as the common *Mooi Indië* style.

A derivative of this spilled into the photographic aesthetic as well. Karen Strassler, who authored a monograph on 20th-century photography in the Dutch East Indies, observed the following: 'In the Indies, amateur photography was closely allied with a painting genre known as *Mooi Indië*, which celebrated untainted, pre-industrial tropical landscapes featuring peaceful, terraced fields, palm trees, and volcanic grandeur.'[3] In a specific reference to Java, where much of the colonial imaging occurred, historian Tony Day commented, 'The photographed scene, because of the way it is framed, is almost one dimensionally flat.'[4]

Motion picture is arguably less flat and a more versatile visual record of a colonial-era moment; film can introduce us to the space in which it occurred as well as provide a richer, more sensory experience of it. Roving documentary footage is typically unable to maintain a sense of aesthetic abstraction for long. The complexities of framing 'picturesquely' for 16 to 24 frames a second over several minutes are difficult—sooner or later a more realistic sense of the surroundings will invariably emerge. Dutch propaganda films were non-fiction in spirit, and no effort was ever made to create Potemkin-like backdrops. Even when Father Buis filmed his fictive stories in Flores, he used natural locations. There were never scenes or props in the Dutch colonial efforts of informational cinema. While there have been some studies devoted to the aesthetics of colonial-era paintings and photographs in the East Indies, these films have mostly yet to be formally reviewed by art historians.

It is important to acknowledge, however, that in several of Lamster's early films, a sense of 'picturesqueness' is actually remarkably maintained even in the cinematic form. Through very careful camera placement, looking at the Javanese landscapes and people with the gaze of an

---

[3] Karen Strassler, *Refracted Visions: Popular Photography and National Modernity in Java* (Durham: Duke University Press, 2010), p. 39.

[4] Tony Day, '"Landscape" in Early Java', in *Recovering the Orient: Artists, Scholars, Appropriations*, ed. Andrew Gerstle and Anthony Milner (Chur: Harwood Academic Publishers, 1994), p. 175.

18th-century Romance-era painter combined with deft editing, Lamster did manage a pleasing, agreeable look for the colony in some of his films. De Bussy and the several cameramen who came after him clearly departed from this method.

Those early Dutch filmmakers, entrusted by their government and other commissioning bodies, did create a significant body of work showcasing the positive aspects of colonial rule that strived to be aesthetically pleasing. But soon they began to capture a darker, 'unpicturesque' vision of everyday life in the Indonesian archipelago. This lack of the picturesque in some of the filmed material bodes well for a more robust inquiry of the spatial history of that time and place. I argue that documentary film footage from this period can help create a heightened sense of that colonial environment. By closely observing these primary sources, the historian is able to re-enter the landscapes and encounters of a century ago in a manner that is significantly different from paintings, still photographs and written descriptions. And yet they remained understudied perhaps because of the indignation, embarrassment, guilt and discomfort associated with colonial rule. In 2004 Nico de Klerk wrote:

> There aren't even a handful of substantial articles or monographies [*sic*] dealing with the colossal Dutch colonial film heritage.... Take Indonesia. Over the last decade a number of books on Indonesian national cinema have been published. But its national film history, as with film histories of many other former colonies ... starts at the moment of independence. In other words: at the moment of national film *production*. Typically, the colonial era, presented as something alien, receives a dismissive treatment in just a couple of pages.... It is fair to stress that Indonesian cinema and cinema history reflect a different priority.[5]

While it is indeed surprising that Dutch scholars (from the Netherlands, Indonesia or elsewhere) did not really delve into this material, it may be the case that these films were not as easily accessible to foreign researchers until recently. It is significant to note here that one Indonesian researcher did look into the matter of the colonial propaganda film and hence merits discussion. In his 1993 edition of a well-regarded book on

[5] De Klerk, 'Dark Treasures', p. 437.

early cinema in Indonesia, *Sejarah Film 1900–1950*, veteran film historian and archivist Misbach Yusa Biran wrote cursory remarks on the Dutch propaganda collection. He appeared unimpressed and regarded the entire colonial propaganda filmmaking enterprise as a failure:

> The filmmaker at that time—or, according to the Dutch term, 'movie operator'—was a cameraman who doubled as everything. The operator performed all the tasks needed to record. The style of the film is mainly tropical wild animals, native customs and other objects from the East, the place full of 'mystery'. The filmmaker travelled with a camera that was always rotated by hand. He went to the middle of Borneo to film one of the main Dayak ceremonies, later he followed in the Sumatran elephant hunting, and then he went shooting on the tea plantations in the Dutch East Indies.
>
> Perhaps because of the grim example shown by filmmakers who came from Holland, the people who lived in the Dutch East Indies were not 'turned on' quickly to strive in the field of filmmaking. Moreover, Dutch filmmaking failed not only because of the quality of the films that Dutch produced, but also because the people in the Netherlands were not so concerned with the situation in the tropical colonies.[6]

In the footnotes to the excerpts above, Yusa Biran attributes the information to a sole letter in his archive written in 1972 from a researcher, Geoffrey N. Donaldson, to a B.J. Bertina regarding the work of Dutch cameraman H.W. Metman.[7] There are no more details on the origins of this letter. Yusa Biran also refers to a newspaper article published in *Het Vaderland* in 1921 that describes bloody scenes of the killing of buffalo.[8]

Yusa Biran seems to have been unaware that a significant amount of filming had been accomplished by Lamster and De Bussy by 1921. Their films were in popular demand in the Netherlands. Indeed, there was a cameraman named H.W. Metman, per the Colonial Institute's records, who was an East Indies–born Dutchman and had returned

[6] Misbach Yusa Biran, *Sejarah Film 1900–1950*, 2nd ed. (Depok: Komunitas Bambu, 2009), pp. 54–5.
[7] Ibid., p. 183.
[8] M.C. van Reuvendroy van Nieuwal, 'Indische Films'. *Het Vaderland* (27 Sept. 1921), p. 1.

to his birthplace for a short time and shot a few films. Among these was the film on the Sumatra tea plantation referred to in Chapter 4, *Sumatra Theecultuur*, and the unpopular film referred to by Yusa Biran in *Het Vaderland*. The latter was *De Doodencultus bij de Sadang Toradja's van Midden-Celebes* [The Cult of the Dead among the Sadang (Sa'dan) Toradja of Central Sulawesi]. The write-up that Yusa Biran refers to was truly scathing. Horrified by the film's gore, the reviewer noted sarcastically, 'When will we get an Indies film of the consummation of the death penalty on the gallows?' While the research is accurate, it is oblique and only in partial reference to the filmmaking efforts in the Dutch East Indies in the 1910s. The company that hired Metman was the National Film Factory Bloemendaal, owned by H.W. Robbers. Records at the Eye Filmmuseum indicate that the film was directed by Louis van Vuuren, a filmmaker and the head of the Encyclopedic Office, who had for a long time been trying to make films in the Dutch Indies. He lobbied unsuccessfully to receive funds from the Dutch government to allow him to make films more in line with an encyclopedic approach. Outdone by Lamster's projects, Van Vuuren nonetheless occasionally managed to produce a film. Unable to do the technical work himself, he hired a camera operator. While Van Vuuren's films do make up a small part of the East Indies collection, they are hardly representative of it.

Yusa Biran's assessment that the Dutch East Indies film industry was stunted because of the low quality of colonial films is unfounded. However, it cannot be denied that commercial filmmaking in the colony was late in arriving. Unlike in Yusa Biran's time, it is now relatively easy to at least get a sampling of the vast collection. The archives in the Netherlands are welcoming to researchers who wish to view the well-catalogued, comprehensive collection. There is also a YouTube channel dedicated to the Dutch East Indies collection at the Eye Filmmuseum.[9] The many computer terminals at the Dutch repositories, or individual ones we may create out of our personal screens, transport us, quite amazingly, into fragments of visions from almost a century ago. The ease with which this can be done, and the scope of the material that we can access, was not possible even a decade ago. The marriage of

[9] See Eye Filmmuseum, 'Dutch East Indies', https://www.youtube.com/playlist?list=PLQr5oaajRw8MElYwKeB3AjT23dVTOa3kH, accessed 11 Nov. 2020.

computer advancements and painstaking archival work now assists in democratizing the hundreds of hours of film that were seen only in the captivity of cinema halls in the 1910s and 1920s by a relatively small fraction of Dutch citizens. Indeed, there is an active Facebook group called Indonesia Tempoe Doeloe where Indonesians and Indonesianists regularly upload images and videos from the colonial era, leading to much reflection and discussion.[10] This is digital humanity's shining moment. But we need to consider some aspects of this rather peculiar metaphysical experience—the act of looking at the early 20th century on a computer screen.

This type of situating ourselves in the past has psychological complexities. Let us imagine, for argument's sake, that we were truly taken back to the 1910s while viewing these films via some sort of incredible teleportation. How would we cope with the knowledge we already have of that period? Philosophers have contemplated this crucial issue of a theoretical 'pre' or 'fore' knowledge. David Hunt outlines for us the pitfalls of these conditions in his article 'Two Problems with Knowing the Future'.[11] Hunt argues that *fore*knowledge leads to the dual problem of realizing we have no agency of changing the inevitable, as well as a peculiar sense of infallibility, because knowing the future gives us an unalterable strength. Although these speculations are meant for currently being in the moment and imagining we are looking at the future, seeing old documentary footage does stir in us similar feelings. It evokes a sense of helplessness that historians often feel as professionals—our ever-refining knowledge is, after all, of the past, and, for all practical purposes, useless. Those wrongs can rarely be righted.

While these films are yet to be studied closely, there has been a resurgence in investigating certain aspects of colonial rule. Those efforts have been publicized widely and have revived interest in Dutch colonial rule, especially in the 1945–49 period, which saw much bloodshed. There has been a reopening of specific cases of Dutch atrocities from the late 1940s that has resulted in long litigation and compensation to some victims. Notably, in Sulawesi in 1946, Dutch Captain Raymond

---

[10] See Facebook, 'Facebook Groups', www.facebook.com/groups/indonesiatempo doeloe/, accessed 11 Nov. 2020.

[11] David P. Hunt, 'Two Problems with Knowing the Future', *American Philosophical Quarterly* 34, 2 (Apr. 1997): 273–4.

Westerling ordered the rounding up and murder of about 3,000 to 4,000 Indonesians suspected to be enemy fighters.[12] That case for compensation went to court in 2011, and the survivors of those families were awarded some compensation in 2013. In October 2020, the government of the Netherlands ruled that it would offer limited compensation to the children of Indonesians who had been executed by Dutch soldiers during the Indonesian War of Independence between 1945 and 1950.[13] This has reopened much dialogue about how to deal with the problems of the colonial legacy.[14]

Mass murders such as those ordered by Westerling in Sulawesi, Van Heutz in Aceh, and Christoffel in Flores have been featured in books, articles and newspapers and on television in both countries.[15] In some of these cases, where there are survivors, they have been reopened in trials. There is a sensationalism to them, an acute sense of fixing wrongs from the past that brutally affected the native population. There are, however, no smoking gun scenes in the colonial film archive, no information that would indict anyone for specific atrocity charges. Does this make them of little use for our comprehension of colonial-era subjugation? I suggest not, because one must consider that much of the oppression in the Dutch East Indies was systemic and widespread and not limited to acute violence. While isolated acts of horror are sometimes revisited by historians and legal activists, the reimagination of a mild, daily savagery does not surface easily anymore. That past is occluded and wrapped in a blanket of shame (on both sides) and a lingering awkwardness. It is, however, hoped that the reignition of interest in events of the 20th century might also pave the path to an interest in the general texture of life in the Dutch Indies—a closer reading of the very fabric of the colonial period. This will bring up a plethora of

[12] 'Netherlands Apologizes for Indonesian Colonial Killings', *Jakarta Globe*, 12 Sept. 2013.

[13] 'Netherlands to Compensate Children of Executed Indonesians', *Al Jazeera*, 19 Oct. 2020, https://www.aljazeera.com/news/2020/10/19/netherlands-to-compensate-children-of-executed-indonesia, accessed 12 Nov. 2020.

[14] Paul Bijl's *Emerging Memory: Photographs of Colonial Atrocity in Dutch Cultural Remembrance* (Amsterdam: Amsterdam University Press, 2015) explores this issue, incorporating a variety of perspectives and academic sources.

[15] See Step Vaessen, 'Indonesians to Receive Dutch Apology', *Al Jazeera*, 11 Sept. 2013, https://www.youtube.com/watch?v=_pzeHf-pD84, accessed 12 Nov. 2020.

issues and possibilities. How will the low-level cognition of decades of servitude and indignity factor into our study of visual materials such as these? How have colonialism and evangelism been represented by the people who made these films? Did they inadvertently or knowingly leave us a repository that helps us understand the texture of those long years?

Historians need to understand and not judge how these makers viewed their role. It is to our advantage today, as scribes after the fact, that they often unwittingly gave us a visual glimpse into practices and traditions that are now lost. Key to this method of visual time travel is the inherent understanding that we are looking at materials far removed from the circumstances that shaped them. It takes a certain reconfiguration of our minds to situate ourselves in those conditions when we view these films. It would thus be constructive, perhaps, not to fixate on the wretchedness of colonialism, which is an immediate and understandable reaction, but also to identify these sources as leading us to sites of memories and legacies that can only add to our knowledge of the past. Much of what we see in these films is no more; many of the landscapes have fundamentally altered, taking with them their lifestyles and cultural practices.

Johann Lamster, Willy Mullens, Father Buis, I.A. Ochse and others did not know that the Dutch would be fighting tooth and claw by the mid-1940s to hold on to their colony. Their films capture their historical optimism and hopes for the colonial future. They created documents that show little interest in the burgeoning ideas of emancipation and self-rule of a long-oppressed people. But knowing what we know now, a century later, we can see that contradiction in the films. Scene after scene of labour exploitation, racial segregation and enormous class distinction have an overwhelming sense of impermanence as we anticipate the upheaval and fall of European empires globally. The rough treatment of natives, especially labourers, feels repulsive. We must situate ourselves in those times, to view the world as it was then. The temporariness of much of what we see from those decades may impinge on our patience, our morality and our clear foresight of the changes ahead. Yet, we could strive to slow down those scenes, observe their minutest details and recreate that gradually dimming era of Dutch supremacy over their colony, filmed in patient exposure in the ever-improving focus of those adventurous, talented cinematographers. And we must concede that colonial filmmaking could not have been 'colonial' all the time.

Bibliography

Archives and Libraries

Amsterdam University Library (Universiteitsbibliotheek Amsterdam), Amsterdam
Eye Film Institute Netherlands (Eye Filminstituut Nederland), Amsterdam
Leiden University Library (Universiteitsbibliotheek Leiden), Leiden
National Archives of Indonesia (Arsip Nasional Republik Indonesia), Jakarta
National Archives of the Netherlands (Nationaal Archief), The Hague
National Library of Indonesia (Perpustakaan Nasional Republik Indonesia), Jakarta
National Library of the Netherlands (Koninklijke Bibliotheek), The Hague
National University of Singapore, Central Library, Singapore
Netherlands Institute of Sound and Vision (Beeld en Geluid), Hilversum
Royal Netherlands Institute for Southeast Asian and Caribbean Studies (Koninklijk Instituut voor Taal-, Land- en Volkenkunde, KITLV), Leiden
Royal Tropical Institute (Koninklijk Instituut voor de Tropen, KIT), Amsterdam
Smithsonian Institution, Human Studies Film Archive, Washington, DC
Society of the Divine World Archives, Teteringen

Primary Sources

Films

Bali-Floti, dir. Simon Buis, Johannes van Cleef, H. Limbrock and Willy Rach. Soverdi, 1926. Eye Film Institute, ID #5306.

Berita Film Di Djawa: Disinipoen Medan Perang! [Java Film News: Here Too Is a Battlefield!]. Nippon Eigasja Di Djawa, c. 1944.

Billiton [Belitung], dir. I.A. Ochse. Polygoon, 1926.

Blindeninstituut en Ooglijdersgasthuis te Bandoeng [Institute for the Blind and Eye Hospital in Bandung], dir. J.C. Lamster. Colonial Institute, 1912–13. Eye Film Institute, ID #7970.

De Doodencultus bij de Sadang Toradja's van Midden-Celebes [The Cult of the Dead among the Sadang Toraja (Sa'dan) of Central Celebes], dir. L. van

Vuuren. Nationale Filmfabriek Bloemendaal (Bloemendaal), 1921. Eye Film Institute, ID #16516.

De Pepercultuur [Cultivation of Pepper], dir. J.C. Lamster. Colonial Institute, 1912–13. Eye Film Institute, ID #52121.

De Tabakscultuur op Midden Java [Cultivation of Tobacco in Central Java], dir. I.A. Ochse. Polygoon, 1927. Beeld en Geluid, ID #53736.

De Tabakscultuur op Midden Java Restmateriaal [Cultivation of Tobacco in Central Java Outtakes], dir. I.A. Ochse. Polygoon, 1927. Beeld en Geluid, 1912, ID #527395.

Delhi Durbar, dir. Charles Urban. A.C. Bromhead, 1912.

Die Fortschritte der Zivilisation in Deutsch-Ostafrika [The Progress of Civilization in German East Africa]. Pathé Frères, 1911.

Flores Film, dir. Johannes Bouma, Simon Buis, Johannes van Cleef and H. Limbrock. Soverdi, 1926. Eye Film Institute, ID #21661.

Het Leven der Europeanen in Indië [The Way Europeans Live in the Netherlands East Indies], dir. J.C. Lamster. Colonial Institute, 1912–13.

Het Leven van den inlander in de Desa [The Way Natives Live in the Countryside], dir. J.C. Lamster. Colonial Institute, 1912–13. Eye Film Institute, ID #38176.

Het Nederlandsch-Indische Leger; De Infanterie [The Netherlands Indies Army; Infantry], dir. J.C. Lamster. Colonial Institute, 1912–13. Eye Film Institute, ID #45889.

Immigratie in Deli [Immigration to Deli], dir. L.P.H. de Bussy. Colonial Institute, 1917. Eye Film Institute, ID #30950.

In Djocjacarta [In Yogyakarta], dir. J.C. Lamster. Colonial Institute, 1912–13. Eye Film Institute.

Independence of Indonesia, dir. unknown. 1949.

Inlandsche Huisnijverheid [Native Cottage Industries], dir. J.C. Lamster. Colonial Institute, 1912–13. Eye Film Institute.

Inlandsche Veeartsenschool te Buitenzorg [Veterinary School for Native Students at Bogor], dir. J.C. Lamster. Colonial Institute, 1912–13. Eye Film Institute.

Java-Soemba Film or *Zending van de Gereformeerde Kerken* [Java-Soemba Film or Mission of the Reformed Churches], dir. Iep Ochse. NIFM Polygoon, 1929. Beeld en Geluid, ID #138829.

Jute. Thomas Duff & Co., 1923.

Koepokinenting in de Desa [Cowpox Vaccination in the Countryside], dir. J.C. Lamster. Colonial Institute, 1912–13. Eye Film Institute, ID #35854.

Koffiecultuur op Java [Cultivation of Coffee in Java], dir. J.C. Lamster. Colonial Institute, 1912–13. Beeld en Geluid, ID #118835.

Kolonisatie van Javanen op eene Delische Tabaksonderneming [Settling Javanese Workers on a Deli Tobacco Plantation], dir. L.P.H. de Bussy. Colonial Institute, 1917. Eye Film Institute, ID #35938.

La Croisiere Noire [The Black Car Cruise], dir. Léon Poirier. Société des Etablissements L. Gaumont, 1926.

L'Atlantide [Atlantis], dir. Greg Wilhelm Pabst. Nero-Film AG, 1932.

Mahasoetji Act 3, dir. Iep Ochse. NIFM Polygoon, 1929. Beeld en Geluid, ID# 118825.

Mataram, dir. Tassilo Adam. Amfilmin (Haarlem), 1927.

Meisjesschool de Bandoeng [Girls' School in Bandung], dir. J.C. Lamster. Colonial Institute, 1912–13. Eye Film Institute, ID #41927.

Moeder Dao, de schildpadgelijkende [Mother Dao, the Turtlelike], dir. Vincent Monnikendam. Nederlandse Programma Stichting, 1995.

Pareh, een rijstlied van Java [Pareh, a Rice Song from Java], dir. Mannus Franken, Albert Balink. Java Pacific Film, 1936.

Peche A La Dynamite Dans Les Iles Salomon [Fishing with Dynamite in the Solomon Islands]. Pathé Frères, 1909.

Pest op Java [The Plague on Java], dir. Willy Mullens. Colonial Institute, 1926. Beeld en Geluid, ID #51739, 51742, 51743.

Propagandafilm Van Het Nederlandsch-Indonesisch Verbond [Propaganda Film by the Dutch-Indonesian Alliance], dir. Willy Mullens. Haghefilm, 1930. Eye Film Institute.

Rawana, dir. Henk Alsem. Hispano Filmfabriek (Den Haag), 1932.

Ria Rago, dir. Simon Buis. Soverdi, 1930. Eye Film Institute, ID #57030.

Rubbercultuur op Java [Cultivation of Rubber in Java], dir. J.C. Lamster. Colonial Institute, 1912–13. Eye Film Institute, ID #58285.

Rubberfilm, dir. Willy Mullens. Haghefilm (Den Haag), 1927. Eye Film Institute, ID #58293.

State Minister Solf Visits the German Colony of Togo. 1913.

Strafgevangenis Te Batavia [Prison in Batavia], dir. J.C. Lamster. Colonial Institute, 1912–13. Eye Film Institute, ID #64026.

Suikerrietcultuur op Java [Sugarcane Cultivation in Java], dir. J.C. Lamster. Colonial Institute, 1912–13. Eye Film Institute, ID #64448.

Sumatra Theecultuur [Sumatra Tea Cultivation]. Nationale Filmfabriek Bloemendaal (Bloemendaal), 1921. Eye Film Institute, ID #64499.

Tabakscultuur in Deli [Tobacco Cultivation in Deli], dir. L.P.H. de Bussy. Colonial Institute, 1917. Eye Film Institute.

Tanah Sabrang, het land aan de overkant [Tanah Sabrang, the Land of the Other Side], dir. Mannus Franken. Anifilm, 1938.

The Battle of Manila Bay, dir. J. Stuart Blackton. Vitagraph Company of America, 1898.

The Legend of Suriyothai, dir. Chatrichalerm Yukol. American Zoetrope, Prommitr International Production, 2001.

Through British North Borneo. British North Borneo Company, 1907.

Viering van den Garebeg Moeloed te Solo [Celebration of Garebeg Mulud in Solo], dir. J.C. Lamster. Colonial Institute, 1912–13. Eye Film Institute, ID #71858.

Newspapers

Algemeen Handelsblad
Bataviaasch Nieuwsblad
De Sumatra Post
De Tijd
Eindhovensch Dagblad
Het nieuws van den dag voor Nederlandsch-Indië
Het Vaderland
Het volk: dagblad voor de arbeiderspartij
Limburger Koerier
Nieuwe Rotterdamsche Courant
The Jakarta Globe
The New York Times
The Straits Times
The Times
Tilburgsche Courant

Journals

De Filmwereld
GBG-Nieuws
Geschiedenis Beeld & Geluid
Het Weekblad Cinema et Theater
Kunst en Letteren
Nieuw Weekblad voor de Cinematografie

Unpublished Sources

Beer, Henk de, SVD. 'Pater Simon Buis en zijn inzet voor de Missiefilms van de paters van het Goddelijk Woord- s.v.d. Achtergrond en totstandkoming' [Father Simon Buis and His Commitment to the Mission Films of the Fathers of the Divine Word-SVD Background and Production]. Teteringen: Archivist of the Provincial Archive, 1992.

Beltjens, Piet, SVD. 'Herinneringen aan pater Simon Buis' [Memories of Father Simon Buis]. Teteringen: Archivist of the Provincial Archive, 1992.

Billiton Tin Restmateriaal 5 [Belitung Tin Outtakes #5], dir. I.A. Ochse. Polygoon, 1926. Beeld en Geluid, ID #530017.

Personal Communications

Arps Ben, conversation, Singapore, Asia Research Institute, 29 Aug. 2012.
Barnes, Robert, email correspondence, 4 Aug. 2014.
Barnes, Ruth, email correspondence, 5 Aug. 2014.
De Klerk, Nico, email correspondence, Apr. 2012–Feb. 2015.
Monnikendam, Vincent, email correspondence, 17 Dec. 2013; 30 Apr., 1 May 2014; 29 June, 9 July 2015.
______, conversation, Leiden, Centraal Railway Station, 20 Nov. 2015.
Steenbrink, Karel, email correspondence, 2 May, 28 May, 29 May, 27 Nov. 2014.

Miscellaneous

Catalogue, *Rubber Film*, International Association for Rubber and Other Cultivations in the Netherlands East Indies, c. 1927.
Minutes of the Colonial Institute, 1911–27.
Toelichting: op de Kinematografische opname van, *Het Leven der Europeanen in Indië*, Colonial Institute Amsterdam.

Secondary Sources

Monographs, Books, Chapters, Articles, Conferences

Adam, Tassilo and Raden Mas Noto Soeroto. *Mataram: Een Openbaring van Java's vorstelijke Praal en Volksleven* [Mataram: A Display of Java's Royal Pomp and Popular Life]. Amsterdam: Roxy Theater, 1923.
Aljunied, Syed Muhd Khairudin. 'Films as Social History: P. Ramlee's "Seniman Bujang Lapok" and Malays in Singapore (1950s–160s)', *Heritage Journal* 2, 1 (2005): 1–21.
Appels, Eddy. 'Mission to Flores: Father Simon Buis and His Flores Films, 1925–1934'. Film and Science Foundation, Audiovisual Archive, Amsterdam, 1997.
Barnard, Timothy P. 'Film *Melayu*: Nationalism, Modernity and Film in a Pre-World War Two Malay Magazine', *Journal of Southeast Asian Studies* 41, 1 (2010): 47–70.
______. 'Protecting the Dragon: Dutch Attempts at Limiting Access to Komodo Lizards in the 1920s and 1930s', *Indonesia* 92 (2011): 97–123.
Barnes, R.H. 'Lamalerap: A Whaling Village in Eastern Indonesia', *Indonesia* 17 (1974): 137.
______. 'Construction Sacrifice, Kidnapping and Head-Hunting Rumors on Flores and Elsewhere in Indonesia', *Oceania* 64, 2 (1993): 149.

———. *Sea Hunters of Indonesia: Fishers and Weavers of Lamalera*. Oxford: Clarendon Press, 1996.

———. 'Marriage by Capture', *Journal of the Royal Anthropological Institute* 5, 1 (1999): 57–9.

Barnes, Ruth. 'Without Cloth We Cannot Marry: The Textiles of the Lamaholot in Transition. Papers from "The Walrus Said", the MEG Meeting on Materials and Techniques Held at the Pitt Rivers Museum on 2 October 1987 and Papers from the MEG Meetings at Brighton and Durham in 1988', *Journal of Museum Ethnography* 2 (1991): 95–112.

Barnouw, Erik. *Documentary: A History of the Non-fiction Film*. Oxford: Oxford University Press, 1983.

Benda, Harry J. 'The Communist Rebellion of 1927 Indonesia', *Pacific Historical Review* 24, 2 (May 1955): 139–52.

Ben-Ghiat, Ruth. *Italian Fascism's Empire Cinema*. Bloomington: Indiana University Press, 2015.

Bhabha, Homi. 'Difference, Discrimination, and the Discourse of Colonialism', in *The Politics of Theory: Proceedings from the Essex Conference on the Sociology of Literature July 1982*, ed. Francis Barker et al. Colchester: University of Essex, 1983.

Bhagwan, Manu. 'Demystifying the "Ideal Progressive": Resistance through Mimicked Modernity in Princely Baroda, 1900–1913', *Modern Asian Studies* 35, 2 (2001): 385–409.

Bijl, Paul. *Emerging Memory: Photographs of Colonial Atrocity in Dutch Cultural Remembrance*. Amsterdam: Amsterdam University Press, 2015.

Bloembergen, Marieke. *Colonial Spectacles: The Netherlands and the Dutch East Indies at the World Exhibitions, 1880–1931*, trans. Beverley Jackson. Singapore: NUS Press, 2006.

Bloom, Peter. *French Colonial Documentary: Mythologies of Humanitarianism*. Minneapolis: University of Minnesota Press, 2008.

Boomgaard, Peter. 'The Making and Unmaking of Tropical Science: Dutch Research on Indonesia, 1600–2000', *Bijdragen tot de Taal-, Land- en Volkenkunde* 162, 2/3 (2006): 206.

Bottomore, Stephen. '"Have You Seen the Gaekwar Bob?": Filming the 1911 Delhi Durbar', *Historical Journal of Film, Radio and Television* 17, 3 (Aug. 1997): 309–45.

———. *The* Titanic *and Silent Cinema*. Hastings: Projection Box, 2000.

Breman, Jan. *Koelies, Planters en Koloniale Politiek* [Coolies, Planters and Colonial Politics]. Dordrecht: Foris, 1987.

———. *Taming the Coolie Beast: Plantation Society and the Colonial Order in Southeast Asia*. Oxford: Oxford University Press, 1989.

Buis, Simon. 'Pas Op Voor De Scholen' [Beware of the Schools], *Het Mahomedanisme Op Flores* [The Mohammedanism of Flores] 1 (1925).

______. 'Beleedigende Taal' [Offensive Language], *Het Mahomedanisme op Flores* [The Mohammedanism of Flores] 3 (1926).

______. 'De Kroning van Koning Baroek van Manggarai' [The Crowning of Alexander Baroek in Manngarai], *Katholieke Missiën* 56 (1930): 104–9.

Burke, Peter. *Eyewitnessing: The Uses of Images as Historical Evidence.* Ithaca: Cornell University Press, 2008.

Chapman, James. *Film and History: Theory and History.* Basingstoke and New York: Palgrave Macmillan, 2013.

Cohen, Eric. *Explorations in Thai Tourism: Collected Case Studies.* Bingley: Emerald Group Publishing, 2008.

Cohen, Sol. 'An Innocent Eye: The "Pictorial Turn," Film Studies, and History', *History of Education Quarterly* 43, 2 (2003): 250–61.

Cohn, Bernard S. *Colonialism and Its Forms of Knowledge: The British in India.* Princeton: Princeton University Press, 1990.

Comaroff, John L. and Jean Comaroff. *Ethnography and the Historical Imagination.* Boulder: Westview Press, 1992.

Cooper, David E. 'Anthropology and Translation', *Proceedings of the Aristotelian Society* 86 (1985–86): 51–68.

Coperius, Louis. *De Stille Kracht* [The Hidden Force]. 17th ed. Utrecht: Veen Uitgevers, 1982.

Cosandey, Roland and François Albéra. *Cinéma sans frontiers, 1896–1918: Aspects de L'internationalité Dans Le Cinéma Mondial: Représentations, Marchés, Influences Et Réception* [Cinema without Borders 1896–1918: Aspects of Internationality in World Cinema: Representations, Markets, Influences and Reception. Lausanne: Payot Lausanne, 1995.

Coté, Joost. 'Romancing the Indies: The Literary Construction of Tempo Doeloe 1880–1930', in *Recalling the Indies: Colonial Culture & Postcolonial Identities*, ed. Joost Coté and Loes Westerbeek. Amsterdam: Aksant Academic Publishers, 2005.

Curson, Peter. *Border Conflicts in a German African Colony: Jakob Morengo and the Untold Tragedy of Edward Presgrave.* St. Edmunds: Arena Books, 2012.

Day, Tony. '"Landscape" in Early Java', in *Recovering the Orient: Artists, Scholars, Appropriations*, ed. Andrew Gerstle and Anthony Milner. Chur: Harwood Academic Publishers, 1994.

De Klerk, Nico. 'Tesori nascosti: ritrovare I film coloniali'/'Dark Treasures: Rediscovering Colonial Films', *Cinegrafie* 17 (2004): 214–25/431–41.

______. 'Home Away from Home', in *Mining the Home Movie: Excavations in Histories and Memories*, ed. Karen L. Ishizuka and Patricia R. Zimmermann. Berkeley: University of California Press, 2008.

______. 'Sand Proft pour Eux: Dierenopnamen in vroege commerciële cinema, 1891–1911' [Without Profit for Them: Animal Recordings in Early Commercial Cinema, 1891–1911], *Tijdschrift voor Mediageschiedenis* 12, 2 (2009): 83–104.

———. 'A 1912 Cinematographic Reconstruction of the 1898 Pedir Expedition, Aceh', read at 'Sight and Sound: Challenges and Ethics of Visual Representations of War and Conflict in Asia' conference, Singapore, 29 Mar. 2018.

Del Mundo, Clodualdo. *Native Resistance: Philippine Cinema and Colonialism, 1898–1941*. Manila: De La Salle University Press, 1991.

Deocampo, Nick. *Cine: Spanish Influences on Early Cinema in the Philippines*. Manila: National Commission for Culture and the Arts, 2003.

Dijk, Janekke van V., Jaap de Jonge and Nico de Klerk. *J.C. Lamster, an Early Dutch Filmmaker in the Netherland East Indies*. Amsterdam: KIT Publishers, 2010.

Fledelius, Karsten. 'Film and History: An Introduction to the Theme', in *History and the Audio-visual Media*, ed. Karsten Fledelius et al. Copenhagen: University of Copenhagen, 1979.

Florida, Nancy. *Writing the Past, Inscribing the Future: History as Prophesy in Colonial Java*. Durham: Duke University Press, 1995.

Fossati, Giovanna. *From Grain to Pixel: The Archival Life of Film in Transition*. Amsterdam: Amsterdam University Press, 2010.

Franken, Mannus. *The Land on the Other Side*. Amsterdam: A.J.G. Strengholt's Publishing Company, 1946.

Fuhrmann, Wolfgang. 'Patriotism, Spectacle, and Reverie: Colonialism in Early Cinema', in *German Colonialism, Visual Culture, and Modern Memory*, ed. Volker Langbehn. New York: Routledge, 2010.

Furnivall, J.S. *Netherlands India: A Study of Plural Economy*. Cambridge: Cambridge University Press, 1939.

Galgano, Michael J. *Doing History: Research and Writing in the Digital Age*. Stamford: Cengage Learning, 2007.

Gately, Iain. *A Cultural History of How an Exotic Plant Seduced Civilization*. New York: Grove Press, 2001.

Gonggrijp, George Francois Elbert. *Schets ener economische geschieldenis van Nederlands-Indie* [Sketch on an Economic History of the Netherlands East Indies]. Haarlem: De Erven F. Bohn, 1949.

Goss, Andrew. 'Decent Colonialism? Pure Science and Colonial Ideology in the Netherlands East Indies, 1910–1929', *Journal of Southeast Asian Studies* 40, 1 (2009): 188.

Gouda, Frances. *Dutch Culture Overseas: Colonial Practice in the Netherlands Indies, 1900–1942*. Jakarta and Kuala Lumpur: Equinox Publishing, 2008.

Gunning, Tom. 'Before Documentary: Early Nonfiction Films and the "View" Aesthetic', in *Uncharted Territory: Essays in Early Nonfiction Film*, ed. Daan Hertogs and Nico de Klerk. Amsterdam: Stichting Nederlands Filmmuseum, 1997.

Hamilton, Roy W. 'Behind the Cloth', in *Gift of the Cotton Maiden: Textiles of Flores and the Solor Islands*, ed. Roy W. Hamilton. Los Angeles: University of California Press, 1994.

Heider, Karl. *Ethnographic Film*. Austin: University of Texas Press, 1976, 2006.

______. *Indonesian Cinema*. Honolulu: University of Hawai'i Press, 1991.

Heidhues, Mary F. Somers. *Bangka Tin and Mentok Pepper: Chinese Settlement on an Indonesian Island*. Singapore: Institute of Southeast Asian Studies, 1992.

Hogenkamp, Bert. *De Nederlandse documentaire film 1920–1940* [The Dutch Documentary Film 1920–1940]. Amsterdam and Utrecht: Stichting Film en Wetenschap, 1988.

Houben, Vincent J.H., J. Thomas Lindblad et al. *Coolie Labour in Colonial Indonesia: A Study of Labour Relations in the Outer Islands, c. 1900–1940*. Wiesbaden: Harrassowitz, 1999.

______. 'Correspondence', *Journal of Southeast Asian Studies* 33, 3 (2002): 559–60.

Hunt, David P. 'Two Problems with Knowing the Future', *American Philosophical Quarterly* 34, 2 (Apr. 1997): 273–4.

Jirattikorn, Amporn. 'Suriyothai: Hybridizing Thai National Identity through Film', *Inter-Asia Cultural Studies* 4, 2 (2003): 296–308.

Kartini, R.A. *Letters of a Javanese Princess*. New York: W.W. Norton, 1964.

Kartomi, Margaret J. 'Music in Nineteenth Century Java: A Precursor to the Twentieth Century', *Journal of Southeast Asian Studies* 20, 1 (1990): 1–34.

Kathirithamby-Wells, J. 'The Islamic City: Melaka to Yogyakarta, c. 1500–1800', *Modern Asian Studies* 20, 2 (1986): 333–51.

Kohl, Karl-Heinz. *Der Tod der Reisjungfrau: Mythen, Kulte und Allianzen in einer ostindonesischen Lokalkultar* [The Death of the Rice Maiden: Myths, Cults and Alliances in an East Indonesian Local Culture], Vol. 1. Stuttgart: Kohlammer, Religionsethnologische Studien des Frobenuis-Instituts Frankfurt am Main, 1998.

Kusters, Paul. 'Expressions of Impressions: Filmmaking in the Dutch East Indies', *GBG-Nieuws* 33 (Summer 1995): 28.

Lagny, Michèle. 'Film History: Or History Expropriated', *Film History* 6, 1 (1994): 30.

Lamster, J.C. *The East Indies: Giving a Description of the Native Population of Netherlands-Indies and of Its Civilization*. Haarlem: Droste, 1929.

Landman, Jane and Chris Ballard. 'An Ocean of Images: Film and History in the Pacific', *Journal of Pacific History* 45, 1 (2010).

Langbehn, Volker. *German Colonialism, Visual Culture, and Modern Memory*. London: Routledge, 2010.

Lloyd, Nick. 'Losing the Game: Propaganda and Influence in the British Raj, 1917–1947', in *British Propaganda and Wars of Empire*, ed. Greg Kennedy and Christopher Tuck. Farnham and Burlington: Ashgate, 2014.

Locher-Scholten, Elsbeth. *Ethiek in fragmenten: vijf studies over koloniaal denken en doen van Nederlanders in de Indonesische archipel, 1877–1942* [Ethics in Fragments: Five Studies on Colonial Thinking and Actions of the Dutch in the Indonesian Archipelago, 1877–1942]. Utrecht: HES Publishers, 1981.

Loiperdinger, Martin. 'World War I Propaganda Films and the Birth of the Documentary', in *Uncharted Territory: Essays in Early Nonfiction Film*, ed. Daan Hertogs and Nico de Klerk. Amsterdam: Stichting Nederlands Filmmuseum, 1997.

Lokin, Stef. 'Een gesprek met beeldresearcher Rogier Smeele, Oude beelden en een nieuwe visie' [A Conversation with Image Researcher Rogier Smeele, Old Images and a New Vision], *GBG-Nieuws* 33 (1995): 35–8.

Martins, Roberts. 'Indonesia: The Movie', in *Cinema and Nation*, ed. Mette Hjort and Scott Mackenzie. London: Routledge, 2000, pp. 173–88.

Marwick, Arthur. *The Nature of History*. 3rd ed. London: Macmillan, 1989.

Matuszewski, Boleslas, Laura U. Marks and Diane Koszarski. 'A New Source of History', *Film History* 7, 3 (1995): 322.

Mitchell, W.J.T. *Picture Theory: Essays on Verbal and Visual Representation.* Chicago: University of Chicago Press, 1995.

Moon, Suzanne. *Technology and Ethical Idealism: A History of Development in the Netherlands East Indies*. Leiden: CNWS Publications, 2010.

Morris, Rosalind C. *Photographies East: The Camera and Its Histories in East and Southeast Asia*. Durham: Duke University Press, 2009.

Mrazek, Rudolf. 'Let Us Become Radio Mechanics: Technology and National Identity in Late Colonial Netherlands East Indies', *Comparative Studies in Society and History* 39, 1 (1997): 3–33.

———. *Engineers of Happy Land: Technology and Nationalism in a Colony.* Princeton: Princeton University Press, 2002.

Mullens, Willy. *Tabakscultuur in Deli: groot filmwerk vervaardigd in opdracht van het Tabaksbureau te Amsterdam* [Tobacco Culture in Deli: A Large Film Project Commissioned by the Tobacco Bureau in Amsterdam]. Den Haag: Haghe-film-fabriek, 1927.

———. *Enkele Pagina's Uit Mijn Gulden Boek* [A Few Pages from My Golden Book]. Den Haag: Staatsdrukkerij, 1929.

Mulvey, Laura. 'Compilation Film as "Deferred Action": Vincent Monnikendam's *Mother Dao, the Turtle-like*', in *Projected Shadows: Psychoanalytic Reflections on the Representation of Loss in European Cinema*, ed. Andrea Sabbadini. New York: Routledge, 2007.

Musser, Charles. *The Emergence of Cinema: The American Screen to 1907*, Vol. 1. Berkeley: University of California Press, 1994.

Nakamura Mitsuo. *The Crescent Arises over the Banyan Tree: A Study of the Muhammadiyah Movement in a Central Javanese Town, c. 1910s–2010.* Singapore: Institute of Southeast Asian Studies, 2012, pp. 73–7.

Nieuwenhuys, Rob. *Oost-Indische Spiegel* [East Indies Mirror]. London: Fontana, 1978.

Noordegraaf, Julia. '*Facing Forward* with Found Footage: Displacing Colonial Footage in *Mother Dao* and the Work of Fiona Tan', in *Technologies of Memory in the Arts*, ed. Liedeke Plate and Anneke Smelik. Basingstoke: Palgrave Macmillan, 2009.

Noordegraaf, Julia J. and Elvira Pouw. 'Extended Family Films Home Movies in the State-Sponsored Archive', *Moving Image* 9, 1 (2009): 87.

Norindr, Panivong. *Phantasmic Indochina*. Durham: Duke University Press, 1996.

Oksiloff, Assenka. *Picturing the Primitive: Visual Culture, Ethnography and Early German Cinema*. New York: Palgrave, 2001.

Onghokham. *The Thugs, the Curtain Thief, and the Sugar Lord: Power, Politics, and Culture in Colonial Java*. Jakarta: Metafor Publishing, 2003.

Ouroussoff, Nicolai. 'Heaven, Hell and Purgatory, Encased in Glass', *New York Times*, 26 May 2007.

Pattynama, Pamela. '(Un)happy endings: Nostalgia in Postimperial and Post-memory Dutch Films', in *The Postcolonial Low Countries: Literature, Colonialism, Multiculturalism*, ed. E. Boehmer and S. De Mul. Lanham: Lexington Books, 2012, pp. 97–122.

______. *Bitterzoet Indie: Herinneringen en nostalgie in Literatuur, Foto's en Film* [Bittersweet Indies: Memories and Nostalgia in Literature, Photos and Film]. Amsterdam: Prometheus, Bert Bakker, 2014.

Pemberton, John. *On the Subject of 'Java'*. Ithaca: Cornell University Press, 1994.

Peterson, Jennifer. 'Truth Is Stranger than Fiction: Travelogues from the 1910s in the Nederlands Filmmuseum', in *Uncharted Territory: Essays in Early Nonfiction Film*, ed. Daan Hertogs and Nico de Klerk. Amsterdam: Stichting Nederlands Filmmuseum, 1997.

Protschky, Susie, ed. *Photography, Modernity and the Governed in Late-Colonial Indonesia*. Amsterdam: Amsterdam University Press, 2015.

Rafael, Vicente L. *White Love*. Manila: Ateneo de Manila University Press, 2000.

Reid, Anthony. *Verandah of Violence: The Background to the Aceh Problem*. Singapore: NUS Press, 2006.

Reksadipura. *Pratelan Miyos Dalem Ingkang Sinuhun Kangjeng Susuhunan Paku-buwana VII Kaprabon Garebeg Mulud ing Dal 1775* [The Birth Statement of Kangjeng Susuhunan Pakubuwana VII Kaprabon Garebeg Mulud in Dal 1775] (composed and inscribed Surakarta, 1847/8). Ms. RP H42; SMP MN 271C.

Rosen, Philip. *Change Mummified: Cinema, Historicity, Theory*. Minneapolis: University of Minnesota Press, 2001.

Rosenstone, Robert A. 'History in Images/History in Words: Reflections on the Possibility of Really Putting History onto Film', *American Historical Review* 93, 5 (1988): 1174.

———. *Visions of the Past: The Challenge of Film to Our Idea of History*. Cambridge: Harvard University Press, 1995.

———. *History on Film/Film on History*. Harlow: Longman/Pearson, 2006.

Rotha, Paul. *Documentary Film*. New York: Hastings House, 1952.

Russell, Catherine. *Experimental Ethnography*. Durham: Duke University Press, 1999.

Schroeter, Susanne. 'The Indigenization of Catholicism in Flores', in *Christianity in Indonesia: Perspectives of Power*, ed. Susanne Schroeter. Berlin: Lit Verlag, 2010.

Schulte Nordholt, Henk. 'Modernity and Middle Class in the Netherlands Indies', in *Photography, Modernity and the Governed in Late-Colonial Indonesia*, ed. Susie Protschky. Amsterdam: Amsterdam University Press, 2015.

Schulte Nordholt, Henk and Fridus Steijlen. 'Don't Forget to Remember Me: An Audiovisual Archive of Everyday Life in Indonesia in the 21st Century', *Indonesia Studies Working Papers* 1 (2007): 1–24.

Shiraishi Takashi. *An Age in Motion: Popular Radicalism in Java, 1912–1926*. Ithaca: Cornell University Press, 1990.

Siregar, Bakri. *Sejarah Sastera Indonesia Modern* [History of Modern Indonesian Literature], Vol. 1. Jakarta: Akademi Sastera dan Bahasa Multatuli, 1964.

Slavin, Henry David. *Colonial Cinema and Imperial France 1919–1939: White Blind Spots, Male Fantasies, Settler Myths*. Baltimore: Johns Hopkins University Press, 2001.

Soegiarto, Jugiarie. 'Wacana Kolonial Dalam Film Moeder Dao de schildpadgelijkende' [Colonial Discourse in the Film *Mother Dao, the Turtlelike*], *Wacana, Journal of the Humanities of Indonesia* 10, 2 (2008): 317–47.

Sorlin, Pierre. *The Film in History: Restaging the Past*. Oxford: Basil Blackwell, 1980.

———. 'How to Look at an "Historical" Film', in *The Historical Film: History and Memory in Media*, ed. Marcia Landy. New Brunswick: Rutgers University Press, 2001.

Steenbrink, Karel. *Catholics in Indonesia, 1808–1942: A Documented History*, Vol. 2: *The Spectacular Growth of a Self-confident Minority, 1903–1942*. Leiden: KITLV Press, 2007.

———. 'Dutch Colonial Containment of Islam in Manggarai, West Flores, in Favor of Catholicism, 1909–1942', *Bijdragen tot de Taal-, Land- en Volkenkunde* 169 (2013): 108.

Stoler, Ann Laura. *Capitalism and Confrontation in Sumatra's Plantation Belt, 1870–1979*. New Haven: Yale University Press, 1985.

______. 'Making Empire Respectable: The Politics of Race and Sexual Morality in 20th-Century Colonial Cultures', *American Ethnologist* 16, 4 (1989): 634–60.

Strangio, Carinda. 'Standplaats Soekaboemi: De Lamster-collectie van het Filmmuseum' [Sukabumi Station: The Lamster Collection of the Filmmuseum], *Tijdschrift Voor Mediageschiedenis* 2 (1999): 23–35.

Strassler, Karen. *Refracted Visions: Popular Photography and National Modernity in Java*. Durham: Duke University Press, 2010.

Sudjojono, S. 'Seni Loekis di Indonesia Sekarang Dan Jang Akan Datang' [Painting in Indonesia: Now and in the Future], *Keboedajaan dan Masjarakat*, No. 6, Oct. 1939.

Taylor, Jean Gelman. 'Aceh Photo Narratives', in *Mapping the Acehnese Past*, ed. Michael Feener, Patrick Daly and Anthony Reid. Leiden: KITLV Press, 2011, pp. 199–239.

______. 'Ethical Policies in Moving Pictures', in *Photography, Modernity and the Governed in Late-Colonial Indonesia*, ed. Susie Protschky. Amsterdam: Amsterdam University Press, 2015.

Tideman, J. *De Huisvesting der contractkoelies ter Oostkust van Sumatra* [Housing of Contract Coolies on the East Coast of Sumatra]. Weltevreden: Albrecht, 1919.

Tofighian, Nadi. 'José Nepomuceno and the Creation of a Filipino National Consciousness', *Film History* 20 (2008): 77–94.

Usai, Paolo Cherchi. 'An Archival View', in *Film and the First World War*, ed. Karel Dibbets and Bert Hogenkamp. Amsterdam: University of Amsterdam Press, 1995.

Van den Berg, Jurrien. 'Tin Island: Labour Conditions of Coolies in the Billiton Mines in the Nineteenth and Early Twentieth Centuries', in Vincent J.H. Houben, J. Thomas Lindblad et al., *Coolie Labour in Colonial Indonesia: A Study of Labour Relations in the Outer Islands, c. 1900–1940*. Wiesbaden: Harrassowitz, 1999.

Van den Brand, Johannes. *De millioenen uit Deli* [The Millions from Deli]. Amsterdam: Pretoria, 1902.

Van Neil, Robert. 'The Legacy of the Cultivation System for Subsequent Economic Development', in *Indonesian Economic History in the Dutch Colonial Era*, ed. Anne Booth, W.J. O'Malley and Anna Weidemann. New Haven: Yale University Southeast Asia Studies, 1990.

Vandenbosch, Amry. *The Dutch East Indies: Its Government, Problems and Politics*. Berkeley and Los Angeles: University of California Press, 1942.

Vaughn, Dai. *For Documentary: Twelve Essays*. Berkeley: University of California Press, 1999, pp. 81–2.

Vergara Jr., Benito M. *Photography and Colonialism in Early-Twentieth-Century Philippines*. Quezon City: University of Philippines Press, 1995.

Veth, Bas. *Het Leven in Nederlandsch Indie* [Life in the Netherlands East Indies]. Amsterdam: Kampen en Zoon, 1900.

Vint, Luc. *Kongo made in Belgium: Beeld van een kolonie in film en Propaganda* [Congo Made in Belgium: Image of a Colony in Film and Propaganda]. Leuven: Kritak, 1984.

Warrington, Marnie-Hughes. *History Goes to the Movies.* New York: Routledge, 2007.

Wertheim, Wim F. 'Conditions on Sugar Estates in Colonial Java: Comparisons with Deli', *Journal of Southeast Asian Studies* 24, 2 (1993): 268–74.

White, Hayden. 'Historiography and Historiophoty', *American Historical Review* 93, 5 (1988): 1197–8.

Willemsen, Marie-Antoinette. 'De *fictive* kracht: De missiefilms van de missionarissen van Steyl (SVD)' [The Fictional Force: The Mission Films of the Steyl Missionaries (SVD)], in *Bewogen missie: het gebruik van het medium film door Nederlandse kloostergemeenschappen* [Moving Mission: The Use of the Film Medium by Dutch Monastic Communities], ed. J.P.A. van Vugt and Marie-Antoinette Willemsen. Hilversum: Stichting Echo, 2012, pp. 62–3.

Winston, Brian. *Claiming the Real: The Griersonian Documentary and Its Legitimations.* London: British Film Institute, 1995.

Winter, J.W. 'Beknopte Beschrijving van het Hof Soerakarta in 1824' [Brief Description of the Surakarta Court in 1824], *Bijdragen tot de Taal-, en Volkenkunde* 54 (1902): 61–4.

Yusa Biran, Misbach. *Sejarah Film 1900–1950.* 2nd ed. Depok: Komunitas Bambu, 2009, pp. 54–5.

Theses and Dissertations

Hendriks, G.A. Jansen. 'Een voorbeeldige kolonie: Nederlands-Indië in 50 jaar overheidsfilms, 1912–1962' [An Imagined Colony: Netherlands East Indies in 50 Years of Government Films, 1912–1962], PhD dissertation, University of Amsterdam, 2014.

Kingston, Jeffrey Burke. 'The Manipulation of Tradition in Java's Shadow: Transmigration, Decentralization and the Ethical Policy in Colonial Lampung', PhD dissertation, Columbia University, 1987.

Pambudi, Adhie Gesit. 'The Audiovisual Battlefield: The Use of Dutch Documentary Films about the Issues of Indonesia, 1945–1949', MA thesis, Leiden University, 2012.

Ruppin, Dafna. 'Early Cinema-Going in Colonial Indonesia, 1896–1914', PhD dissertation, Utrecht University, 2014.

Tofighian, Nadi. 'Blurring the Colonial Binary: Turn-of-the-Century Transnational Entertainment in Southeast Asia', PhD dissertation, Stockholm University, 2013.

Wilson, Donald Dean Jr. 'Colonial Việt Nam on Film: 1896 to 1926', PhD dissertation, City University of New York, 2007.

Websites

Al Jazeera, 'Netherlands to Compensate Children of Executed Indonesians', 19 Oct. 2020. https://www.aljazeera.com/news/2020/10/19/netherlands-to-compensate-children-of-executed-indonesia, accessed 12 Nov. 2020.

American Library Association. 'Primary Sources on the Web: Finding, Evaluating, Using'. http://www.ala.org/rusa/sections/history/resources/primarysources, accessed 11 Nov. 2020.

Appels, Eddy. 'Faraway Places and Exotic Cultures in a Movie Mission'. Cultuur Wijzer. https://static.kunstelo.nl/ckv2/cultuurwijzer/cultuurwijzer/www/cultuurwijzer.nl/cultuurwijzer.nl/i000741.html, accessed 11 Nov. 2020.

Artwis. 'The Cartographic Representation of the Netherlands East Indies and West Indies on Dutch School Wall Maps'. A.M. Brouwer, 1930, published by P. Noordhoff, 70 × 130 cm, scale 1:4.000.000. http://www.artwis.com/articles/the cartographic-representation-of-the-netherlands-east-and-west-indies-on-dutch school-wall-maps/4/, accessed, 1 July 2015.

Berita Film Di Djawa: Disinipoen Medan Perang! YouTube. http://www.youtube.com/watch?v=bJ-rhWRJD00, accessed 11 Nov. 2020.

Cinema Context. 'Film in the Netherlands from 1896'. http://www.cinema context.nl, accessed 6 Nov. 2020.

Colonial Film. Moving Images of the British Empire. http://www.colonialfilm.org.uk/, accessed 6 Nov. 2020.

Eye Filmmuseum, 'Dutch East Indies', https://www.youtube.com/playlist?list=PLQr5oaajRw8MElYwKeB3AjT23dVTOa3kH, accessed 11 Nov. 2020.

Facebook. 'Facebook Groups'. www.facebook.com/groups/indonesiatempodoeloe/, accessed 11 Nov. 2020.

Forgasc, Peter. 'Looming Fire: Stories from the Dutch East Indies 1900–1940'. Installation, EYE, Amsterdam, 5 Oct.–1 Dec. 2013. https://www.eyefilm.nl/en/exhibition/péter-forgács---looming-fire, accessed 11 Nov. 2020.

Indonesian War of Independence 1945–1949. YouTube. https://www.youtube.com/watch?v=8U2QImMSzwE, accessed 11 Nov. 2020.

Rahman, Lisabona. 'Lembah Ndona di Dunia Maya: Roman Adat-Relijius ala Flores tahun 1930-an' [Valley of Ndona in Maya's World: Traditional-Religious Romance in Flores in the 1930s]. Film Indonesia, Oct. 2013. http://filmindonesia.or.id/article/lembah-ndona-di-dunia-maya-roman-adat-relijius-ala-flores-tahun-1930-an#.U6W_so2SzCl, accessed 14 Jan. 2021.

Steenbrink, Karel. 'Sandeep Ray and Colonial Movies'. Relindonesia. http://relindonesia.blogspot.nl/2014/05/sandeep-ray-and-colonial-movies.html, accessed 11 Nov. 2020.

University of Chicago, Film Studies Center. 'Colonial Imaging: Mother Dao the Turtlelike'. http://filmstudiescenter.uchicago.edu/events/1997/colonial-imaging- mother-dao-turtlelike, accessed 7 Nov. 2019.

Vaessen, Step. 'Indonesians to Receive Dutch Apology'. *Al Jazeera. YouTube*, 11 Sept. 2013. https://www.youtube.com/watch?v=_pzeHf-pD84, accessed 12 Nov. 2020.

Yale-New Haven Teachers Institute. 'Mohandas Gandhi: The Art of Non-violence', Unit 98.03.05. http://www.yale.edu/ynhti/curriculum/units/1998/3/98.03.05.x.html, accessed 4 Jan. 2021.

Index